STAR WARS

THE CLONE WARS

SLAVES OF THE REPUBLIC

SCRIPT **HENRY GILROY**

INKS **DAN PARSONS**

COLORS **MICHAEL E. WIGGAM**

PENCILS **SCOTT HEPBURN**
RAMÓN K. PÉREZ
LUCAS MARANGON

LETTERING **MICHAEL HEISLER**

COVER ART **LUCAS MARANGON**

DESIGNER **STEPHEN REICHERT**

ASSISTANT EDITOR **FREDDYE LINS**

EDITOR **RANDY STRADLEY**

PUBLISHER **MIKE RICHARDSON**

Special thanks to Elaine Mederer, Jann Moorhead, David Anderman, Leland Chee, Sue Rostoni, and Carol Roeder at Lucas Licensing.

Published by Dark Horse Books, a division of Dark Horse Comics, Inc.
10956 SE Main Street, Milwaukie, OR 97222

darkhorse.com | starwars.com

To find a comics shop in your area, call the Comic Shop Locator Service toll-free at 1.888.266.4226
First edition: November 2009 | ISBN 978-1-59582-349-6

10 9 8 7 6 5 4 3 2 1
Printed in China

 The events in these stories take place sometime during the Clone Wars.

STAR WARS: THE CLONE WARS—SLAVES OF THE REPUBLIC

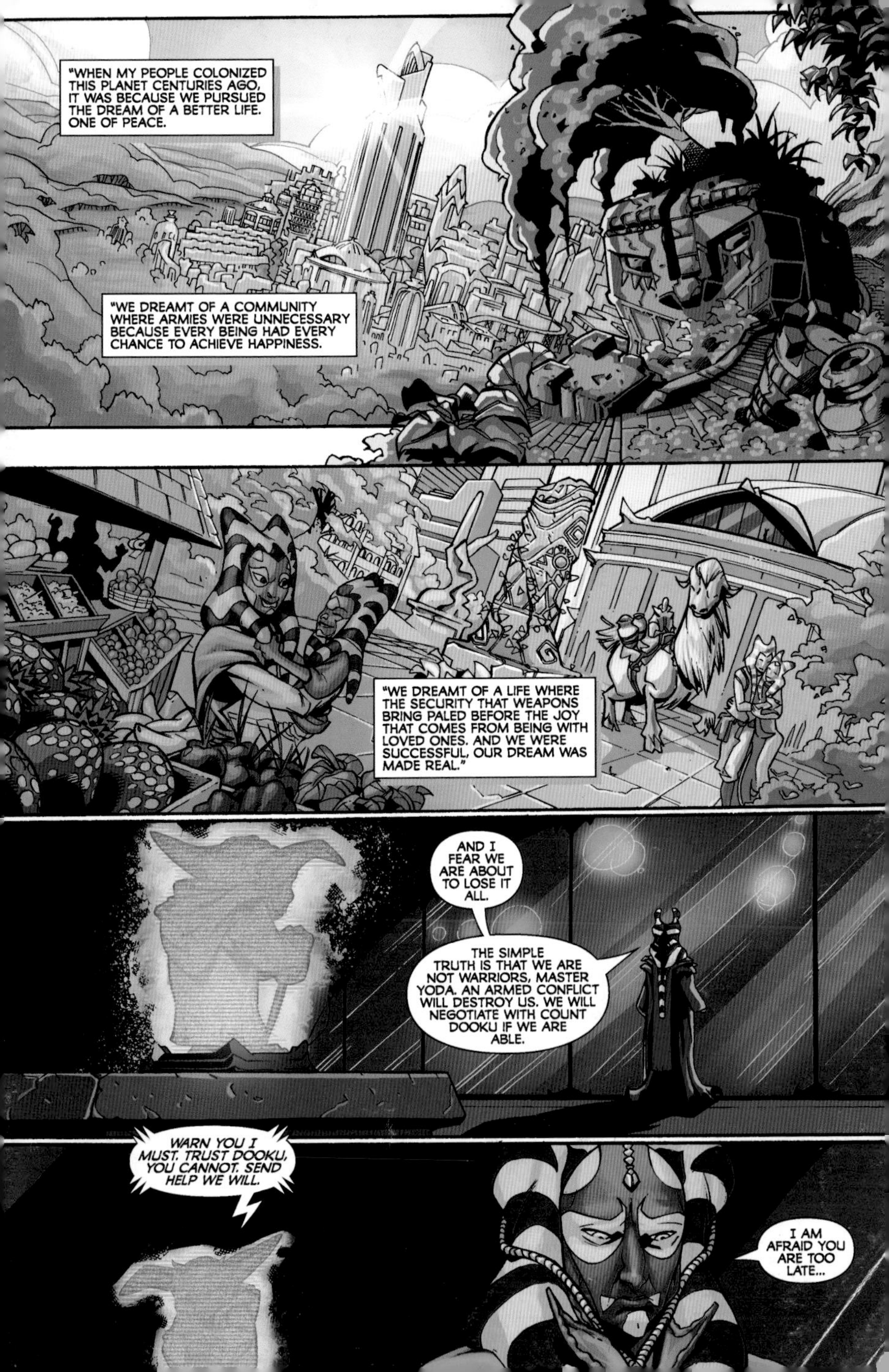
"WHEN MY PEOPLE COLONIZED THIS PLANET CENTURIES AGO, IT WAS BECAUSE WE PURSUED THE DREAM OF A BETTER LIFE. ONE OF PEACE.
"WE DREAMT OF A COMMUNITY WHERE ARMIES WERE UNNECESSARY BECAUSE EVERY BEING HAD EVERY CHANCE TO ACHIEVE HAPPINESS.
"WE DREAMT OF A LIFE WHERE THE SECURITY THAT WEAPONS BRING PALED BEFORE THE JOY THAT COMES FROM BEING WITH LOVED ONES. AND WE WERE SUCCESSFUL, OUR DREAM WAS MADE REAL."
AND I FEAR WE ARE ABOUT TO LOSE IT ALL.
THE SIMPLE TRUTH IS THAT WE ARE NOT WARRIORS, MASTER YODA. AN ARMED CONFLICT WILL DESTROY US. WE WILL NEGOTIATE WITH COUNT DOOKU IF WE ARE ABLE.
WARN YOU I MUST. TRUST DOOKU, YOU CANNOT. SEND HELP WE WILL.
I AM AFRAID YOU ARE TOO LATE...

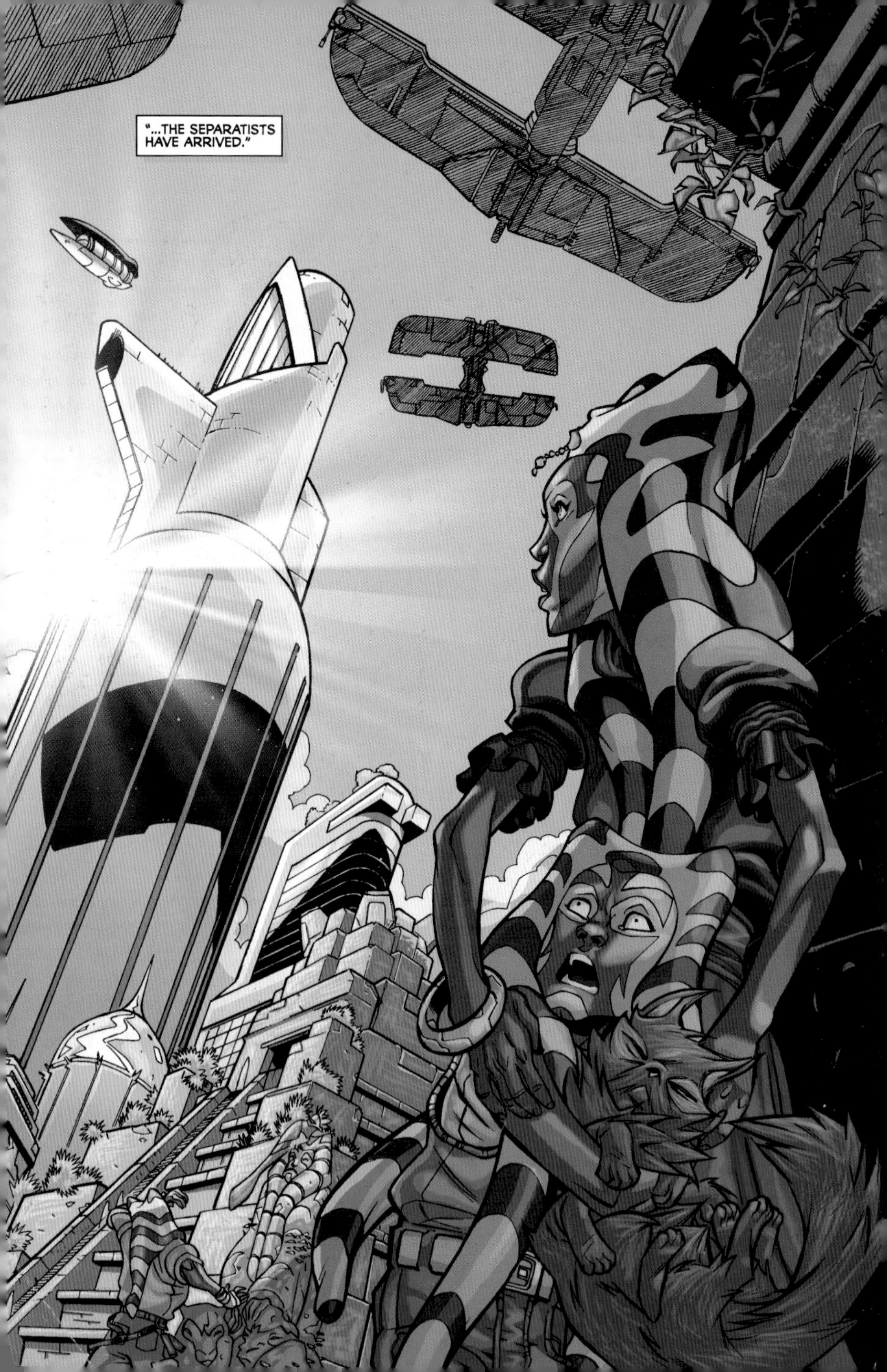
"...THE SEPARATISTS HAVE ARRIVED."

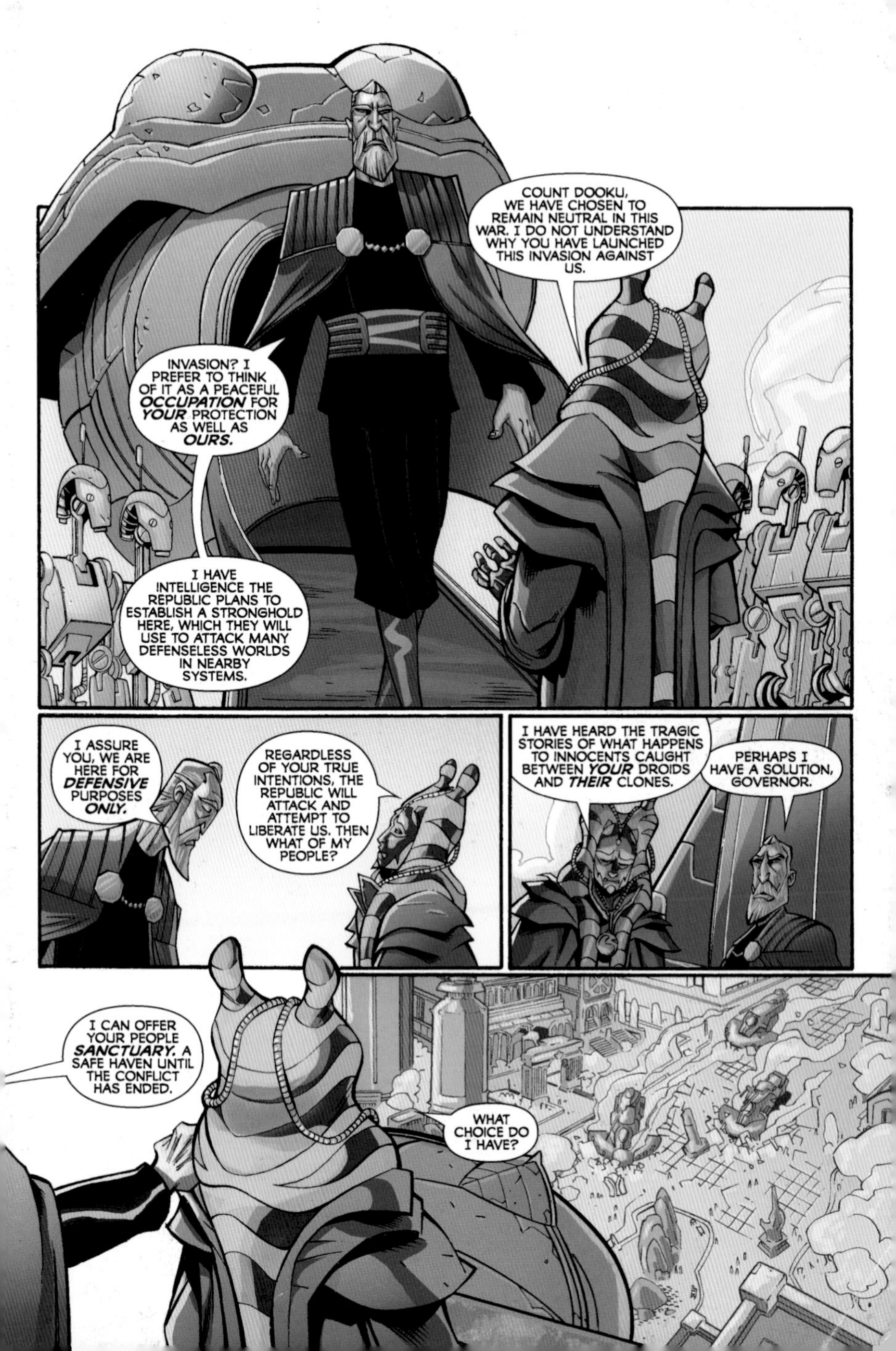
COUNT DOOKU, WE HAVE CHOSEN TO REMAIN NEUTRAL IN THIS WAR. I DO NOT UNDERSTAND WHY YOU HAVE LAUNCHED THIS INVASION AGAINST US.
INVASION? I PREFER TO THINK OF IT AS A PEACEFUL *OCCUPATION* FOR *YOUR* PROTECTION AS WELL AS *OURS.*
I HAVE INTELLIGENCE THE REPUBLIC PLANS TO ESTABLISH A STRONGHOLD HERE, WHICH THEY WILL USE TO ATTACK MANY DEFENSELESS WORLDS IN NEARBY SYSTEMS.
I ASSURE YOU, WE ARE HERE FOR *DEFENSIVE* PURPOSES *ONLY.*
REGARDLESS OF YOUR TRUE INTENTIONS, THE REPUBLIC WILL ATTACK AND ATTEMPT TO LIBERATE US. THEN WHAT OF MY PEOPLE?
I HAVE HEARD THE TRAGIC STORIES OF WHAT HAPPENS TO INNOCENTS CAUGHT BETWEEN *YOUR* DROIDS AND *THEIR* CLONES.
PERHAPS I HAVE A SOLUTION, GOVERNOR.
I CAN OFFER YOUR PEOPLE *SANCTUARY.* A SAFE HAVEN UNTIL THE CONFLICT HAS ENDED.
WHAT CHOICE DO I HAVE?

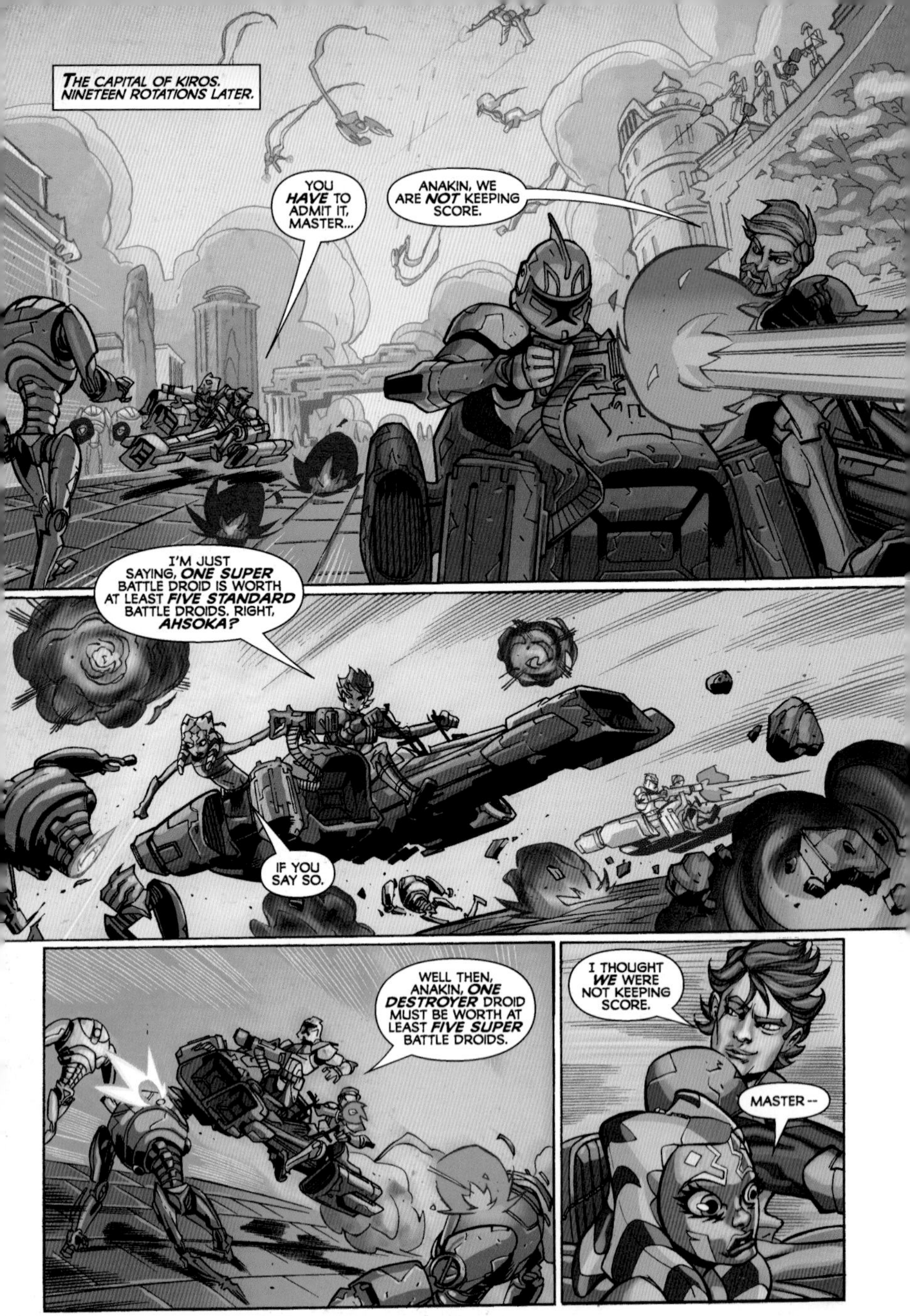
THE CAPITAL OF KIROS. NINETEEN ROTATIONS LATER.
YOU *HAVE* TO ADMIT IT, MASTER...
ANAKIN, WE ARE *NOT* KEEPING SCORE.
I'M JUST SAYING, *ONE SUPER* BATTLE DROID IS WORTH AT LEAST *FIVE STANDARD* BATTLE DROIDS. RIGHT, *AHSOKA?*
IF YOU SAY SO.
WELL THEN, ANAKIN, *ONE DESTROYER* DROID MUST BE WORTH AT LEAST *FIVE SUPER* BATTLE DROIDS.
I THOUGHT *WE* WERE NOT KEEPING SCORE.
MASTER --

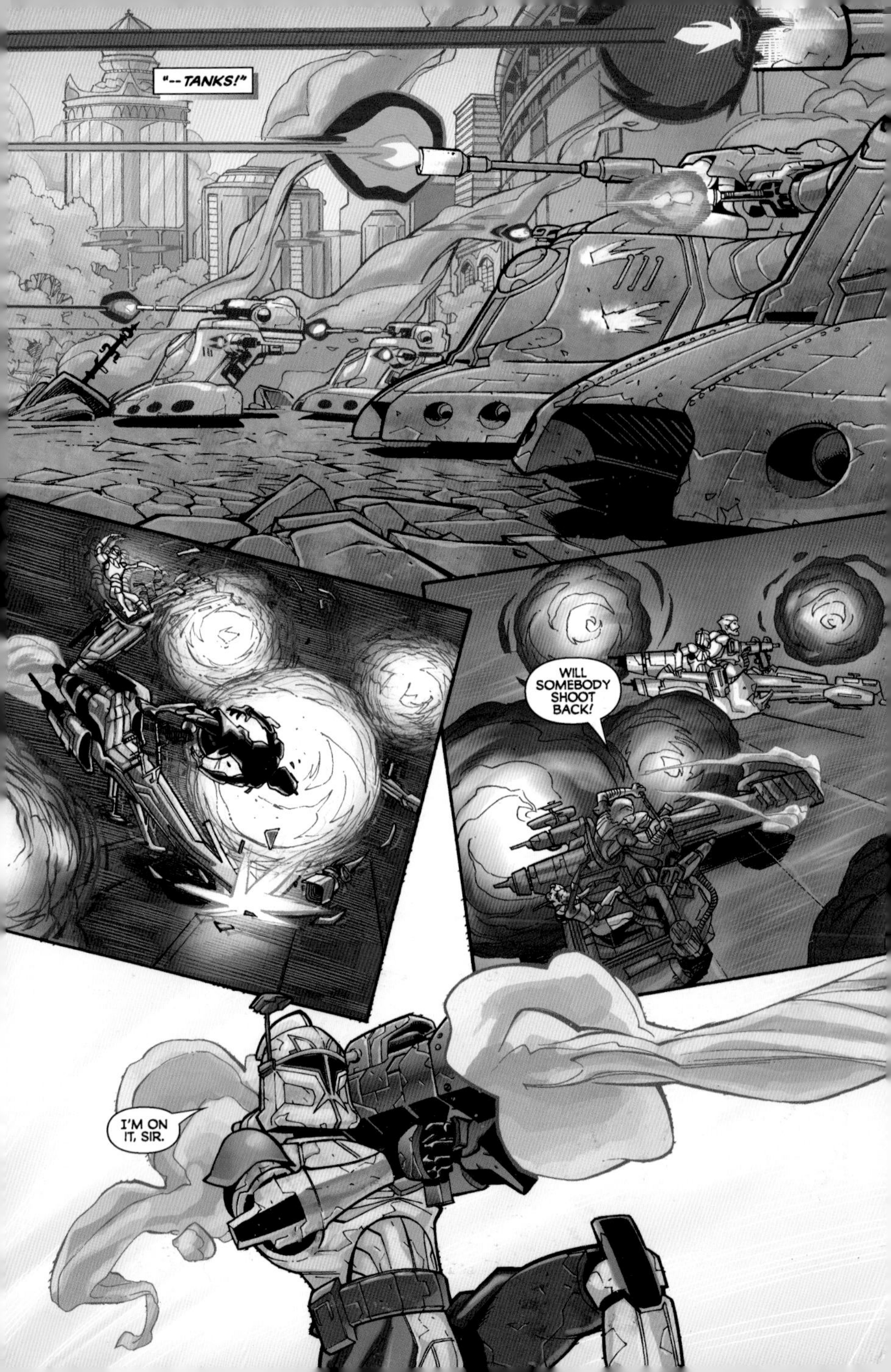
"--TANKS!"
WILL SOMEBODY SHOOT BACK!
I'M ON IT, SIR.

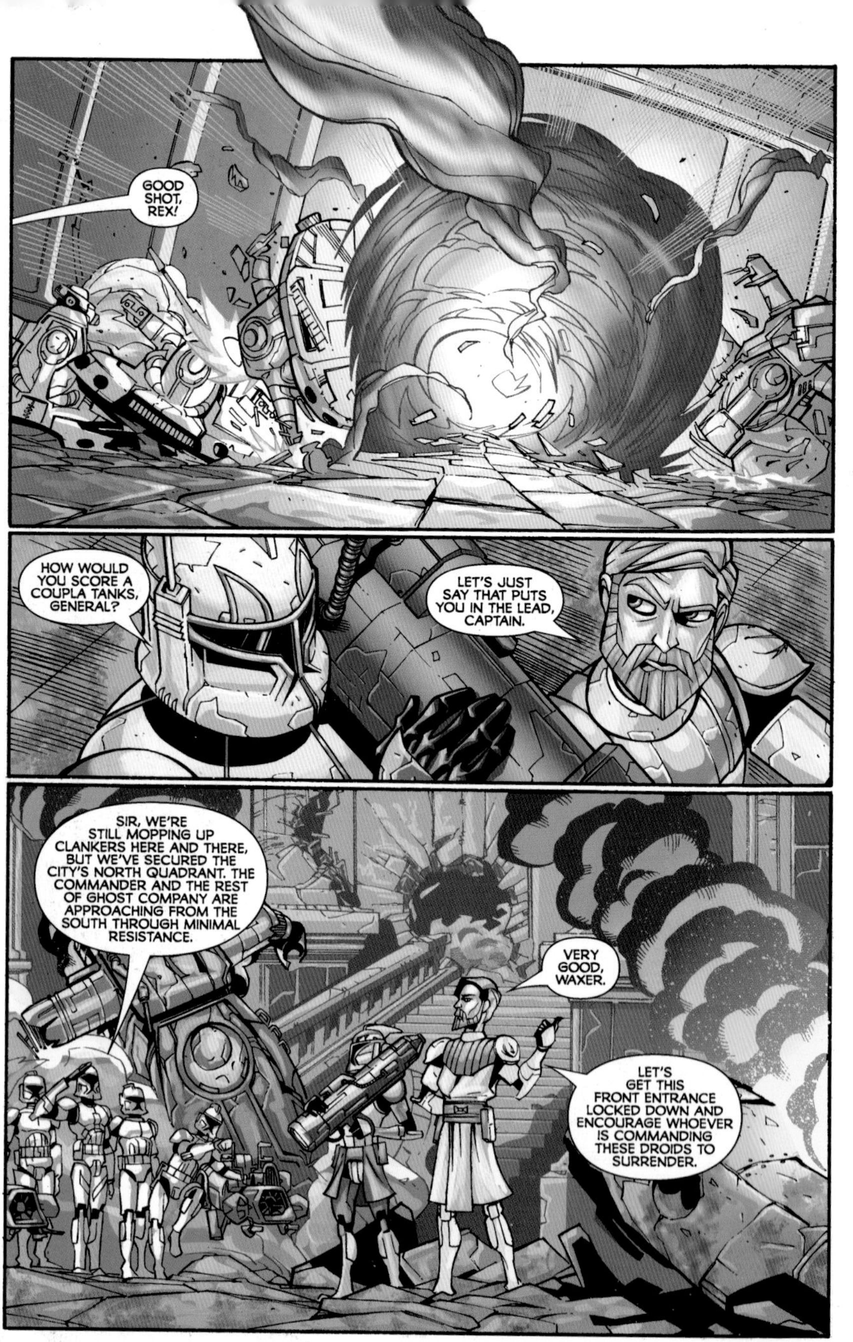
GOOD SHOT, REX!
HOW WOULD YOU SCORE A COUPLA TANKS, GENERAL?
LET'S JUST SAY THAT PUTS YOU IN THE LEAD, CAPTAIN.
SIR, WE'RE STILL MOPPING UP CLANKERS HERE AND THERE, BUT WE'VE SECURED THE CITY'S NORTH QUADRANT. THE COMMANDER AND THE REST OF GHOST COMPANY ARE APPROACHING FROM THE SOUTH THROUGH MINIMAL RESISTANCE.
VERY GOOD, WAXER.
LET'S GET THIS FRONT ENTRANCE LOCKED DOWN AND ENCOURAGE WHOEVER IS COMMANDING THESE DROIDS TO SURRENDER.

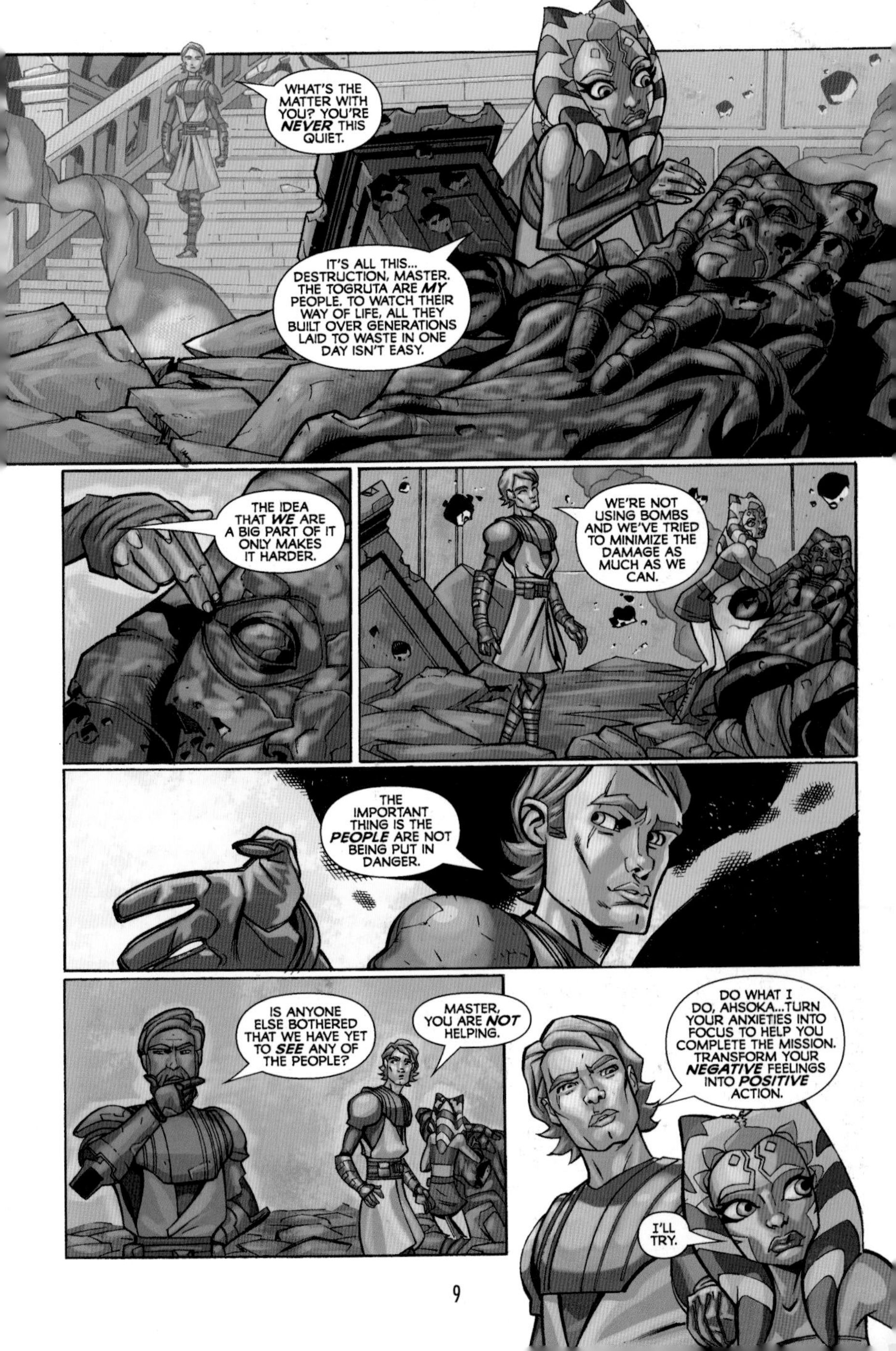
WHAT'S THE MATTER WITH YOU? YOU'RE NEVER THIS QUIET.
IT'S ALL THIS... DESTRUCTION, MASTER. THE TOGRUTA ARE MY PEOPLE. TO WATCH THEIR WAY OF LIFE, ALL THEY BUILT OVER GENERATIONS LAID TO WASTE IN ONE DAY ISN'T EASY.
THE IDEA THAT WE ARE A BIG PART OF IT ONLY MAKES IT HARDER.
WE'RE NOT USING BOMBS AND WE'VE TRIED TO MINIMIZE THE DAMAGE AS MUCH AS WE CAN.
THE IMPORTANT THING IS THE PEOPLE ARE NOT BEING PUT IN DANGER.
IS ANYONE ELSE BOTHERED THAT WE HAVE YET TO SEE ANY OF THE PEOPLE?
MASTER, YOU ARE NOT HELPING.
DO WHAT I DO, AHSOKA...TURN YOUR ANXIETIES INTO FOCUS TO HELP YOU COMPLETE THE MISSION. TRANSFORM YOUR NEGATIVE FEELINGS INTO POSITIVE ACTION.
I'LL TRY.

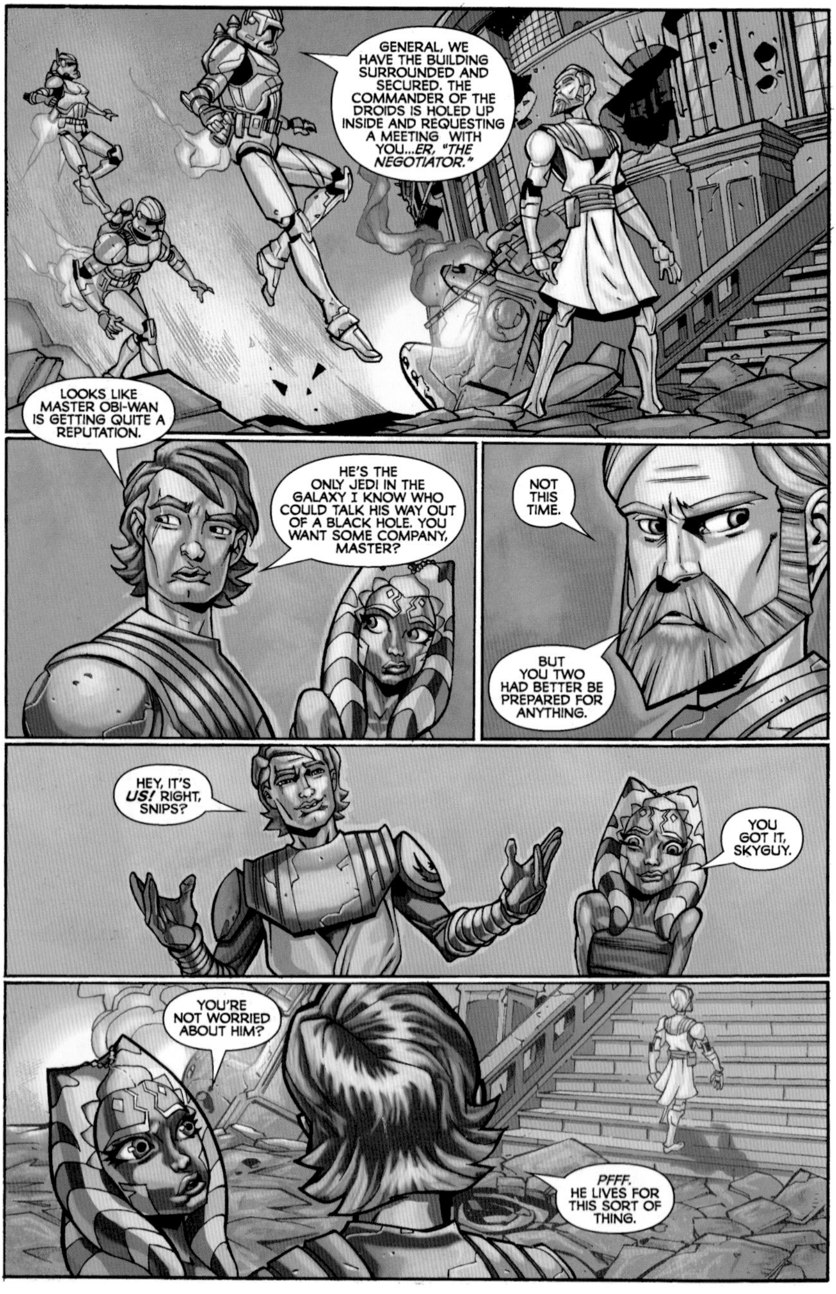
GENERAL, WE HAVE THE BUILDING SURROUNDED AND SECURED. THE COMMANDER OF THE DROIDS IS HOLED UP INSIDE AND REQUESTING A MEETING WITH YOU...ER, "THE NEGOTIATOR."
LOOKS LIKE MASTER OBI-WAN IS GETTING QUITE A REPUTATION.
HE'S THE ONLY JEDI IN THE GALAXY I KNOW WHO COULD TALK HIS WAY OUT OF A BLACK HOLE. YOU WANT SOME COMPANY, MASTER?
NOT THIS TIME.
BUT YOU TWO HAD BETTER BE PREPARED FOR ANYTHING.
HEY, IT'S US! RIGHT, SNIPS?
YOU GOT IT, SKYGUY.
YOU'RE NOT WORRIED ABOUT HIM?
PFFF. HE LIVES FOR THIS SORT OF THING.

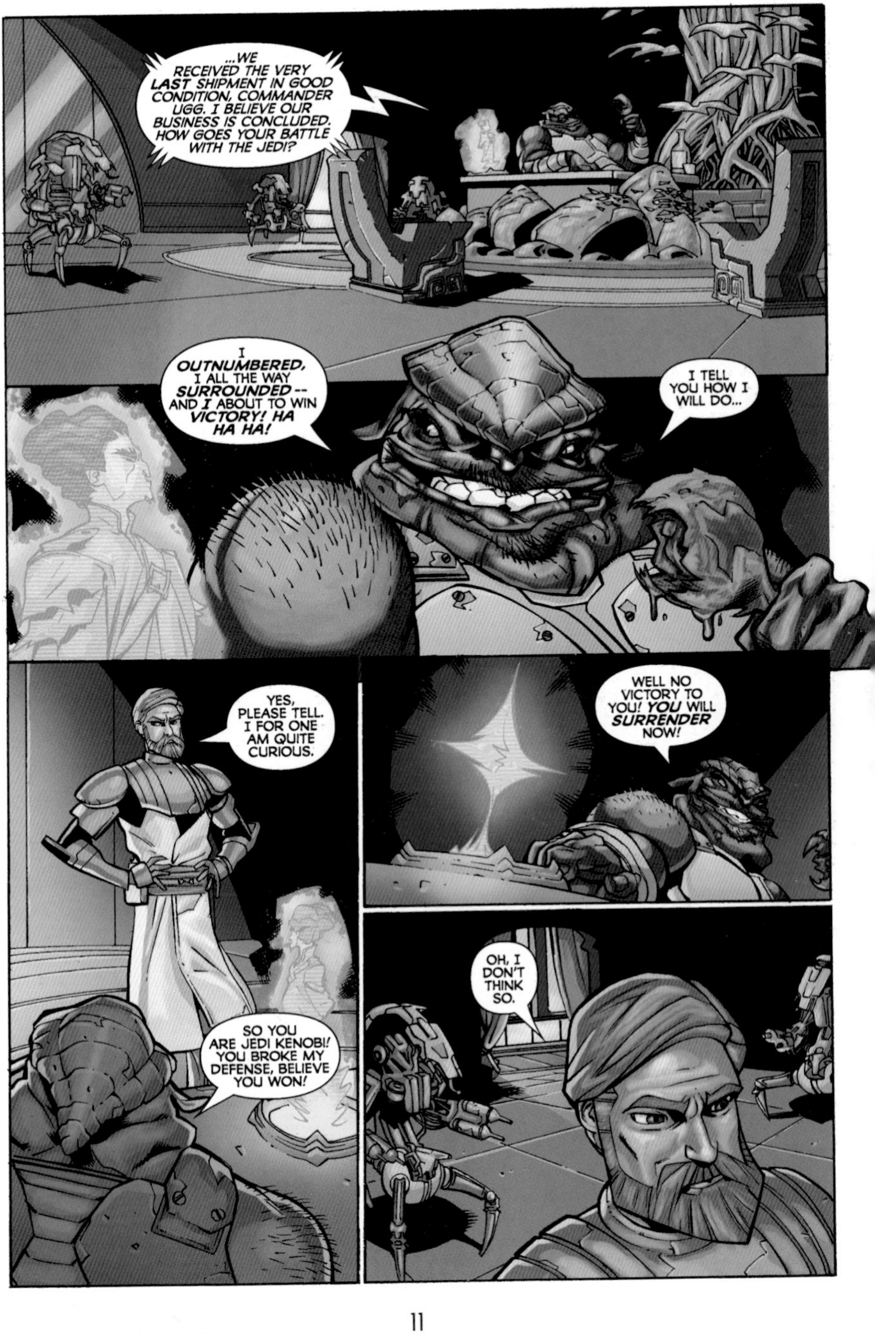
...WE RECEIVED THE VERY LAST SHIPMENT IN GOOD CONDITION, COMMANDER UGG. I BELIEVE OUR BUSINESS IS CONCLUDED. HOW GOES YOUR BATTLE WITH THE JEDI?
I OUTNUMBERED, I ALL THE WAY SURROUNDED -- AND I ABOUT TO WIN VICTORY! HA HA HA!
I TELL YOU HOW I WILL DO...
YES, PLEASE TELL. I FOR ONE AM QUITE CURIOUS.
SO YOU ARE JEDI KENOBI! YOU BROKE MY DEFENSE, BELIEVE YOU WON!
WELL NO VICTORY TO YOU! YOU WILL SURRENDER NOW!
OH, I DON'T THINK SO.

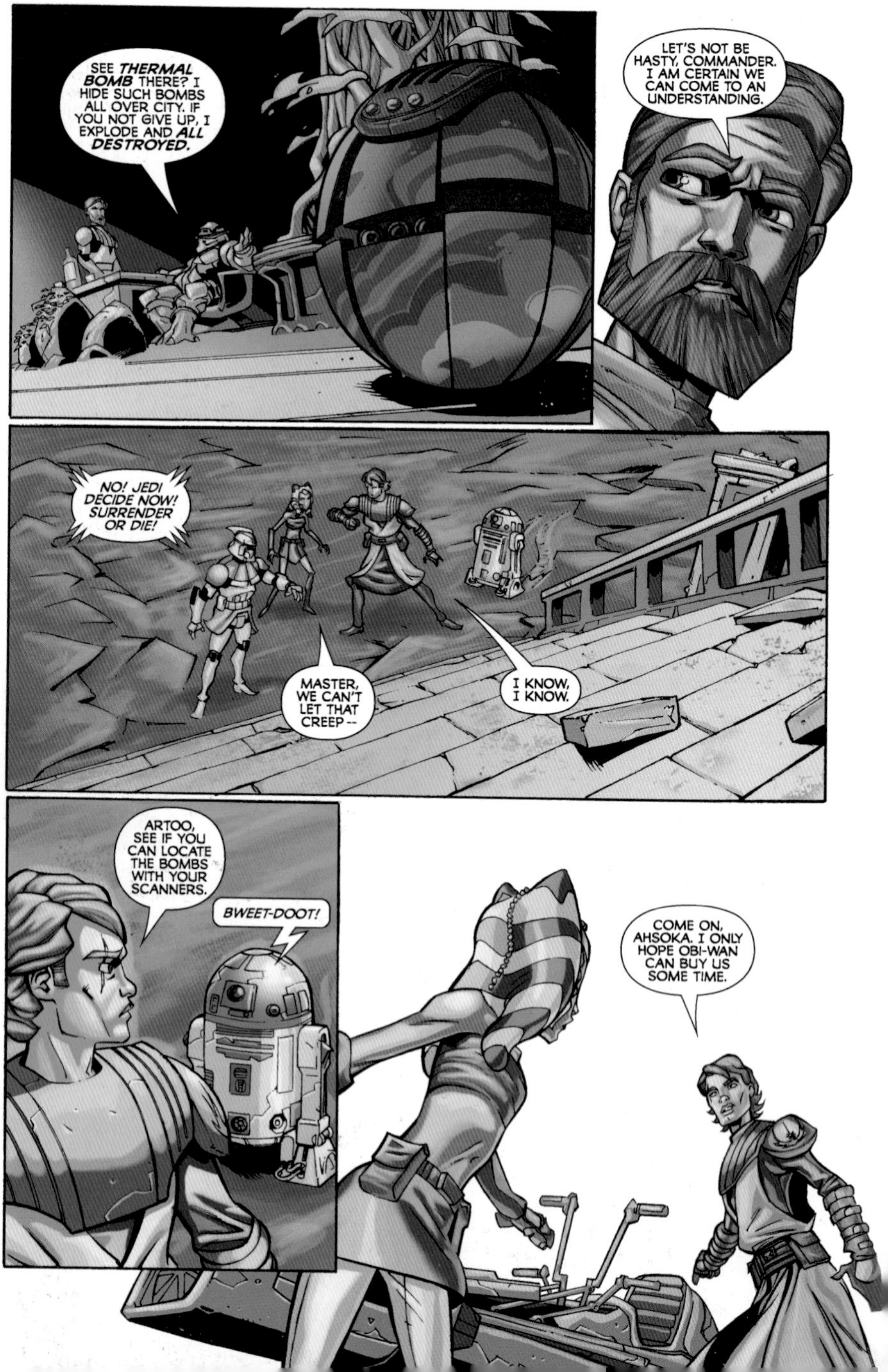
SEE *THERMAL BOMB* THERE? I HIDE SUCH BOMBS ALL OVER CITY. IF YOU NOT GIVE UP, I EXPLODE AND *ALL DESTROYED.*
LET'S NOT BE HASTY, COMMANDER. I AM CERTAIN WE CAN COME TO AN UNDERSTANDING.
NO! JEDI DECIDE NOW! SURRENDER OR DIE!
MASTER, WE CAN'T LET THAT CREEP --
I KNOW, I KNOW.
ARTOO, SEE IF YOU CAN LOCATE THE BOMBS WITH YOUR SCANNERS.
BWEET-DOOT!
COME ON, AHSOKA. I ONLY HOPE OBI-WAN CAN BUY US SOME TIME.

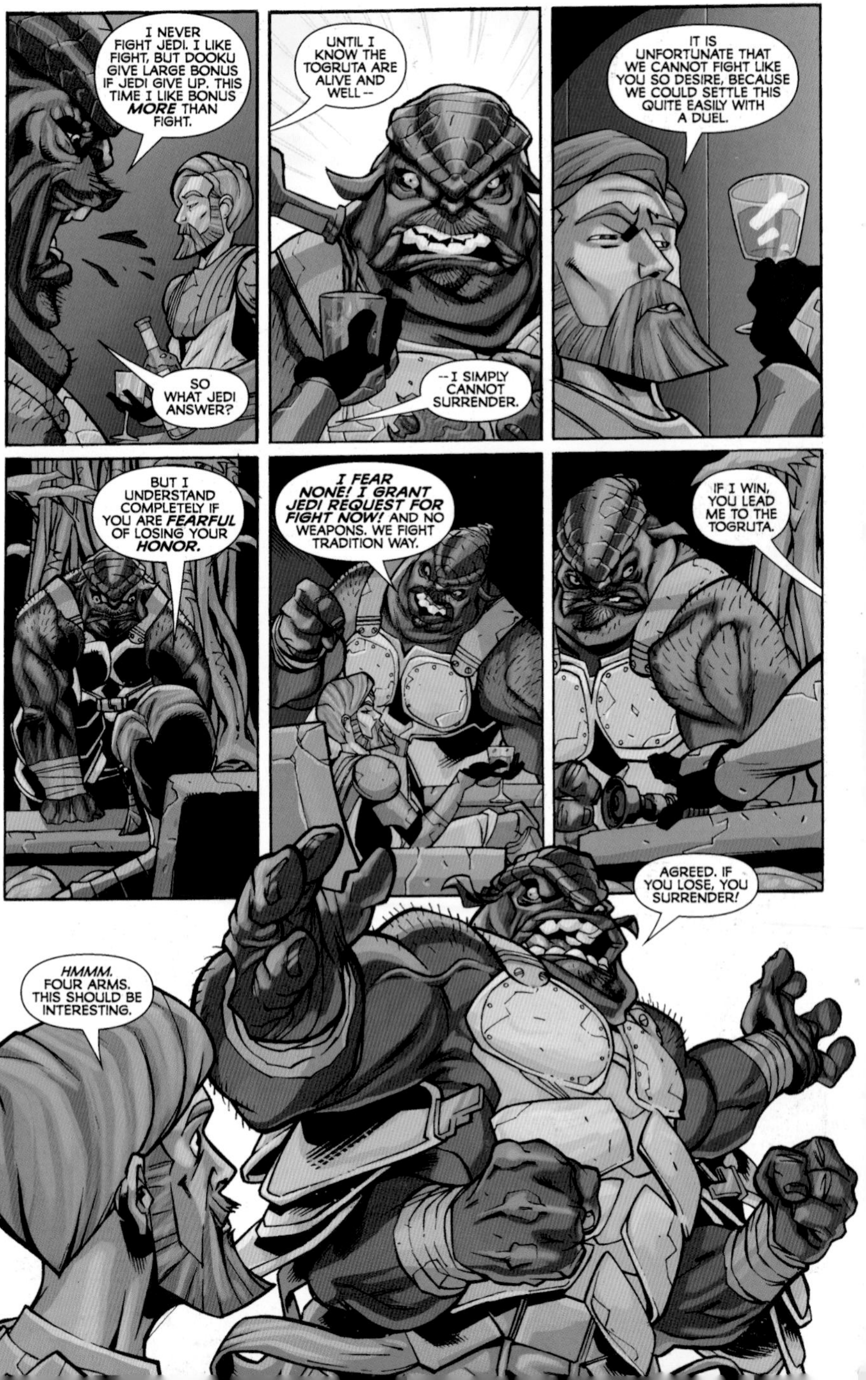
I NEVER FIGHT JEDI. I LIKE FIGHT, BUT DOOKU GIVE LARGE BONUS IF JEDI GIVE UP. THIS TIME I LIKE BONUS *MORE* THAN FIGHT.
SO WHAT JEDI ANSWER?
UNTIL I KNOW THE TOGRUTA ARE ALIVE AND WELL --
--I SIMPLY CANNOT SURRENDER.
IT IS UNFORTUNATE THAT WE CANNOT FIGHT LIKE YOU SO DESIRE, BECAUSE WE COULD SETTLE THIS QUITE EASILY WITH A DUEL.
BUT I UNDERSTAND COMPLETELY IF YOU ARE ***FEARFUL*** OF LOSING YOUR ***HONOR.***
I FEAR NONE! I GRANT JEDI REQUEST FOR FIGHT NOW! AND NO WEAPONS. WE FIGHT TRADITION WAY.
IF I WIN, YOU LEAD ME TO THE TOGRUTA.
AGREED. IF YOU LOSE, YOU SURRENDER!
HMMM. FOUR ARMS. THIS SHOULD BE INTERESTING.

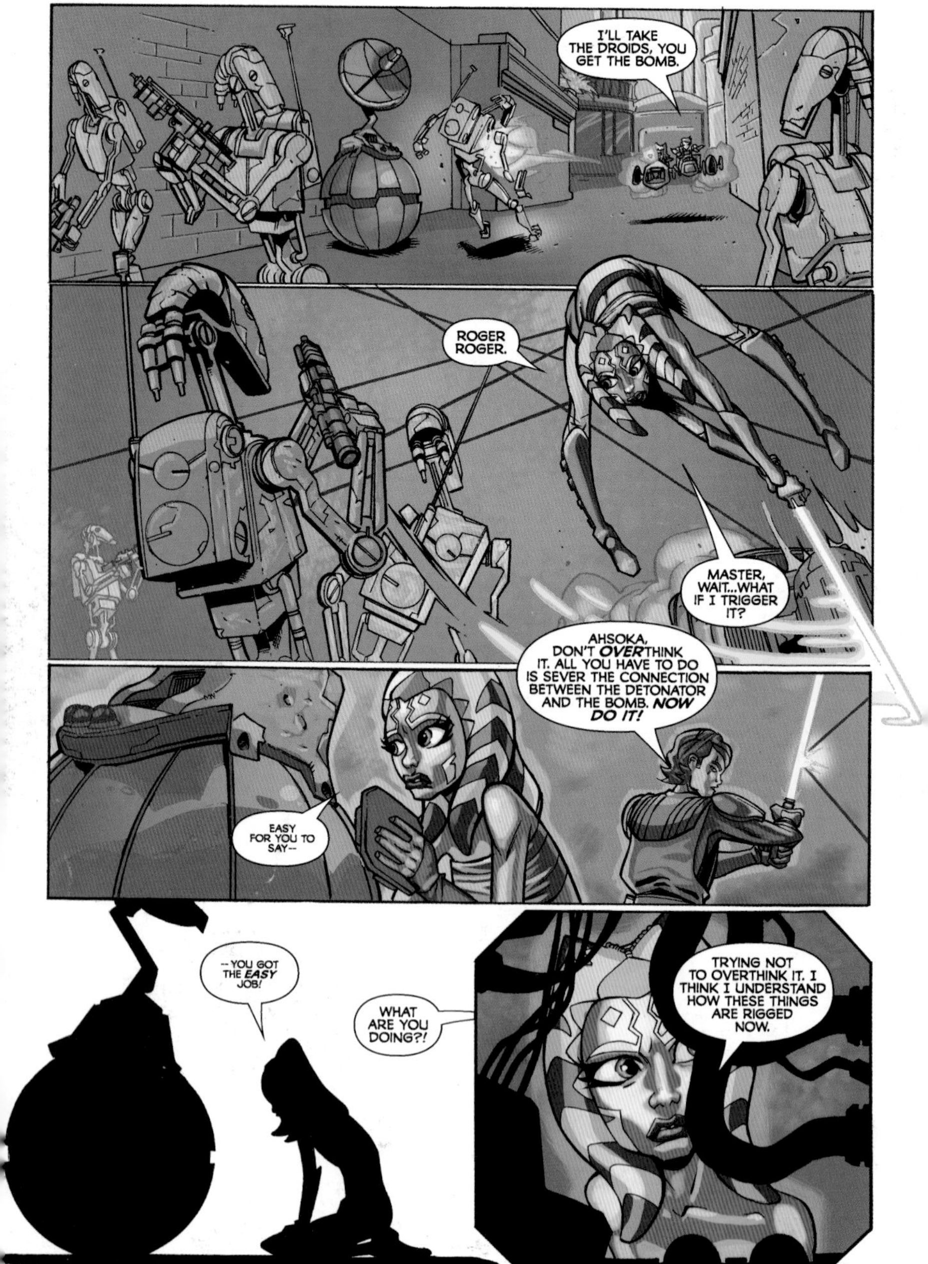
I'LL TAKE THE DROIDS, YOU GET THE BOMB.
ROGER ROGER.
MASTER, WAIT...WHAT IF I TRIGGER IT?
AHSOKA, DON'T ***OVER***THINK IT. ALL YOU HAVE TO DO IS SEVER THE CONNECTION BETWEEN THE DETONATOR AND THE BOMB. ***NOW DO IT!***
EASY FOR YOU TO SAY--
--YOU GOT THE ***EASY*** JOB!
WHAT ARE YOU DOING?!
TRYING NOT TO OVERTHINK IT. I THINK I UNDERSTAND HOW THESE THINGS ARE RIGGED NOW.

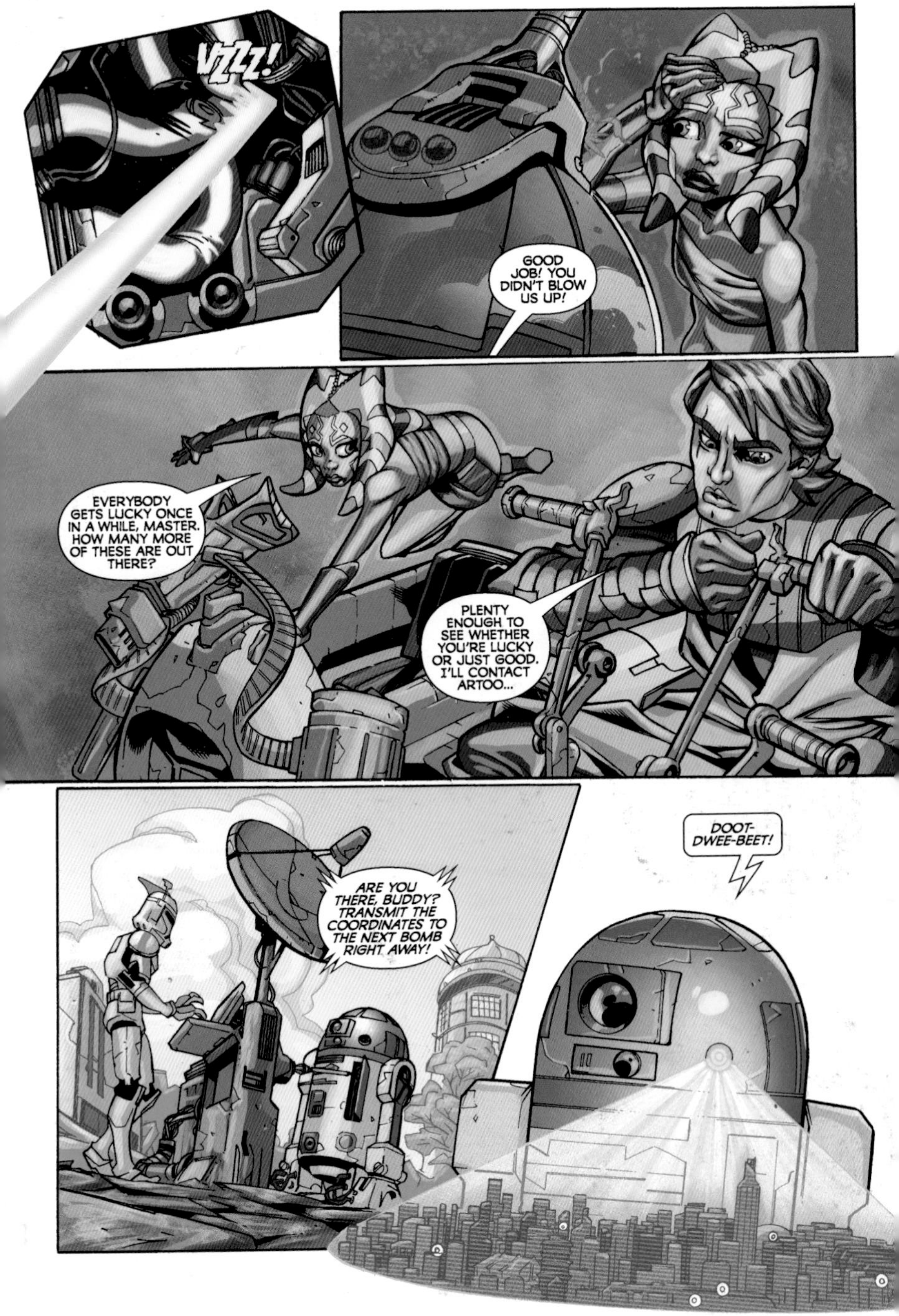
VZZZ!
GOOD JOB! YOU DIDN'T BLOW US UP!
EVERYBODY GETS LUCKY ONCE IN A WHILE, MASTER. HOW MANY MORE OF THESE ARE OUT THERE?
PLENTY ENOUGH TO SEE WHETHER YOU'RE LUCKY OR JUST GOOD. I'LL CONTACT ARTOO...
ARE YOU THERE, BUDDY? TRANSMIT THE COORDINATES TO THE NEXT BOMB RIGHT AWAY!
DOOT-DWEE-BEET!

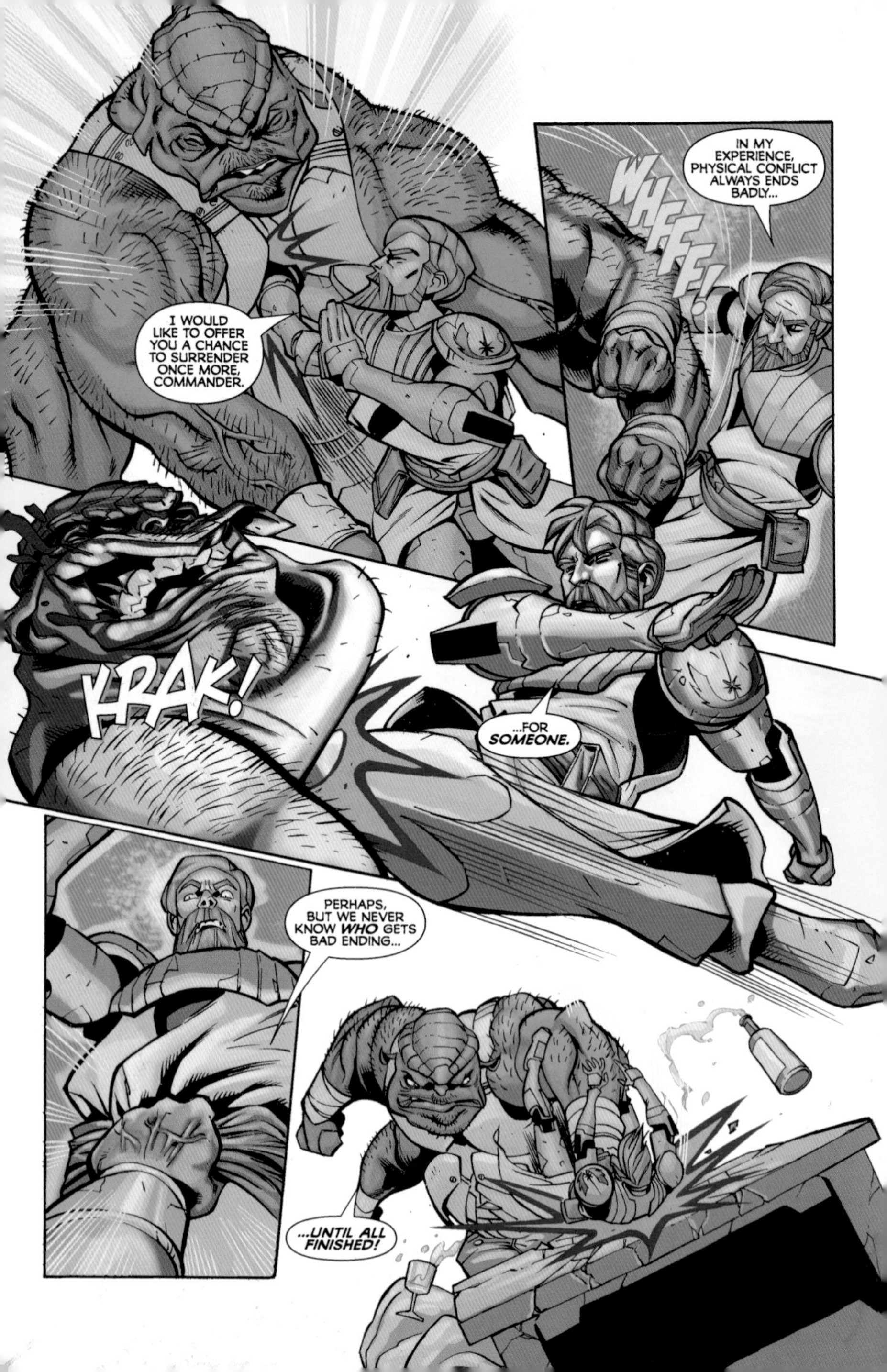

I WOULD LIKE TO OFFER YOU A CHANCE TO SURRENDER ONCE MORE, COMMANDER.
WHFFF!
IN MY EXPERIENCE, PHYSICAL CONFLICT ALWAYS ENDS BADLY...
KRAK!
...FOR *SOMEONE.*
PERHAPS, BUT WE NEVER KNOW *WHO* GETS BAD ENDING...
...UNTIL ALL FINISHED!

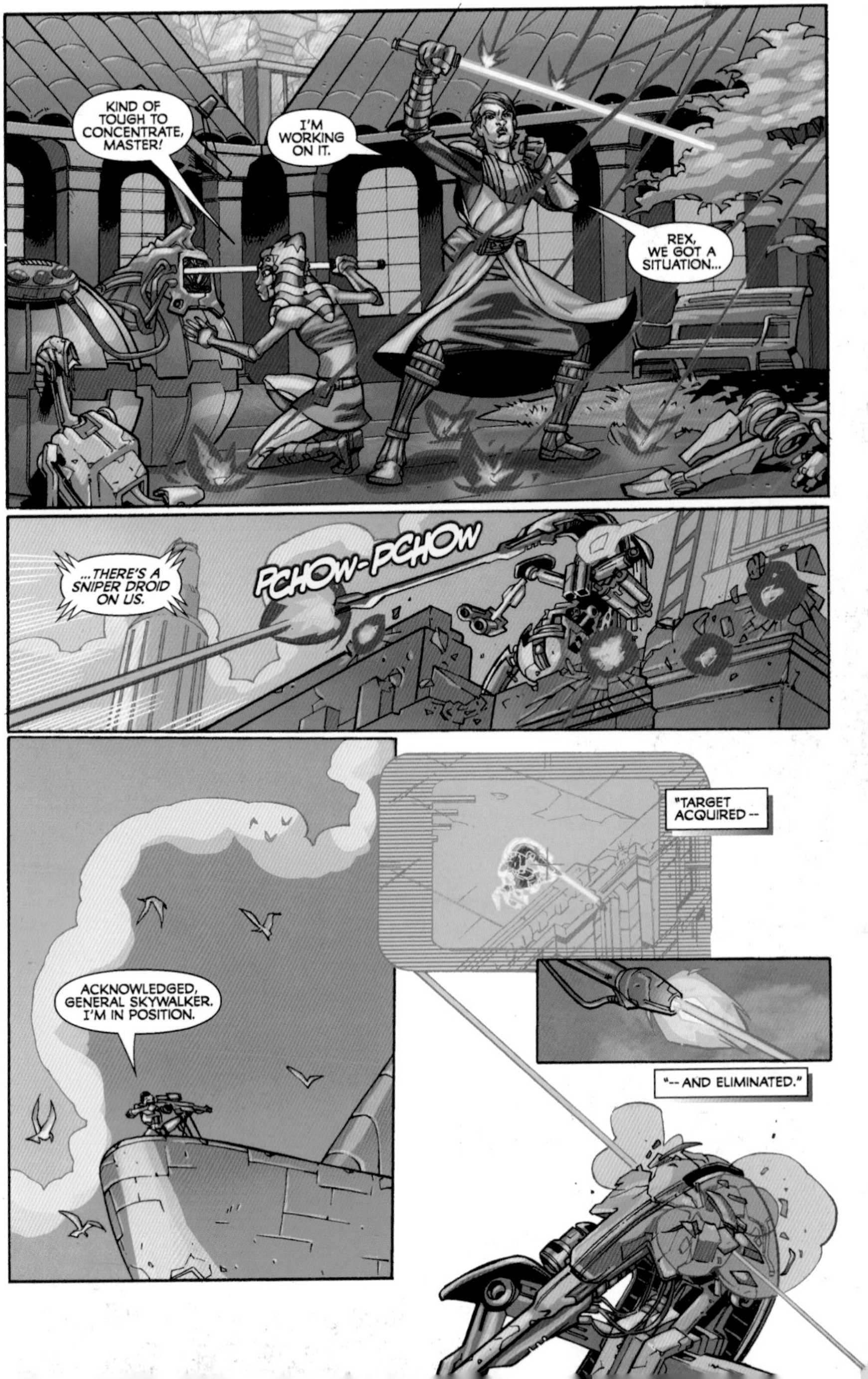
KIND OF TOUGH TO CONCENTRATE, MASTER!
I'M WORKING ON IT.
REX, WE GOT A SITUATION...
...THERE'S A SNIPER DROID ON US.
PCHOW-PCHOW
ACKNOWLEDGED, GENERAL SKYWALKER. I'M IN POSITION.
"TARGET ACQUIRED --
"-- AND ELIMINATED."

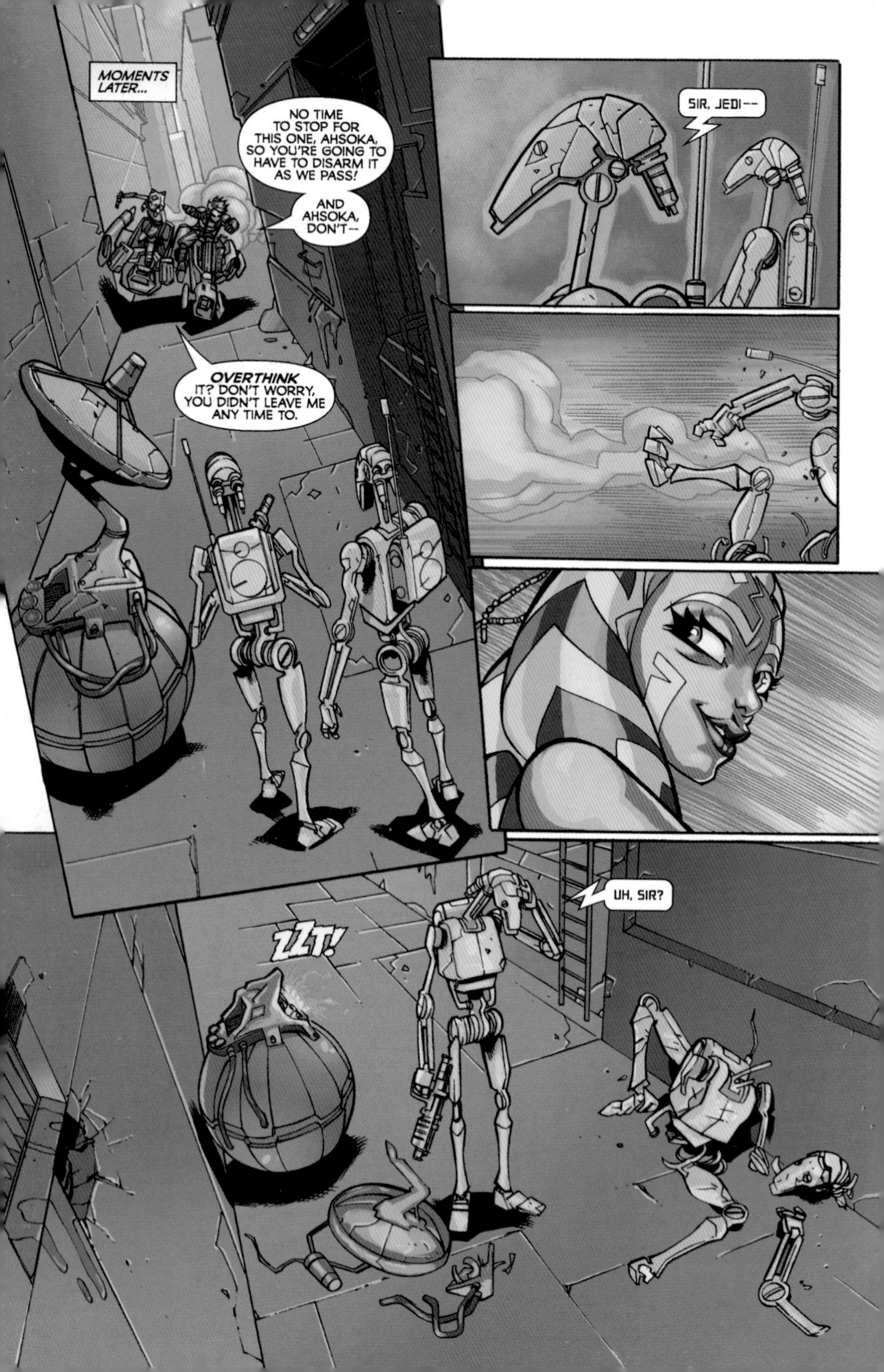
MOMENTS LATER...
NO TIME TO STOP FOR THIS ONE, AHSOKA, SO YOU'RE GOING TO HAVE TO DISARM IT AS WE PASS!
AND AHSOKA, DON'T--
OVERTHINK IT? DON'T WORRY, YOU DIDN'T LEAVE ME ANY TIME TO.
SIR, JEDI--
ZZT!
UH, SIR?

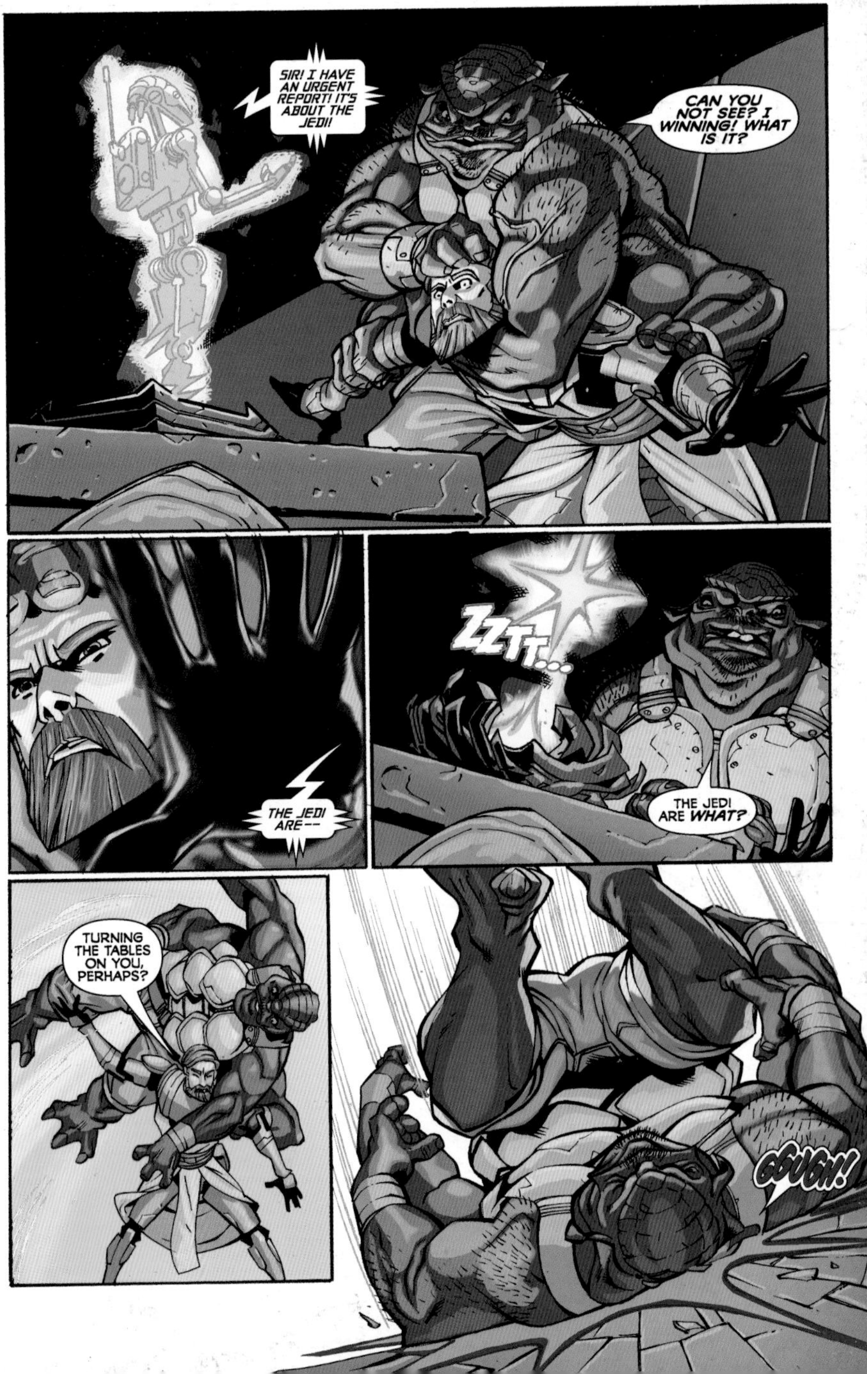
SIR! I HAVE AN URGENT REPORT! IT'S ABOUT THE JEDI!
CAN YOU NOT SEE? I WINNING! WHAT IS IT?
THE JEDI ARE--
ZZTT...
THE JEDI ARE WHAT?
TURNING THE TABLES ON YOU, PERHAPS?
GGUGH!

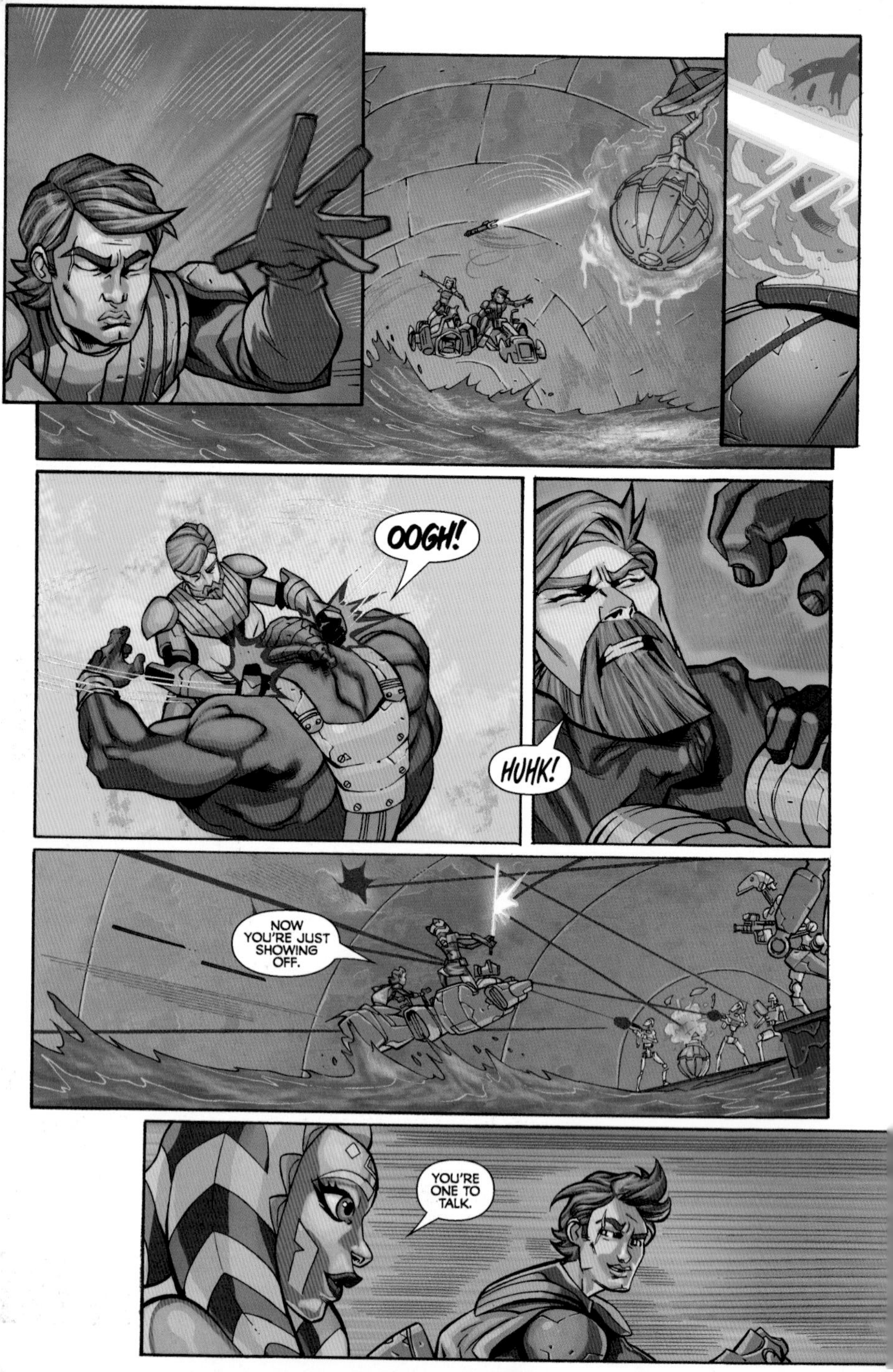
OOGH!
HUHK!
NOW YOU'RE JUST SHOWING OFF.
YOU'RE ONE TO TALK.

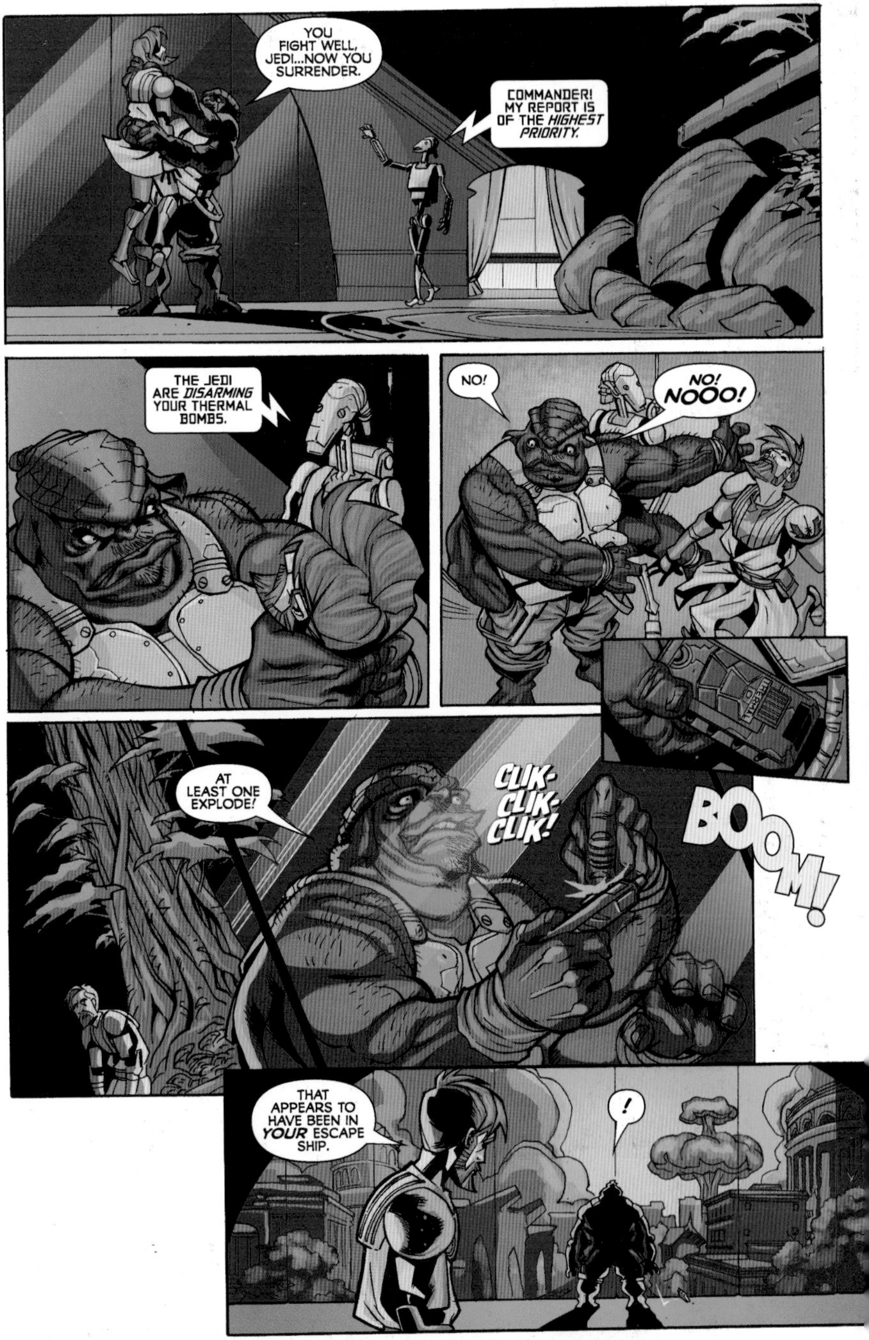
YOU FIGHT WELL, JEDI...NOW YOU SURRENDER.
COMMANDER! MY REPORT IS OF THE HIGHEST PRIORITY.
THE JEDI ARE DISARMING YOUR THERMAL BOMBS.
NO!
NO! NOOO!
THERMAL
AT LEAST ONE EXPLODE!
CLIK-CLIK-CLIK!
BOOM!
THAT APPEARS TO HAVE BEEN IN YOUR ESCAPE SHIP.
!

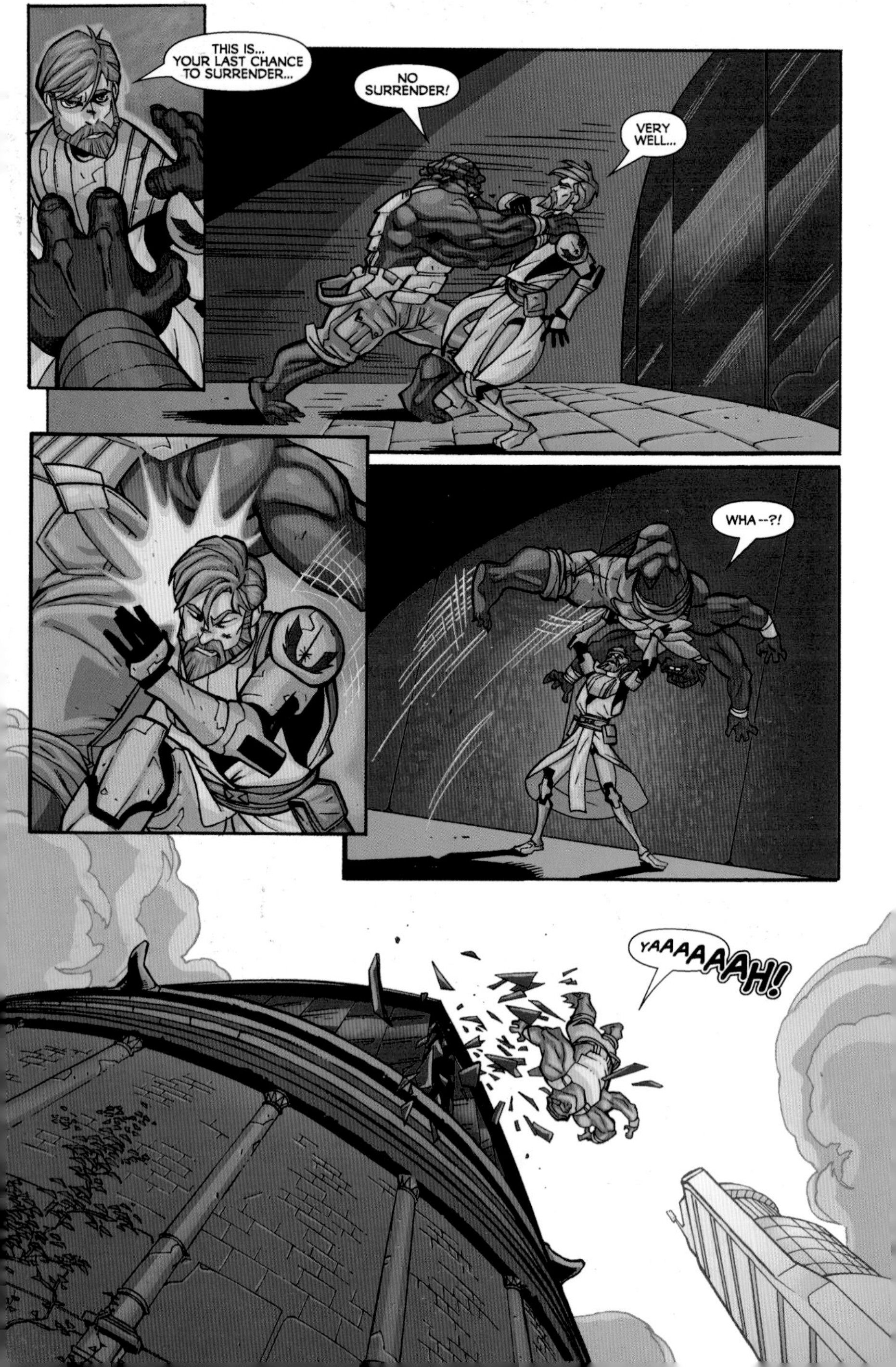
THIS IS... YOUR LAST CHANCE TO SURRENDER...
NO SURRENDER!
VERY WELL...
WHA--?!
YAAAAAAH!

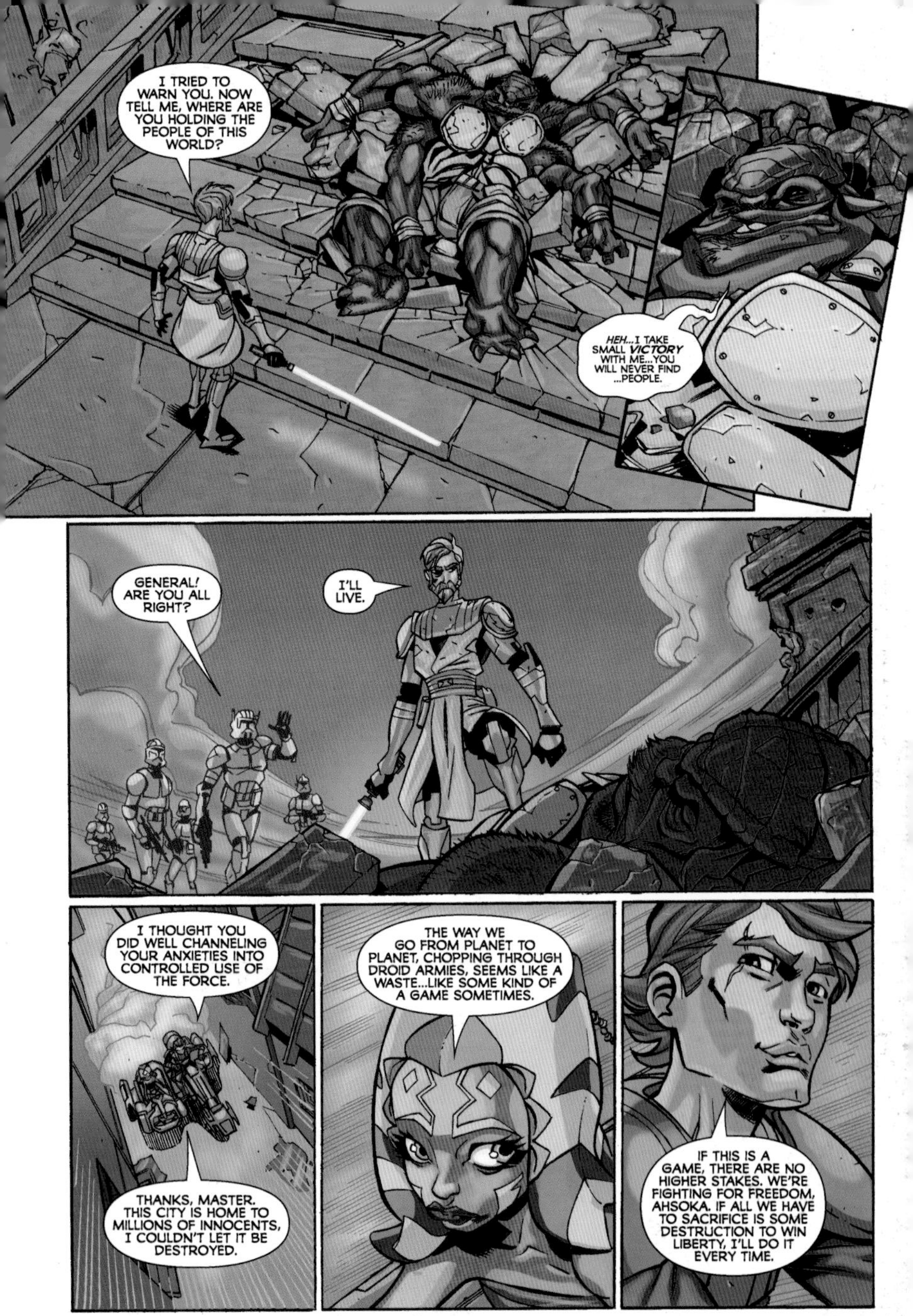

I TRIED TO WARN YOU. NOW TELL ME, WHERE ARE YOU HOLDING THE PEOPLE OF THIS WORLD?
HEH...I TAKE SMALL ***VICTORY*** WITH ME...YOU WILL NEVER FIND ...PEOPLE.
GENERAL! ARE YOU ALL RIGHT?
I'LL LIVE.
I THOUGHT YOU DID WELL CHANNELING YOUR ANXIETIES INTO CONTROLLED USE OF THE FORCE.
THANKS, MASTER. THIS CITY IS HOME TO MILLIONS OF INNOCENTS, I COULDN'T LET IT BE DESTROYED.
THE WAY WE GO FROM PLANET TO PLANET, CHOPPING THROUGH DROID ARMIES, SEEMS LIKE A WASTE...LIKE SOME KIND OF A GAME SOMETIMES.
IF THIS IS A GAME, THERE ARE NO HIGHER STAKES. WE'RE FIGHTING FOR FREEDOM, AHSOKA. IF ALL WE HAVE TO SACRIFICE IS SOME DESTRUCTION TO WIN LIBERTY, I'LL DO IT EVERY TIME.

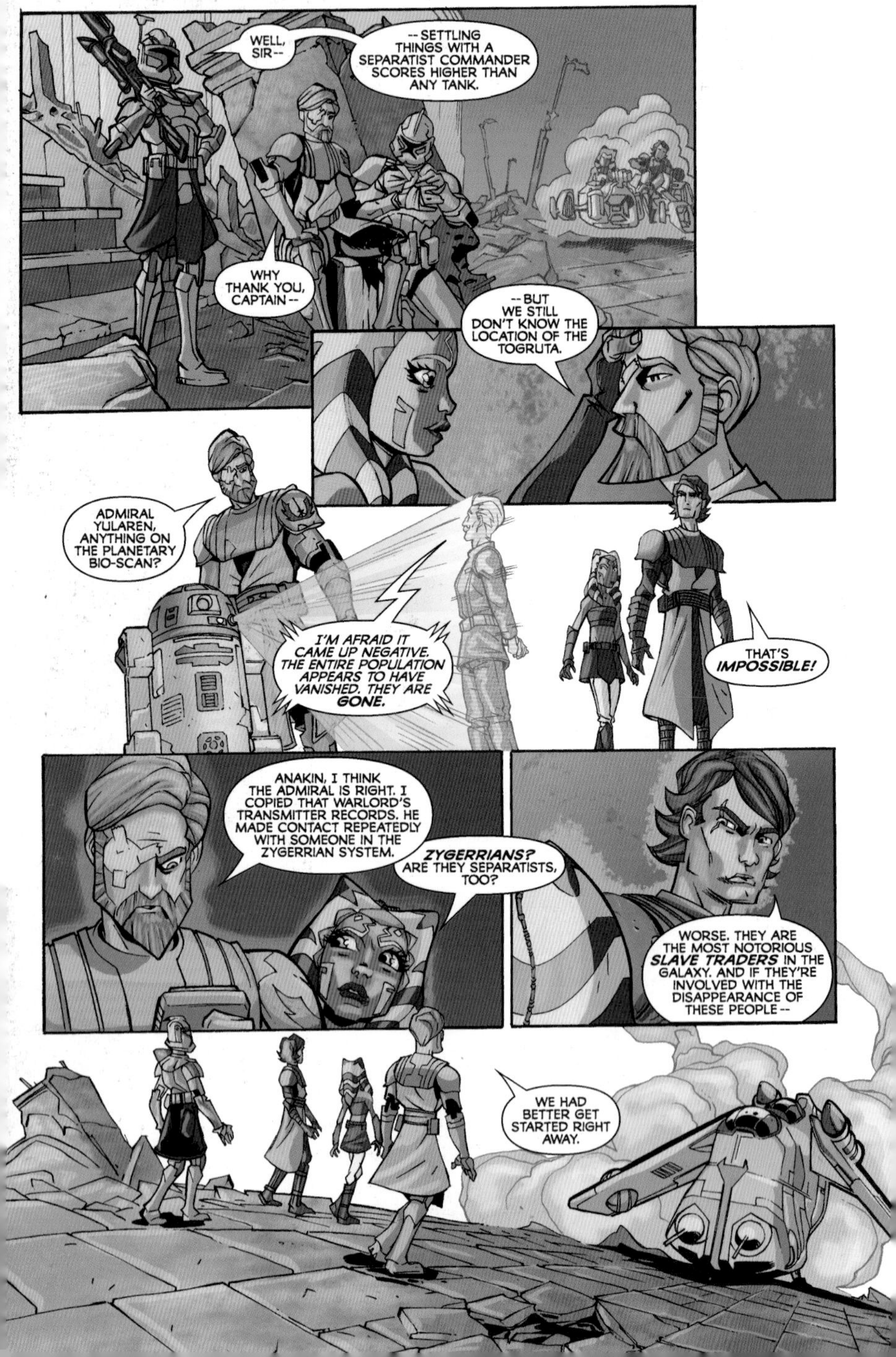
WELL, SIR--
--SETTLING THINGS WITH A SEPARATIST COMMANDER SCORES HIGHER THAN ANY TANK.
WHY THANK YOU, CAPTAIN--
--BUT WE STILL DON'T KNOW THE LOCATION OF THE TOGRUTA.
ADMIRAL YULAREN, ANYTHING ON THE PLANETARY BIO-SCAN?
I'M AFRAID IT CAME UP NEGATIVE. THE ENTIRE POPULATION APPEARS TO HAVE VANISHED. THEY ARE GONE.
THAT'S IMPOSSIBLE!
ANAKIN, I THINK THE ADMIRAL IS RIGHT. I COPIED THAT WARLORD'S TRANSMITTER RECORDS. HE MADE CONTACT REPEATEDLY WITH SOMEONE IN THE ZYGERRIAN SYSTEM.
ZYGERRIANS? ARE THEY SEPARATISTS, TOO?
WORSE. THEY ARE THE MOST NOTORIOUS SLAVE TRADERS IN THE GALAXY. AND IF THEY'RE INVOLVED WITH THE DISAPPEARANCE OF THESE PEOPLE--
WE HAD BETTER GET STARTED RIGHT AWAY.

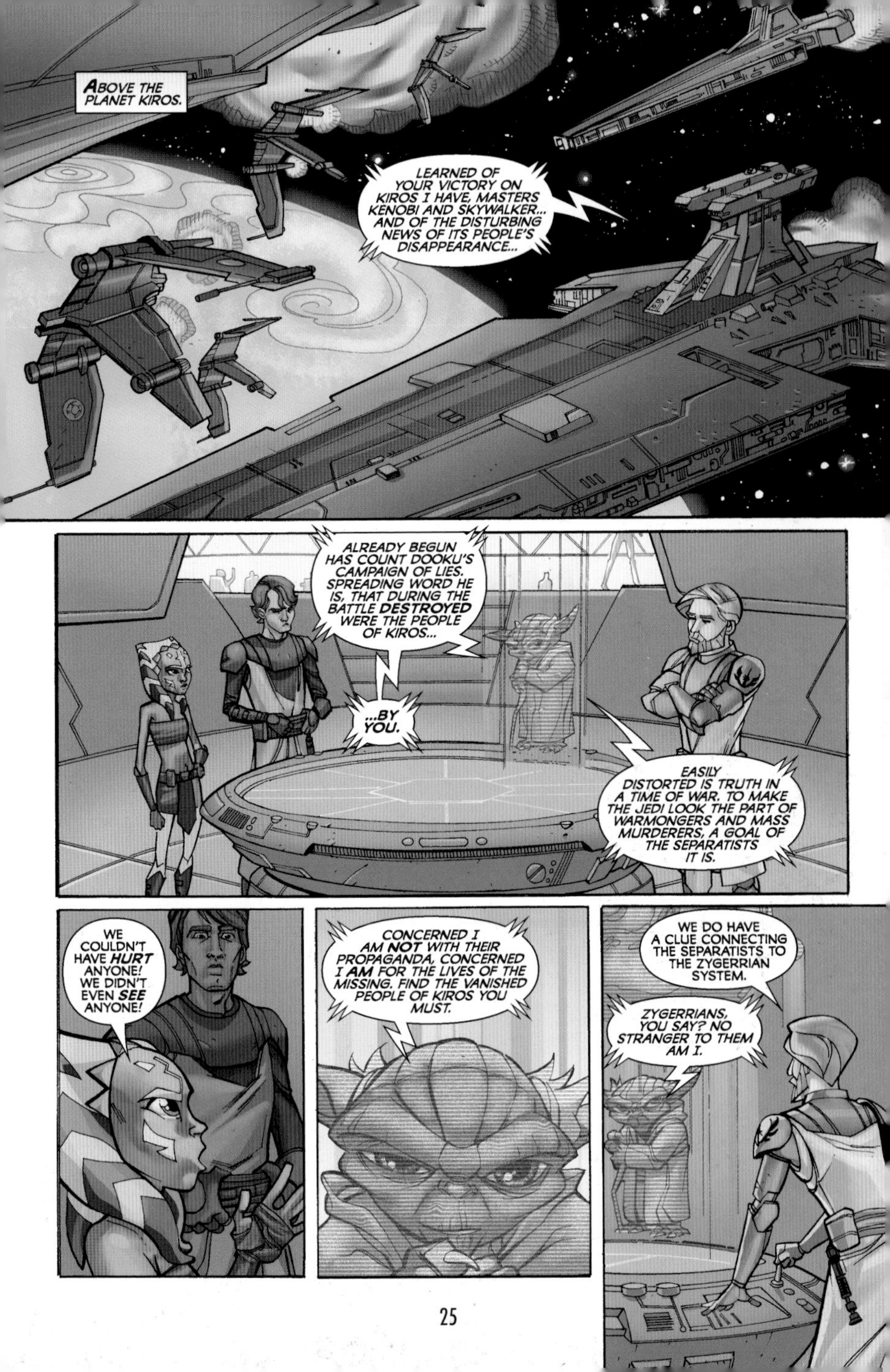
ABOVE THE PLANET KIROS.
LEARNED OF YOUR VICTORY ON KIROS I HAVE, MASTERS KENOBI AND SKYWALKER... AND OF THE DISTURBING NEWS OF ITS PEOPLE'S DISAPPEARANCE...
ALREADY BEGUN HAS COUNT DOOKU'S CAMPAIGN OF LIES. SPREADING WORD HE IS, THAT DURING THE BATTLE DESTROYED WERE THE PEOPLE OF KIROS...
...BY YOU.
EASILY DISTORTED IS TRUTH IN A TIME OF WAR. TO MAKE THE JEDI LOOK THE PART OF WARMONGERS AND MASS MURDERERS, A GOAL OF THE SEPARATISTS IT IS.
WE COULDN'T HAVE HURT ANYONE! WE DIDN'T EVEN SEE ANYONE!
CONCERNED I AM NOT WITH THEIR PROPAGANDA, CONCERNED I AM FOR THE LIVES OF THE MISSING. FIND THE VANISHED PEOPLE OF KIROS YOU MUST.
WE DO HAVE A CLUE CONNECTING THE SEPARATISTS TO THE ZYGERRIAN SYSTEM.
ZYGERRIANS, YOU SAY? NO STRANGER TO THEM AM I.

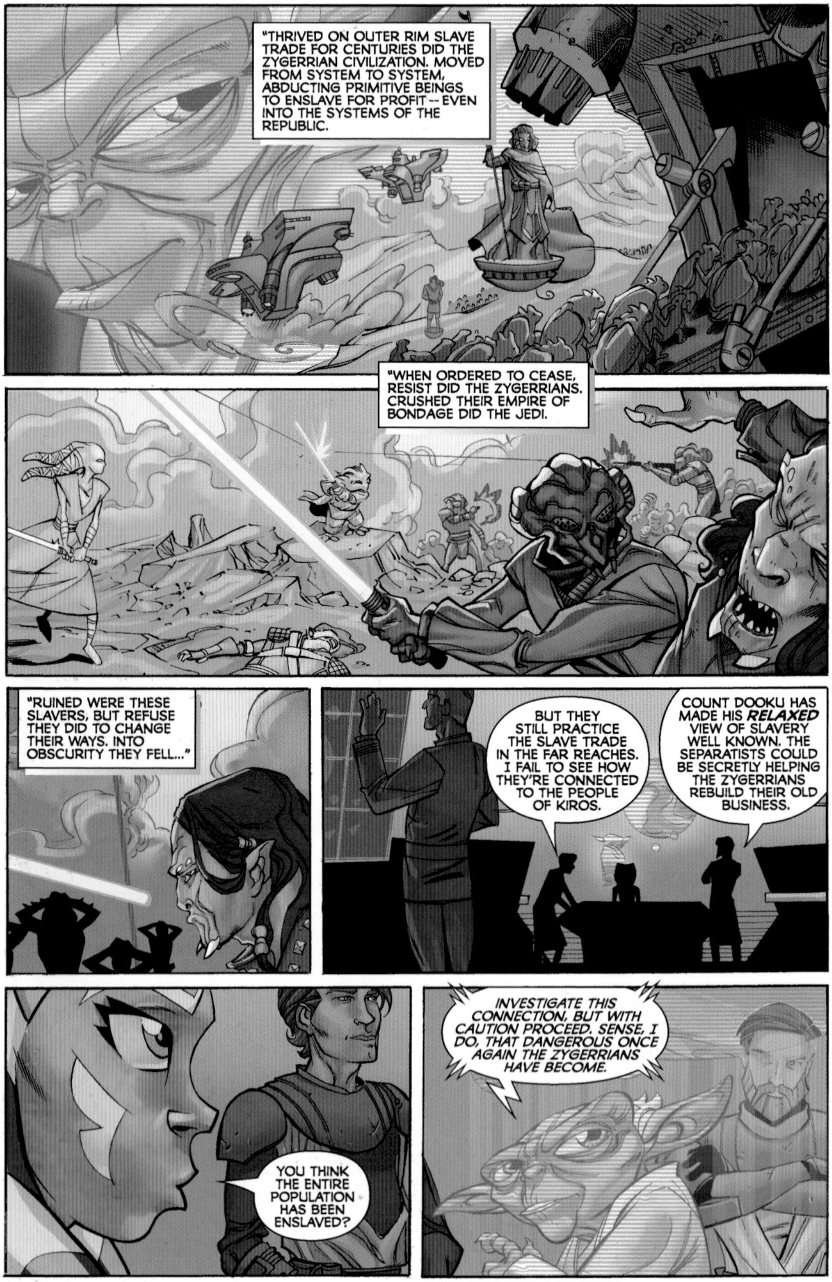
"THRIVED ON OUTER RIM SLAVE TRADE FOR CENTURIES DID THE ZYGERRIAN CIVILIZATION. MOVED FROM SYSTEM TO SYSTEM, ABDUCTING PRIMITIVE BEINGS TO ENSLAVE FOR PROFIT -- EVEN INTO THE SYSTEMS OF THE REPUBLIC.
"WHEN ORDERED TO CEASE, RESIST DID THE ZYGERRIANS. CRUSHED THEIR EMPIRE OF BONDAGE DID THE JEDI.
"RUINED WERE THESE SLAVERS, BUT REFUSE THEY DID TO CHANGE THEIR WAYS. INTO OBSCURITY THEY FELL..."
BUT THEY STILL PRACTICE THE SLAVE TRADE IN THE FAR REACHES. I FAIL TO SEE HOW THEY'RE CONNECTED TO THE PEOPLE OF KIROS.
COUNT DOOKU HAS MADE HIS ***RELAXED*** VIEW OF SLAVERY WELL KNOWN. THE SEPARATISTS COULD BE SECRETLY HELPING THE ZYGERRIANS REBUILD THEIR OLD BUSINESS.
YOU THINK THE ENTIRE POPULATION HAS BEEN ENSLAVED?
INVESTIGATE THIS CONNECTION, BUT WITH CAUTION PROCEED. SENSE, I DO, THAT DANGEROUS ONCE AGAIN THE ZYGERRIANS HAVE BECOME.

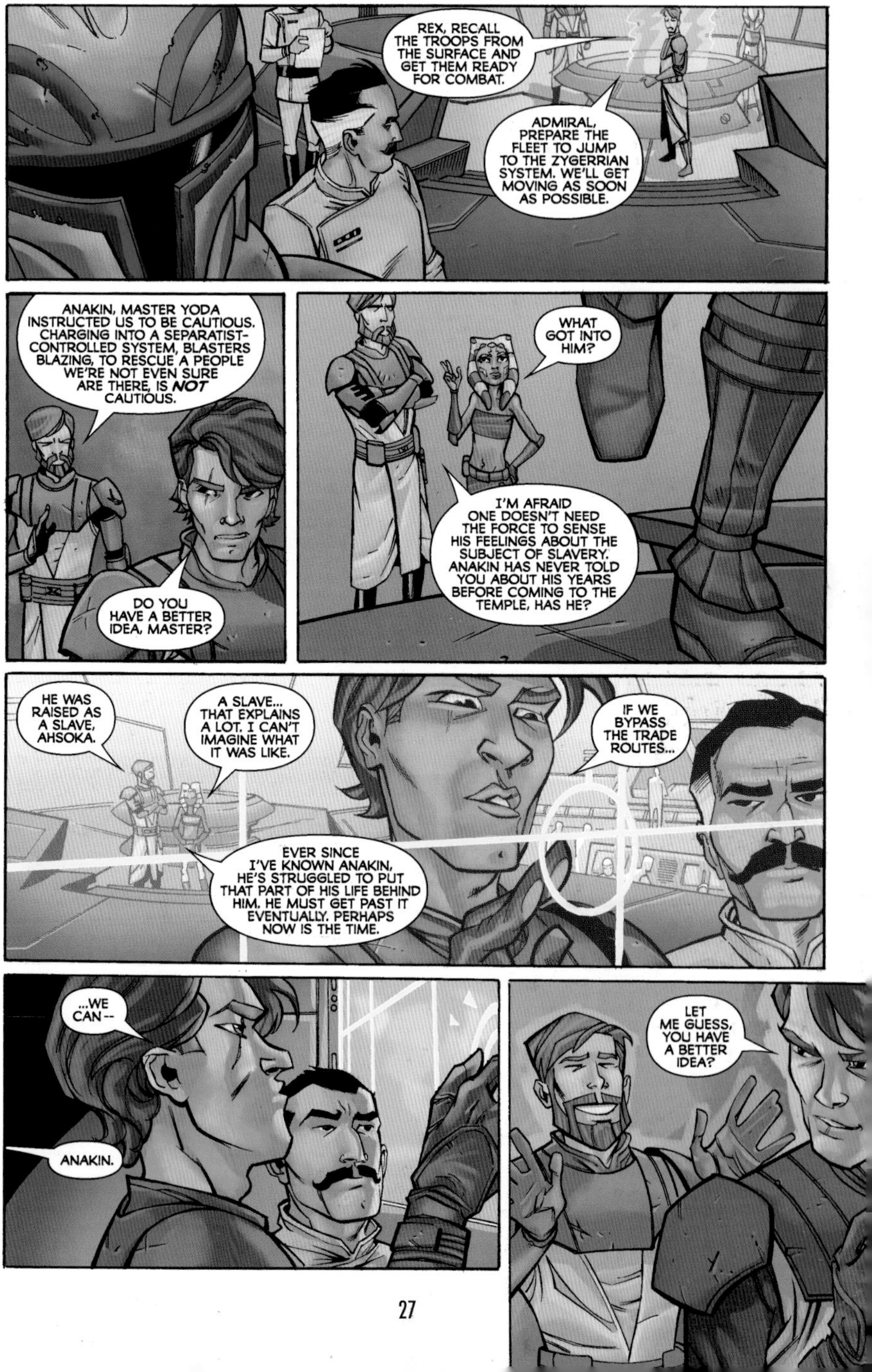
REX, RECALL THE TROOPS FROM THE SURFACE AND GET THEM READY FOR COMBAT.
ADMIRAL, PREPARE THE FLEET TO JUMP TO THE ZYGERRIAN SYSTEM. WE'LL GET MOVING AS SOON AS POSSIBLE.
ANAKIN, MASTER YODA INSTRUCTED US TO BE CAUTIOUS. CHARGING INTO A SEPARATIST-CONTROLLED SYSTEM, BLASTERS BLAZING, TO RESCUE A PEOPLE WE'RE NOT EVEN SURE ARE THERE, IS NOT CAUTIOUS.
DO YOU HAVE A BETTER IDEA, MASTER?
WHAT GOT INTO HIM?
I'M AFRAID ONE DOESN'T NEED THE FORCE TO SENSE HIS FEELINGS ABOUT THE SUBJECT OF SLAVERY. ANAKIN HAS NEVER TOLD YOU ABOUT HIS YEARS BEFORE COMING TO THE TEMPLE, HAS HE?
HE WAS RAISED AS A SLAVE, AHSOKA.
A SLAVE... THAT EXPLAINS A LOT. I CAN'T IMAGINE WHAT IT WAS LIKE.
EVER SINCE I'VE KNOWN ANAKIN, HE'S STRUGGLED TO PUT THAT PART OF HIS LIFE BEHIND HIM. HE MUST GET PAST IT EVENTUALLY. PERHAPS NOW IS THE TIME.
IF WE BYPASS THE TRADE ROUTES...
...WE CAN--
ANAKIN.
LET ME GUESS, YOU HAVE A BETTER IDEA?

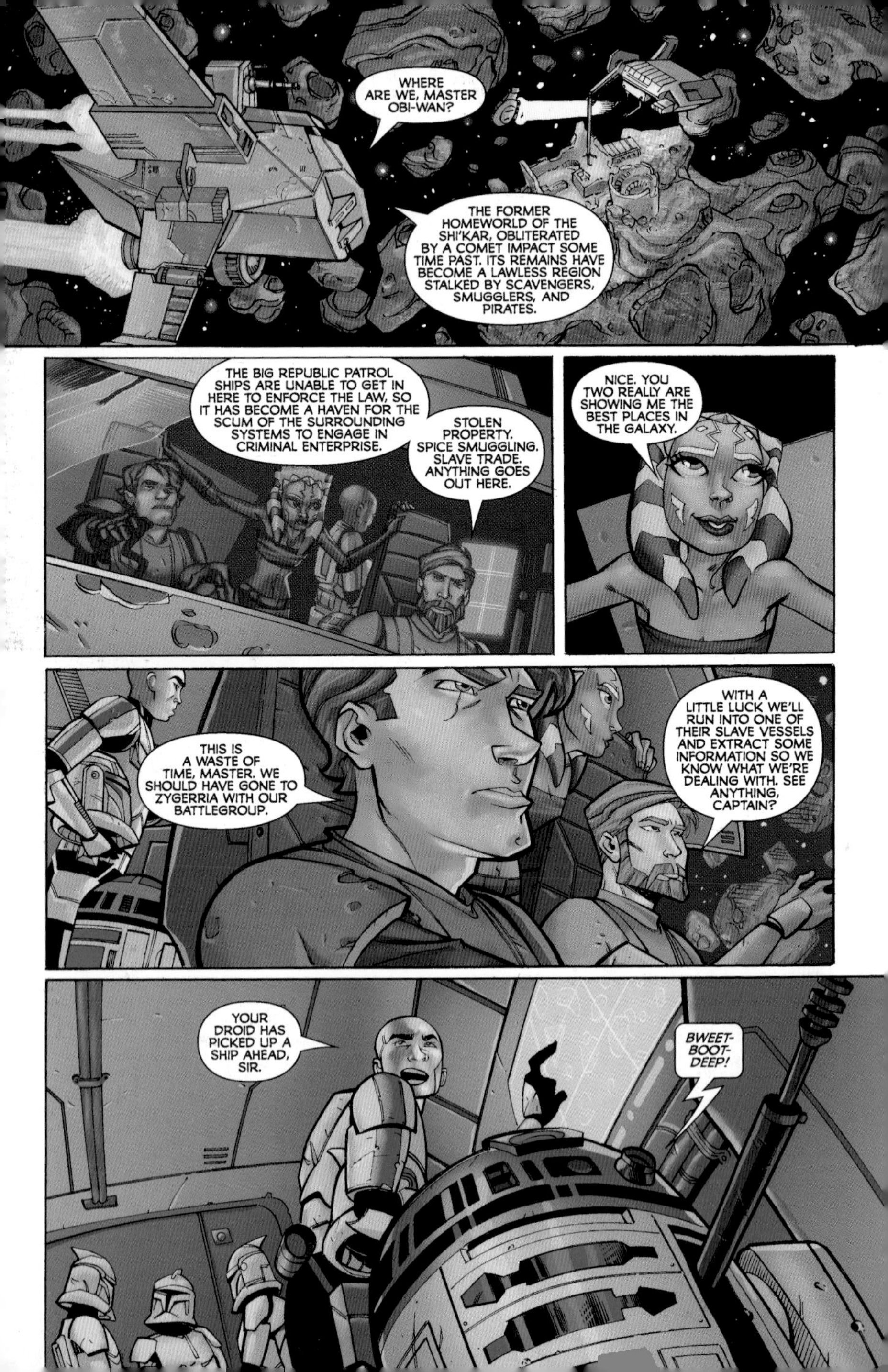
WHERE ARE WE, MASTER OBI-WAN?
THE FORMER HOMEWORLD OF THE SHI'KAR, OBLITERATED BY A COMET IMPACT SOME TIME PAST. ITS REMAINS HAVE BECOME A LAWLESS REGION STALKED BY SCAVENGERS, SMUGGLERS, AND PIRATES.
THE BIG REPUBLIC PATROL SHIPS ARE UNABLE TO GET IN HERE TO ENFORCE THE LAW, SO IT HAS BECOME A HAVEN FOR THE SCUM OF THE SURROUNDING SYSTEMS TO ENGAGE IN CRIMINAL ENTERPRISE.
STOLEN PROPERTY. SPICE SMUGGLING. SLAVE TRADE. ANYTHING GOES OUT HERE.
NICE. YOU TWO REALLY ARE SHOWING ME THE BEST PLACES IN THE GALAXY.
THIS IS A WASTE OF TIME, MASTER. WE SHOULD HAVE GONE TO ZYGERRIA WITH OUR BATTLEGROUP.
WITH A LITTLE LUCK WE'LL RUN INTO ONE OF THEIR SLAVE VESSELS AND EXTRACT SOME INFORMATION SO WE KNOW WHAT WE'RE DEALING WITH. SEE ANYTHING, CAPTAIN?
YOUR DROID HAS PICKED UP A SHIP AHEAD, SIR.
BWEET-BOOT-DEEP!

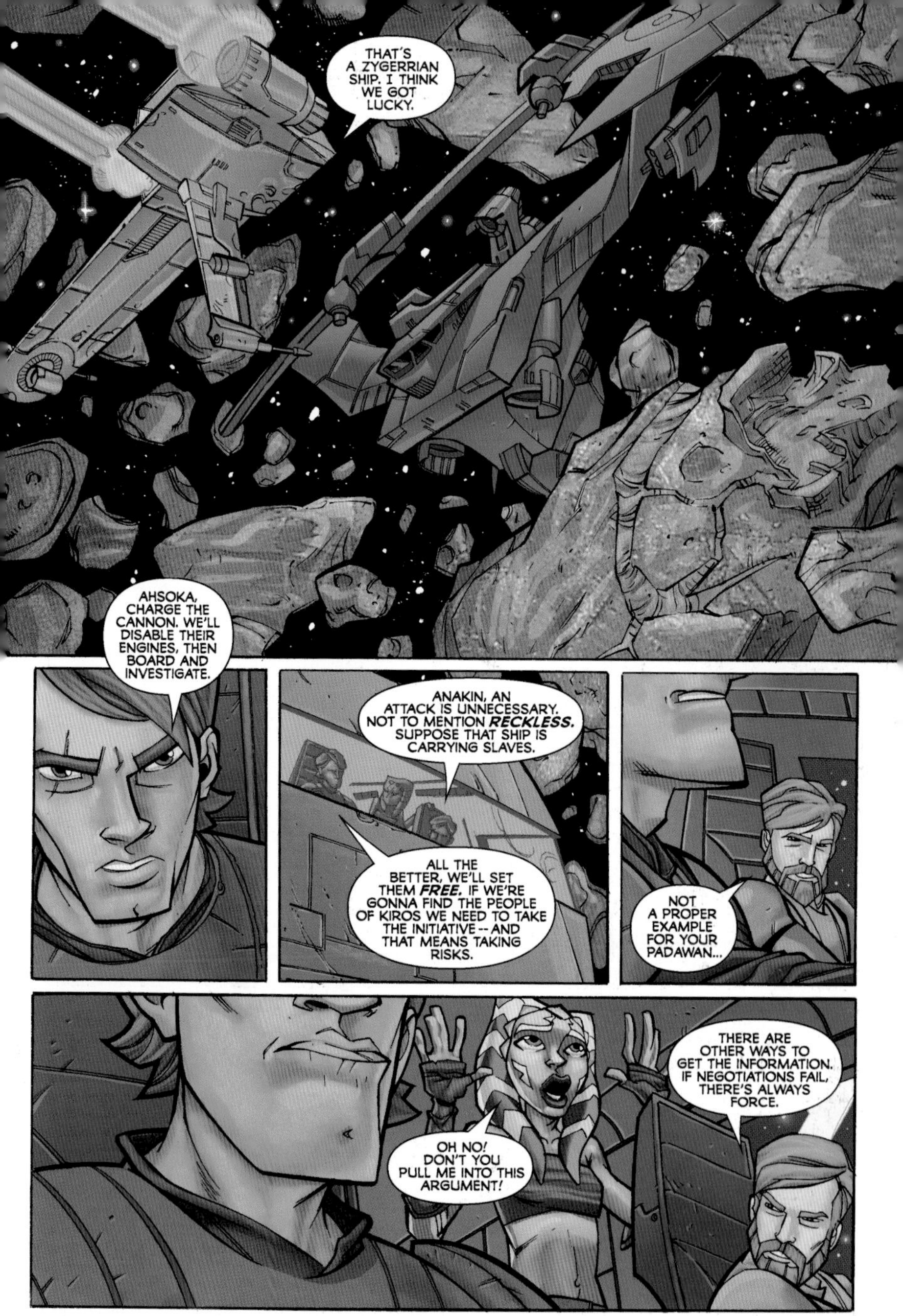
THAT'S A ZYGERRIAN SHIP. I THINK WE GOT LUCKY.
AHSOKA, CHARGE THE CANNON. WE'LL DISABLE THEIR ENGINES, THEN BOARD AND INVESTIGATE.
ANAKIN, AN ATTACK IS UNNECESSARY. NOT TO MENTION *RECKLESS.* SUPPOSE THAT SHIP IS CARRYING SLAVES.
ALL THE BETTER, WE'LL SET THEM *FREE.* IF WE'RE GONNA FIND THE PEOPLE OF KIROS WE NEED TO TAKE THE INITIATIVE -- AND THAT MEANS TAKING RISKS.
NOT A PROPER EXAMPLE FOR YOUR PADAWAN...
THERE ARE OTHER WAYS TO GET THE INFORMATION. IF NEGOTIATIONS FAIL, THERE'S ALWAYS FORCE.
OH NO! DON'T YOU PULL ME INTO THIS ARGUMENT!

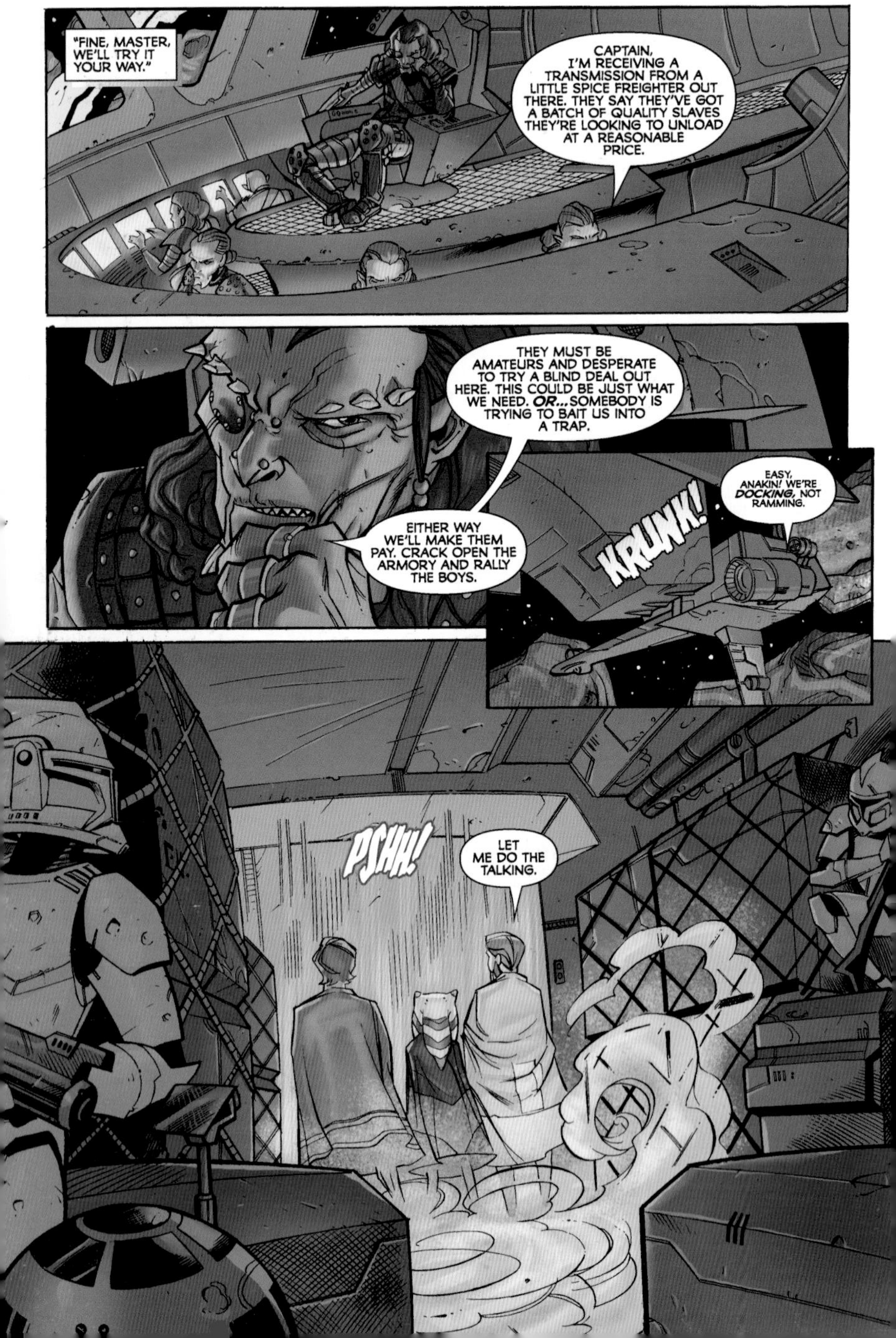
"FINE, MASTER, WE'LL TRY IT YOUR WAY."
CAPTAIN, I'M RECEIVING A TRANSMISSION FROM A LITTLE SPICE FREIGHTER OUT THERE. THEY SAY THEY'VE GOT A BATCH OF QUALITY SLAVES THEY'RE LOOKING TO UNLOAD AT A REASONABLE PRICE.
THEY MUST BE AMATEURS AND DESPERATE TO TRY A BLIND DEAL OUT HERE. THIS COULD BE JUST WHAT WE NEED. OR... SOMEBODY IS TRYING TO BAIT US INTO A TRAP.
EITHER WAY WE'LL MAKE THEM PAY. CRACK OPEN THE ARMORY AND RALLY THE BOYS.
KRUNK!
EASY, ANAKIN! WE'RE DOCKING, NOT RAMMING.
PSHH!
LET ME DO THE TALKING.

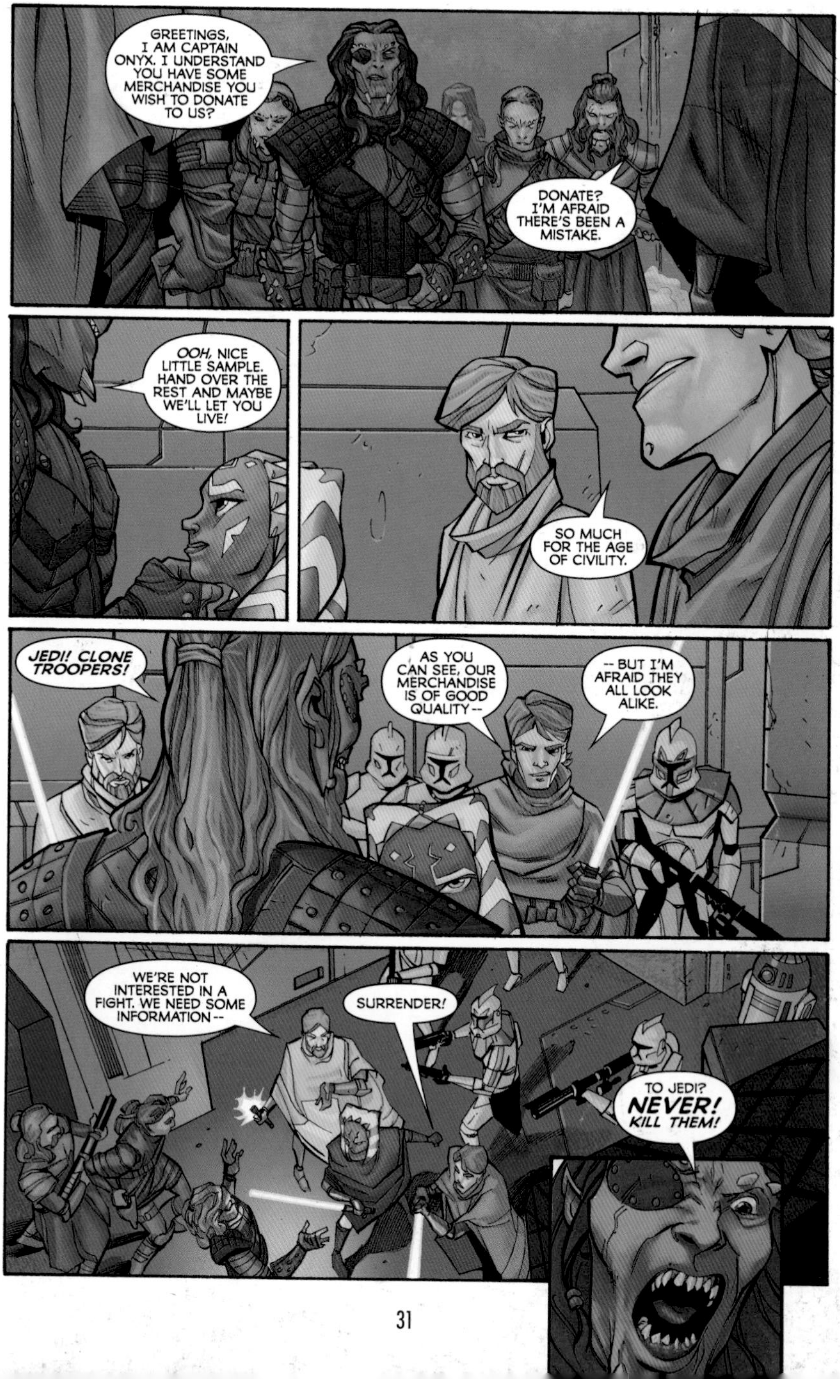
GREETINGS, I AM CAPTAIN ONYX. I UNDERSTAND YOU HAVE SOME MERCHANDISE YOU WISH TO DONATE TO US?
DONATE? I'M AFRAID THERE'S BEEN A MISTAKE.
OOH, NICE LITTLE SAMPLE. HAND OVER THE REST AND MAYBE WE'LL LET YOU LIVE!
SO MUCH FOR THE AGE OF CIVILITY.
JEDI! CLONE TROOPERS!
AS YOU CAN SEE, OUR MERCHANDISE IS OF GOOD QUALITY--
-- BUT I'M AFRAID THEY ALL LOOK ALIKE.
WE'RE NOT INTERESTED IN A FIGHT. WE NEED SOME INFORMATION--
SURRENDER!
TO JEDI? NEVER! KILL THEM!

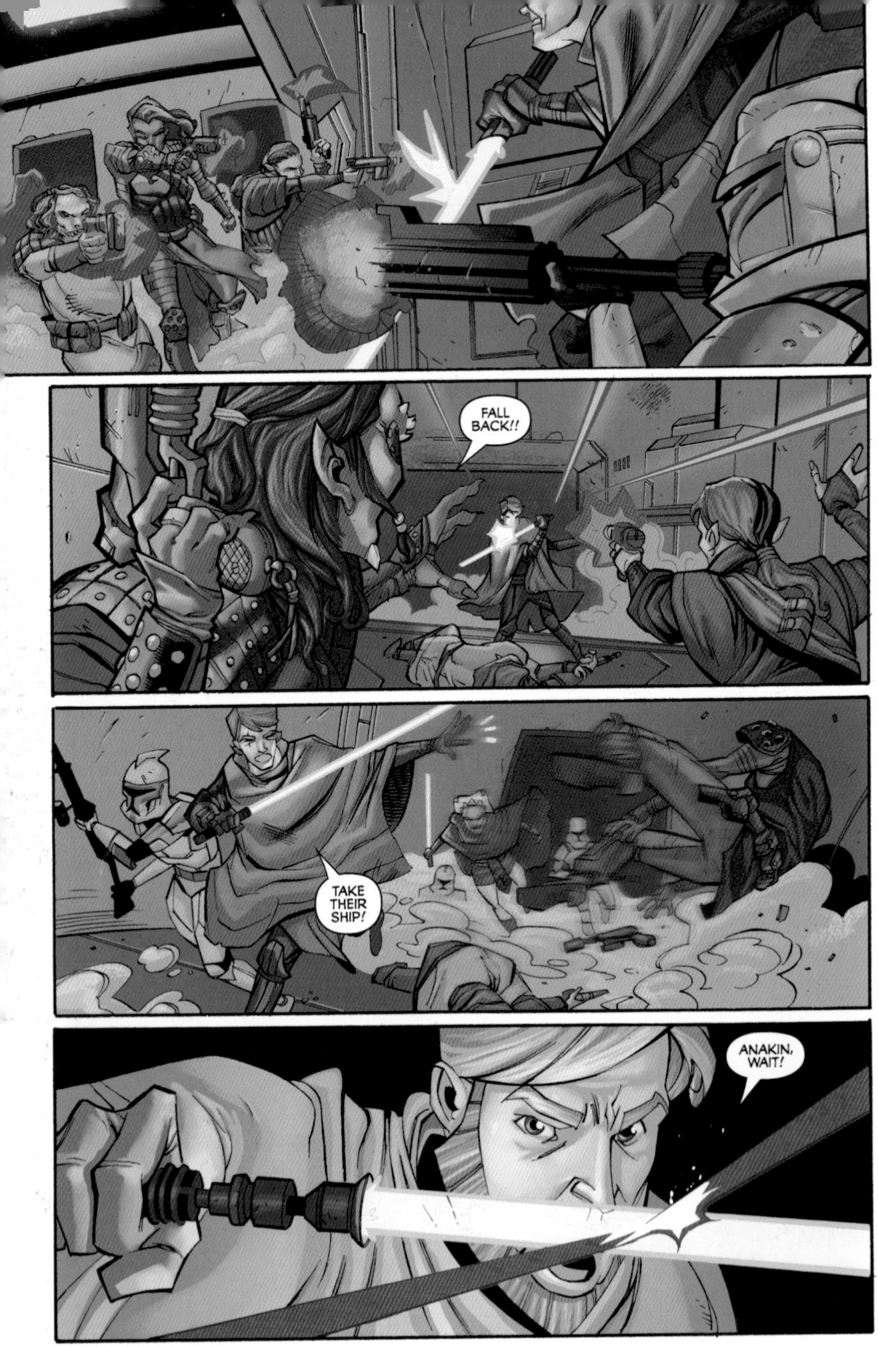
FALL BACK!!
TAKE THEIR SHIP!
ANAKIN, WAIT!

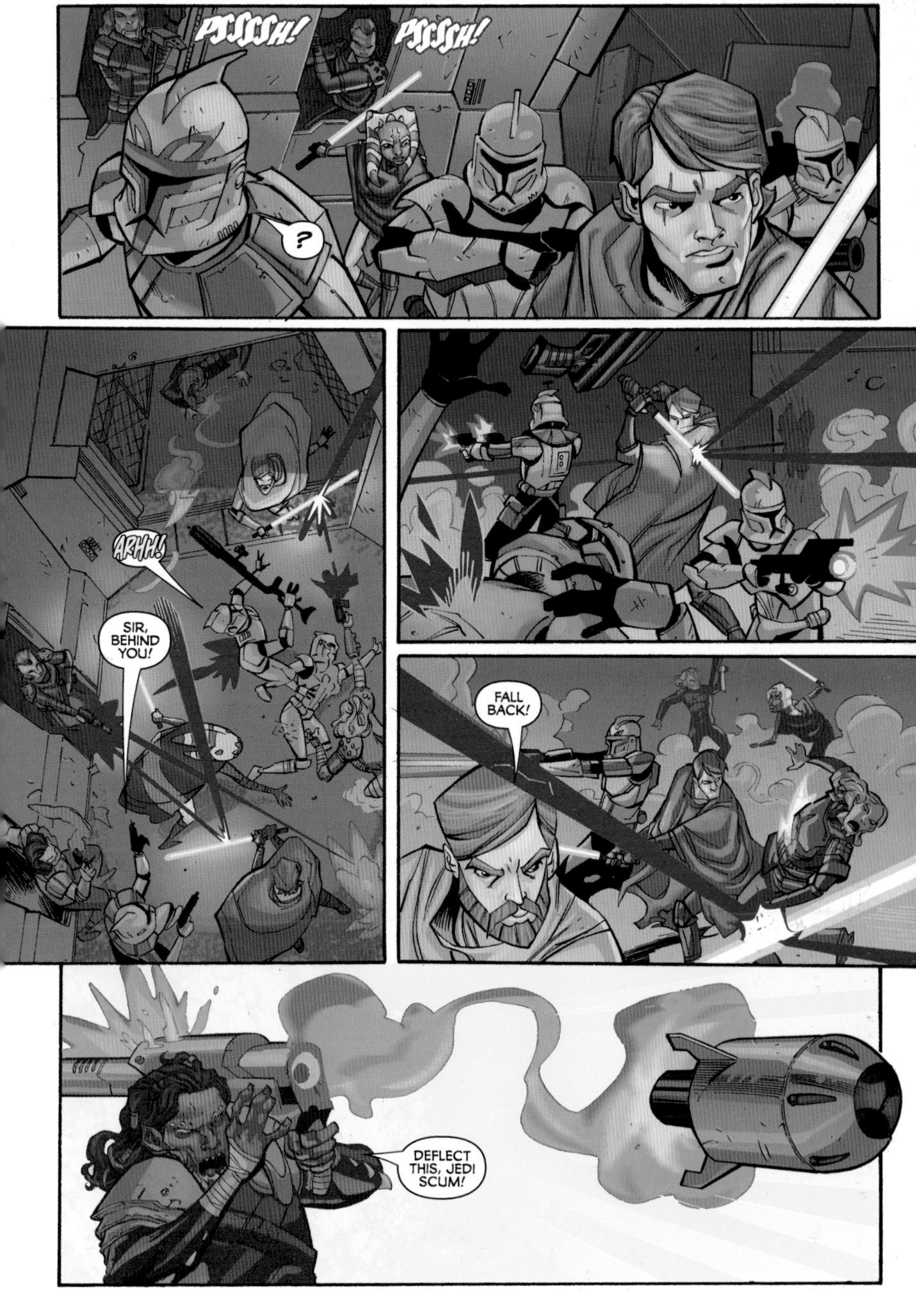
PSSSSH!
PSSSSH!
?
ARHH!
SIR, BEHIND YOU!
FALL BACK!
DEFLECT THIS, JEDI SCUM!

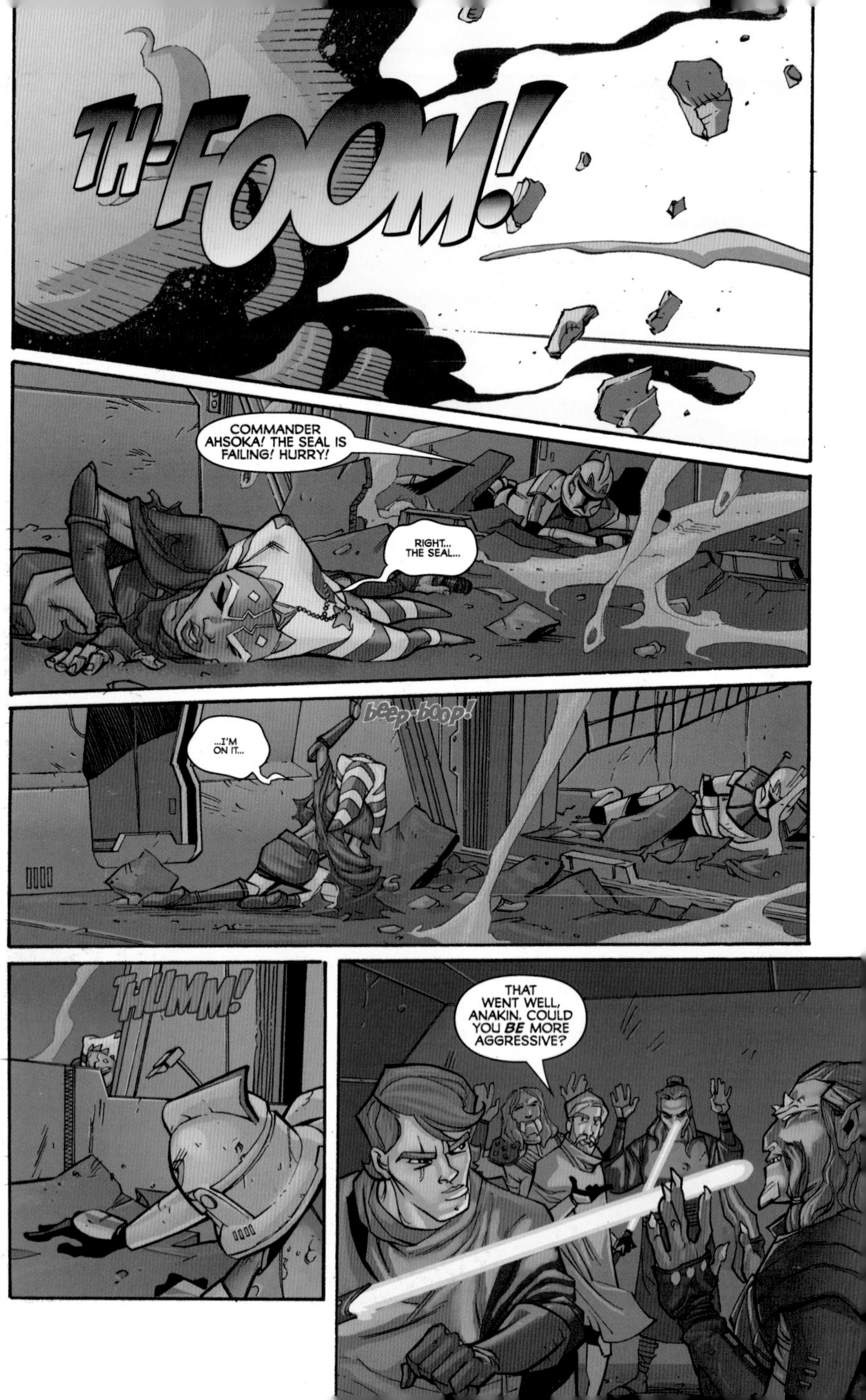
TH-FOOM!
COMMANDER AHSOKA! THE SEAL IS FAILING! HURRY!
RIGHT... THE SEAL...
...I'M ON IT...
beep-boop!
THUMM!
THAT WENT WELL, ANAKIN. COULD YOU *BE* MORE AGGRESSIVE?

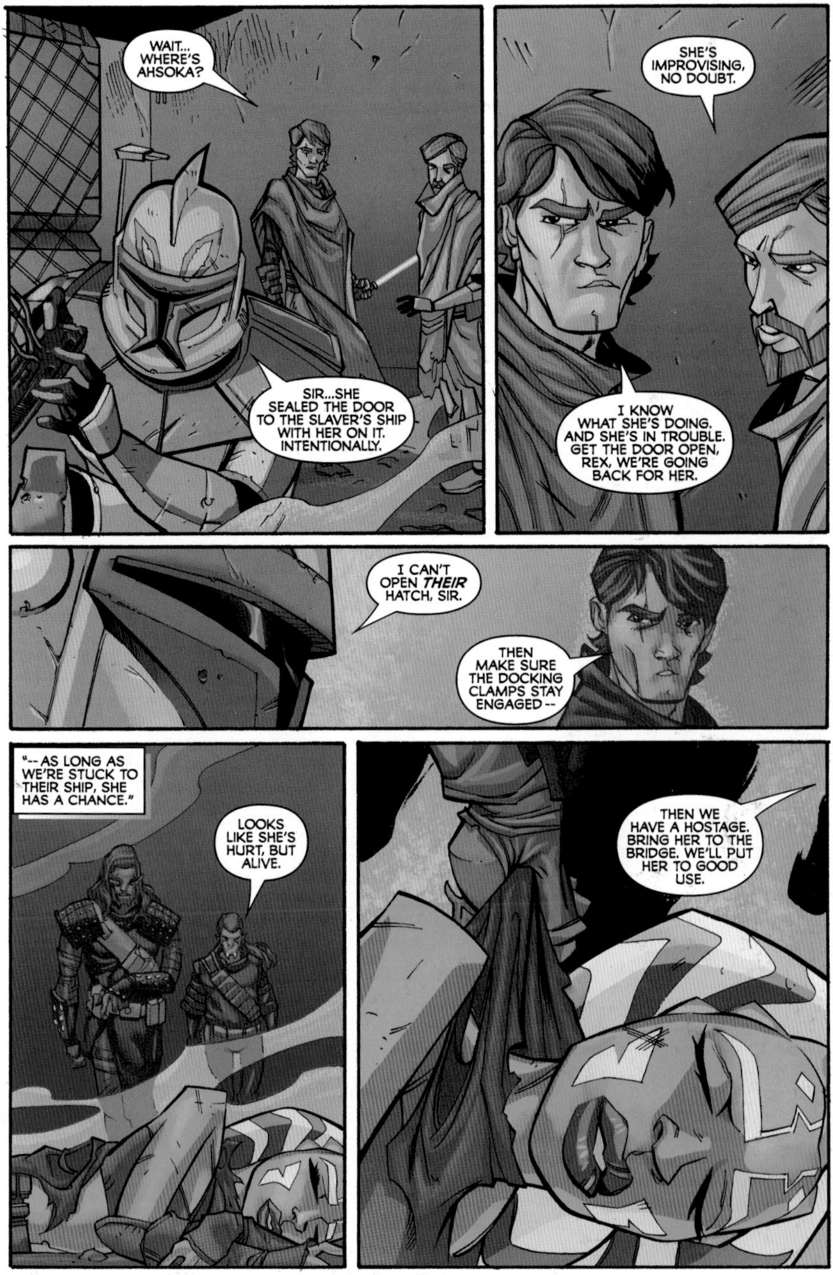
WAIT... WHERE'S AHSOKA?
SIR...SHE SEALED THE DOOR TO THE SLAVER'S SHIP WITH HER ON IT. INTENTIONALLY.
SHE'S IMPROVISING, NO DOUBT.
I KNOW WHAT SHE'S DOING. AND SHE'S IN TROUBLE. GET THE DOOR OPEN, REX, WE'RE GOING BACK FOR HER.
I CAN'T OPEN *THEIR* HATCH, SIR.
THEN MAKE SURE THE DOCKING CLAMPS STAY ENGAGED --
"-- AS LONG AS WE'RE STUCK TO THEIR SHIP, SHE HAS A CHANCE."
LOOKS LIKE SHE'S HURT, BUT ALIVE.
THEN WE HAVE A HOSTAGE. BRING HER TO THE BRIDGE. WE'LL PUT HER TO GOOD USE.

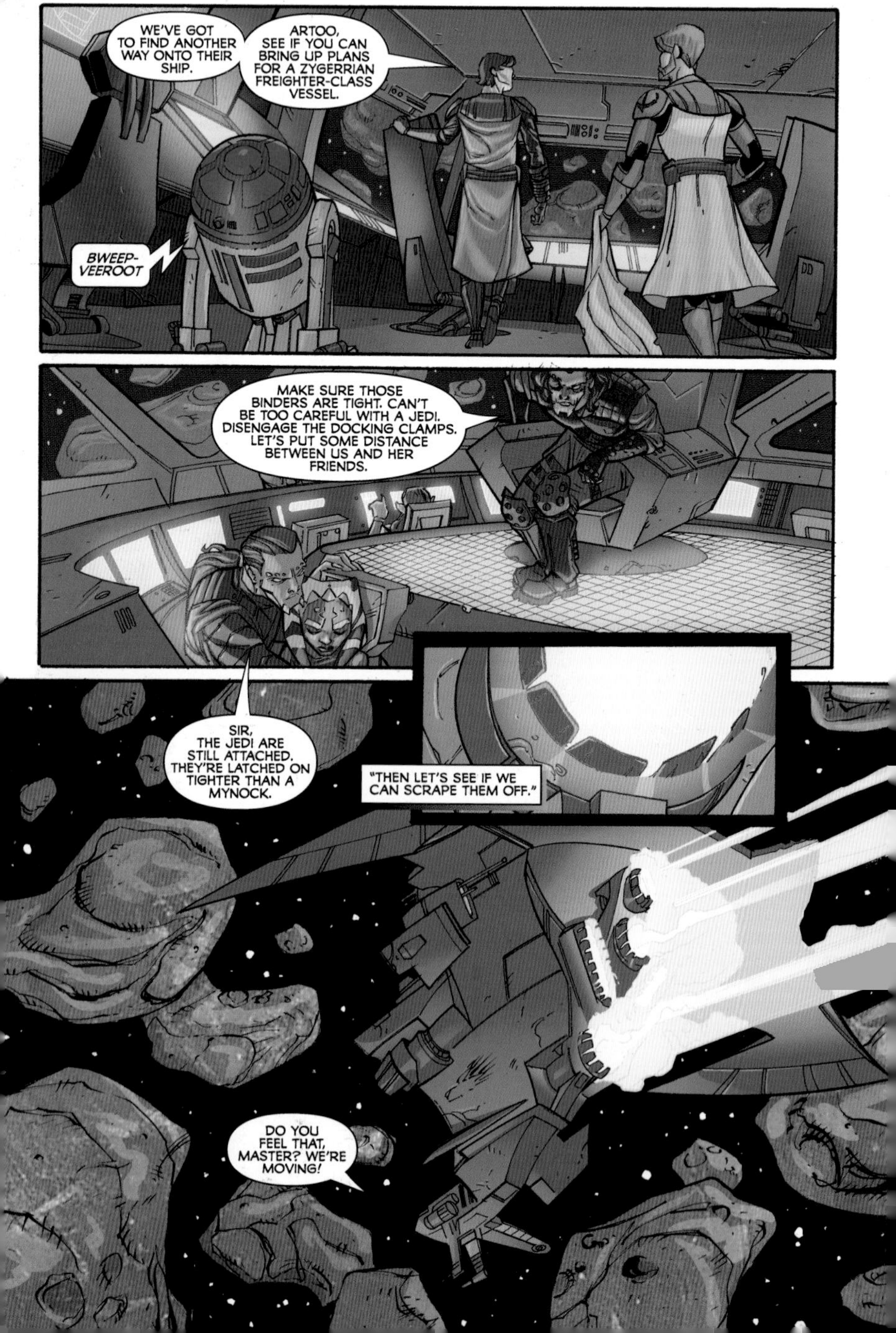
WE'VE GOT TO FIND ANOTHER WAY ONTO THEIR SHIP.
ARTOO, SEE IF YOU CAN BRING UP PLANS FOR A ZYGERRIAN FREIGHTER-CLASS VESSEL.
BWEEP-VEEROOT
MAKE SURE THOSE BINDERS ARE TIGHT. CAN'T BE TOO CAREFUL WITH A JEDI. DISENGAGE THE DOCKING CLAMPS. LET'S PUT SOME DISTANCE BETWEEN US AND HER FRIENDS.
SIR, THE JEDI ARE STILL ATTACHED. THEY'RE LATCHED ON TIGHTER THAN A MYNOCK.
"THEN LET'S SEE IF WE CAN SCRAPE THEM OFF."
DO YOU FEEL THAT, MASTER? WE'RE MOVING!

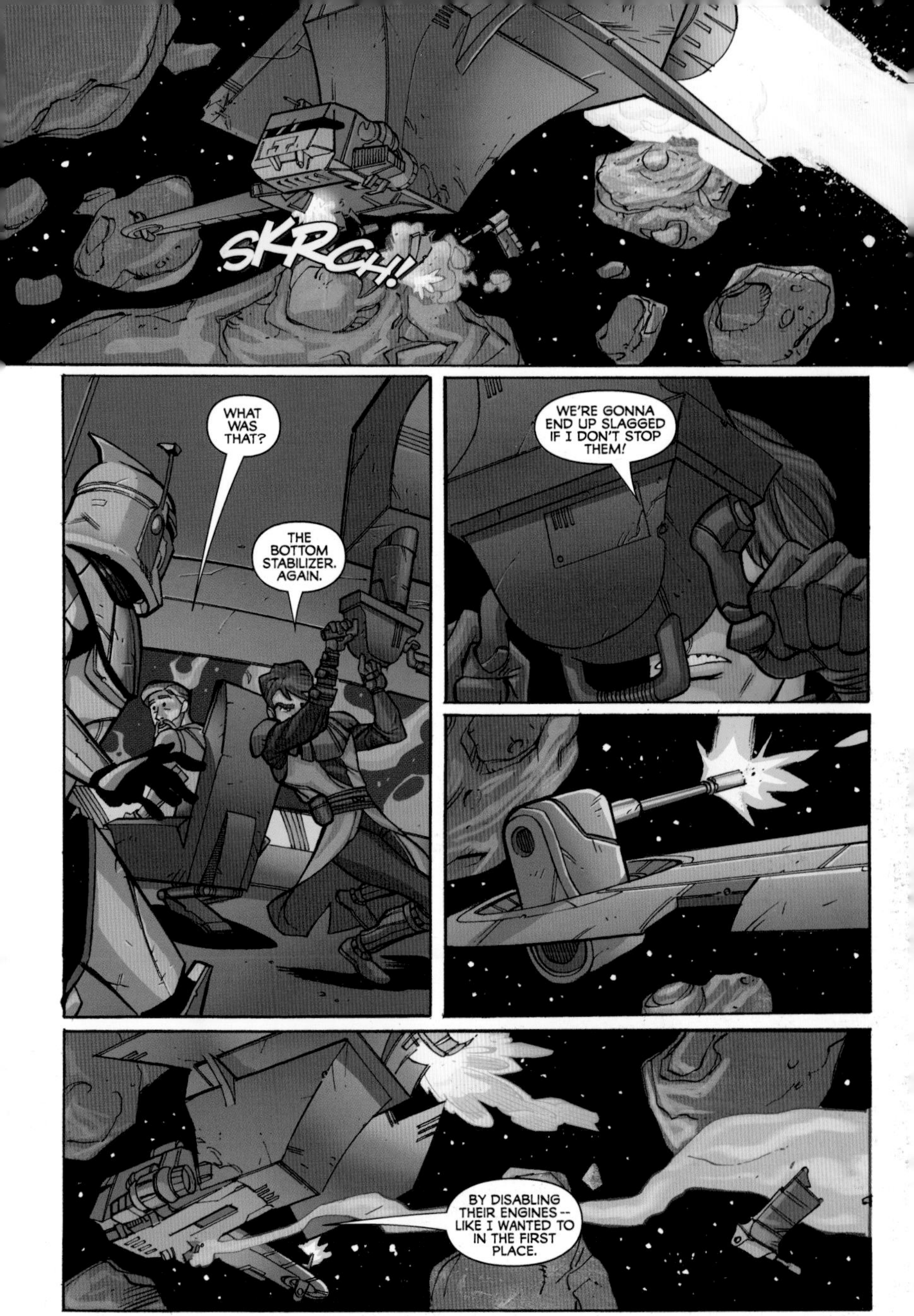
SKRCH!
WHAT WAS THAT?
THE BOTTOM STABILIZER. AGAIN.
WE'RE GONNA END UP SLAGGED IF I DON'T STOP THEM!
BY DISABLING THEIR ENGINES -- LIKE I WANTED TO IN THE FIRST PLACE.

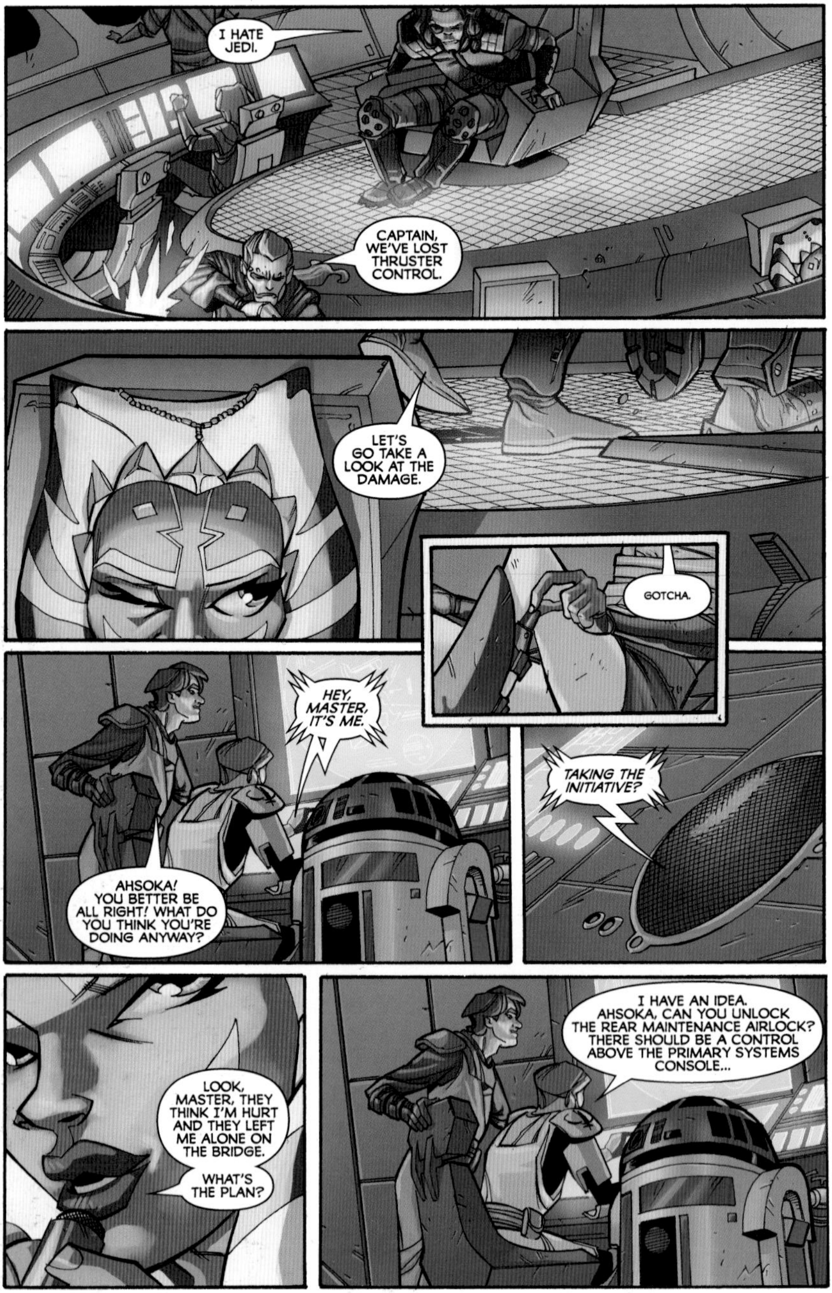
I HATE JEDI.
CAPTAIN, WE'VE LOST THRUSTER CONTROL.
LET'S GO TAKE A LOOK AT THE DAMAGE.
GOTCHA.
HEY, MASTER, IT'S ME.
AHSOKA! YOU BETTER BE ALL RIGHT! WHAT DO YOU THINK YOU'RE DOING ANYWAY?
TAKING THE INITIATIVE?
LOOK, MASTER, THEY THINK I'M HURT AND THEY LEFT ME ALONE ON THE BRIDGE.
WHAT'S THE PLAN?
I HAVE AN IDEA. AHSOKA, CAN YOU UNLOCK THE REAR MAINTENANCE AIRLOCK? THERE SHOULD BE A CONTROL ABOVE THE PRIMARY SYSTEMS CONSOLE...

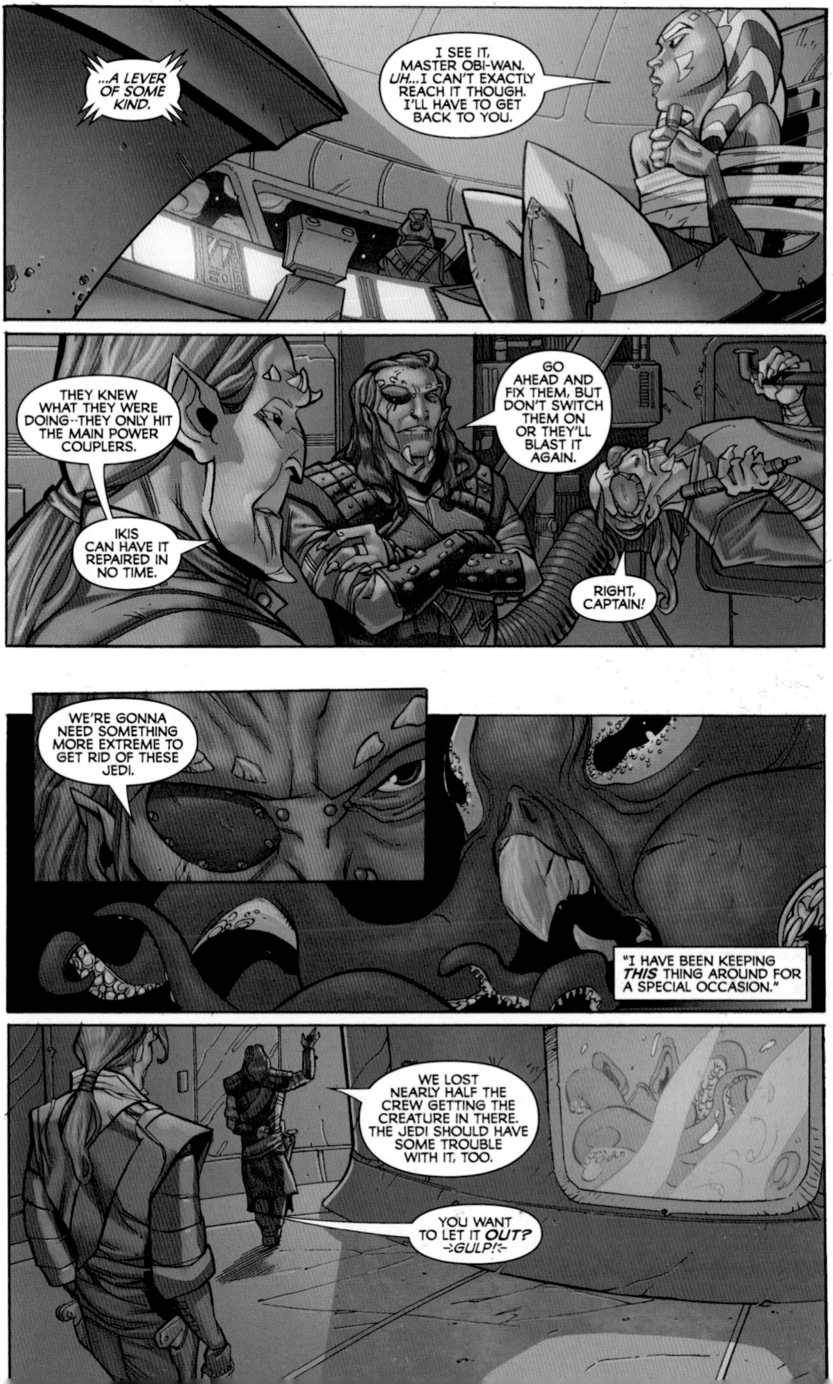
...A LEVER OF SOME KIND.
I SEE IT, MASTER OBI-WAN. UH...I CAN'T EXACTLY REACH IT THOUGH. I'LL HAVE TO GET BACK TO YOU.
THEY KNEW WHAT THEY WERE DOING--THEY ONLY HIT THE MAIN POWER COUPLERS.
IKIS CAN HAVE IT REPAIRED IN NO TIME.
GO AHEAD AND FIX THEM, BUT DON'T SWITCH THEM ON OR THEY'LL BLAST IT AGAIN.
RIGHT, CAPTAIN!
WE'RE GONNA NEED SOMETHING MORE EXTREME TO GET RID OF THESE JEDI.
"I HAVE BEEN KEEPING THIS THING AROUND FOR A SPECIAL OCCASION."
WE LOST NEARLY HALF THE CREW GETTING THE CREATURE IN THERE. THE JEDI SHOULD HAVE SOME TROUBLE WITH IT, TOO.
YOU WANT TO LET IT OUT? -GULP!-

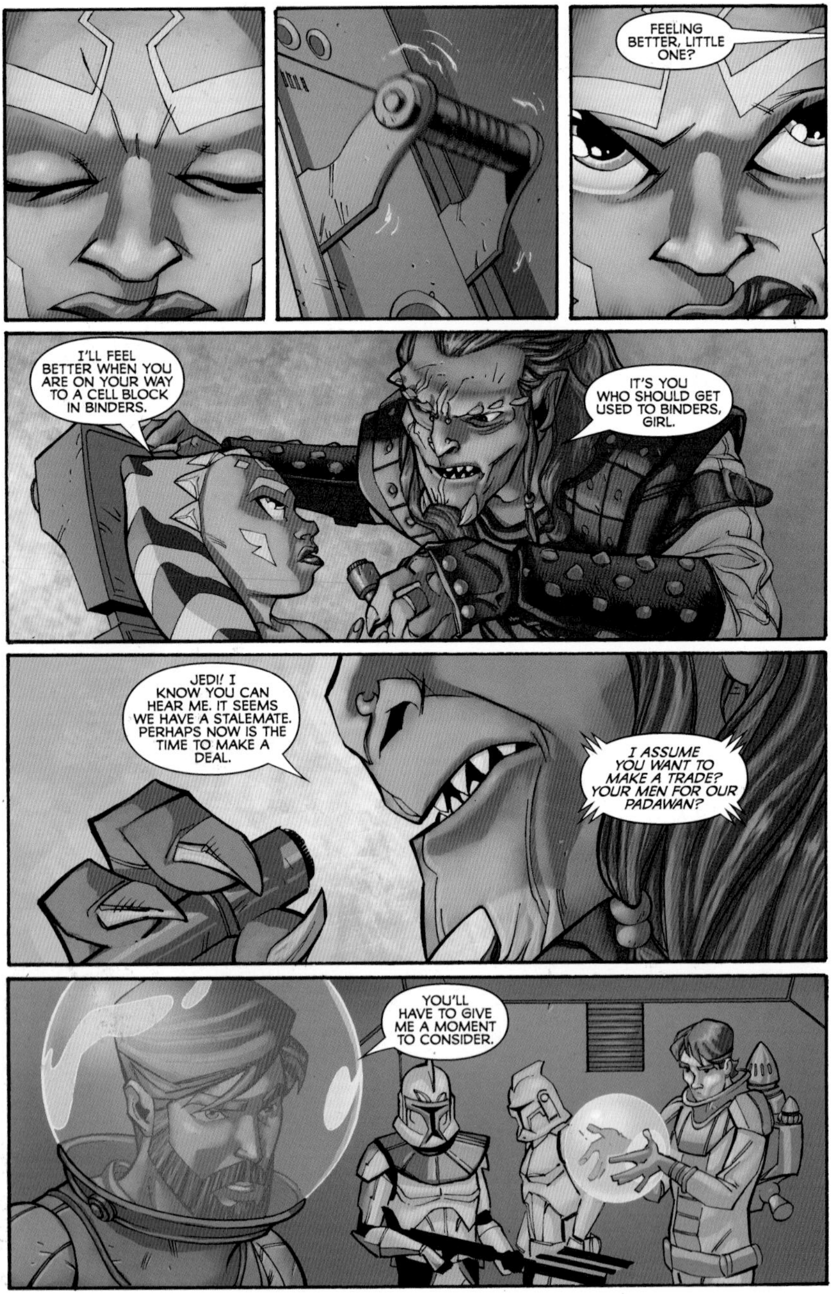

FEELING BETTER, LITTLE ONE?
I'LL FEEL BETTER WHEN YOU ARE ON YOUR WAY TO A CELL BLOCK IN BINDERS.
IT'S YOU WHO SHOULD GET USED TO BINDERS, GIRL.
JEDI! I KNOW YOU CAN HEAR ME. IT SEEMS WE HAVE A STALEMATE. PERHAPS NOW IS THE TIME TO MAKE A DEAL.
I ASSUME YOU WANT TO MAKE A TRADE? YOUR MEN FOR OUR PADAWAN?
YOU'LL HAVE TO GIVE ME A MOMENT TO CONSIDER.

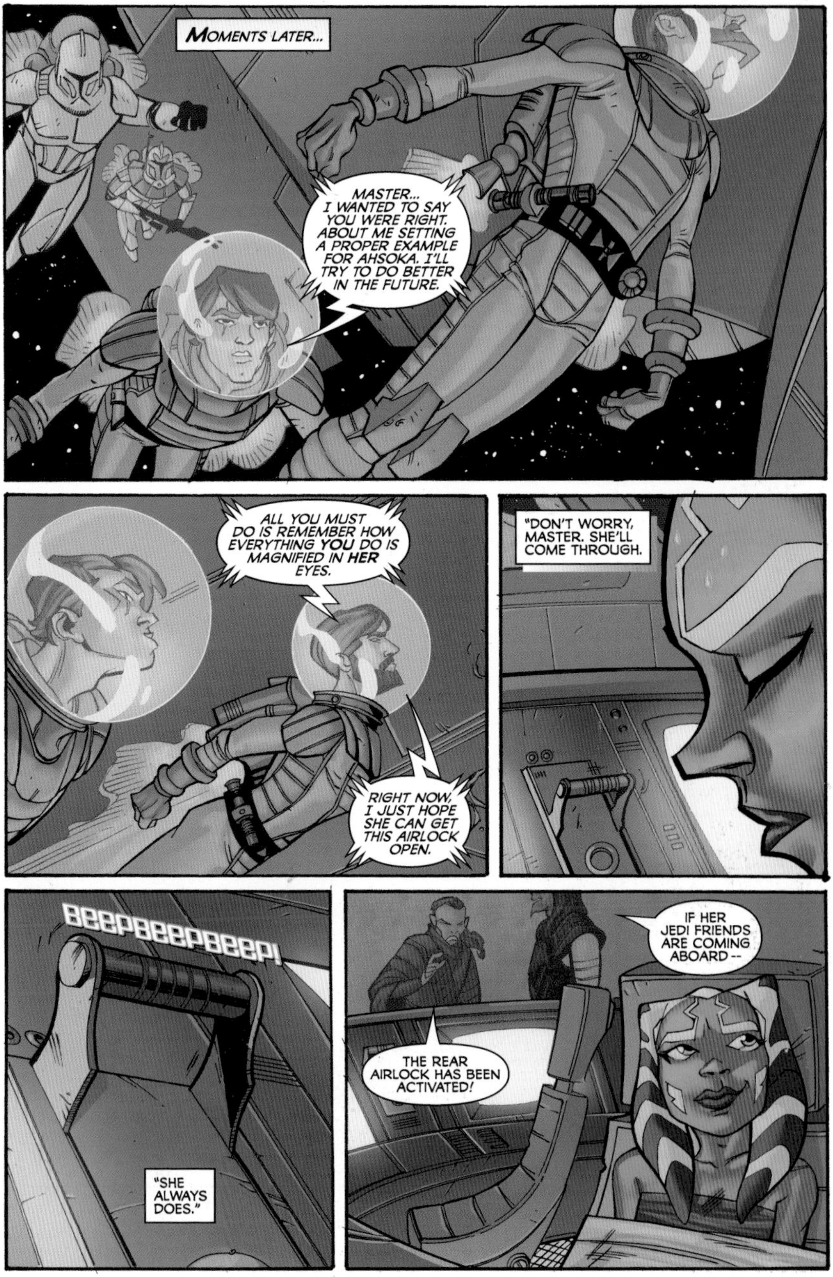
MOMENTS LATER...
MASTER... I WANTED TO SAY YOU WERE RIGHT. ABOUT ME SETTING A PROPER EXAMPLE FOR AHSOKA. I'LL TRY TO DO BETTER IN THE FUTURE.
ALL YOU MUST DO IS REMEMBER HOW EVERYTHING YOU DO IS MAGNIFIED IN HER EYES.
RIGHT NOW, I JUST HOPE SHE CAN GET THIS AIRLOCK OPEN.
"DON'T WORRY, MASTER. SHE'LL COME THROUGH.
BEEPBEEPBEEP!
"SHE ALWAYS DOES."
IF HER JEDI FRIENDS ARE COMING ABOARD --
THE REAR AIRLOCK HAS BEEN ACTIVATED!

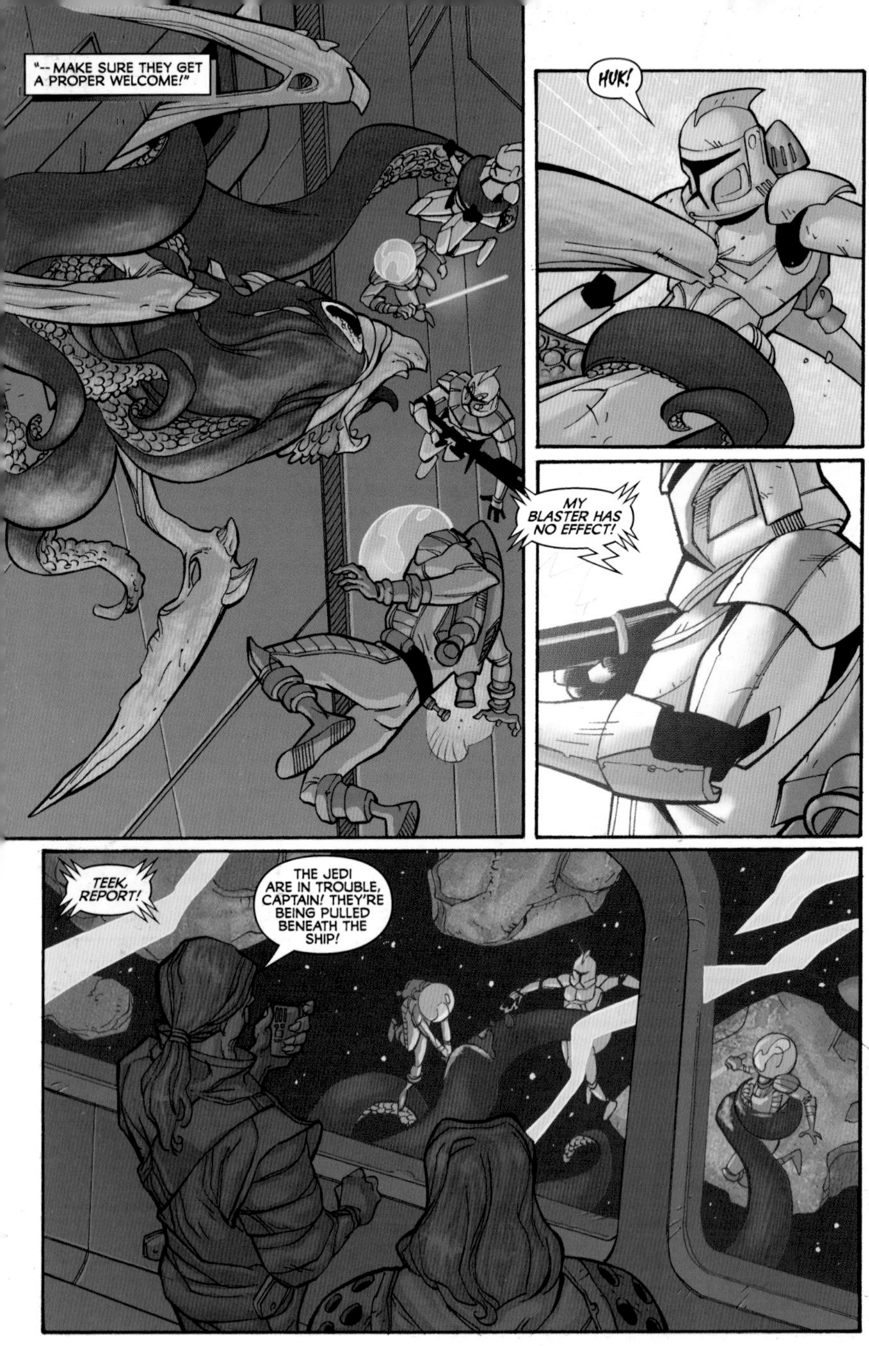
"-- MAKE SURE THEY GET A PROPER WELCOME!"
HUK!
MY BLASTER HAS NO EFFECT!
TEEK, REPORT!
THE JEDI ARE IN TROUBLE, CAPTAIN! THEY'RE BEING PULLED BENEATH THE SHIP!

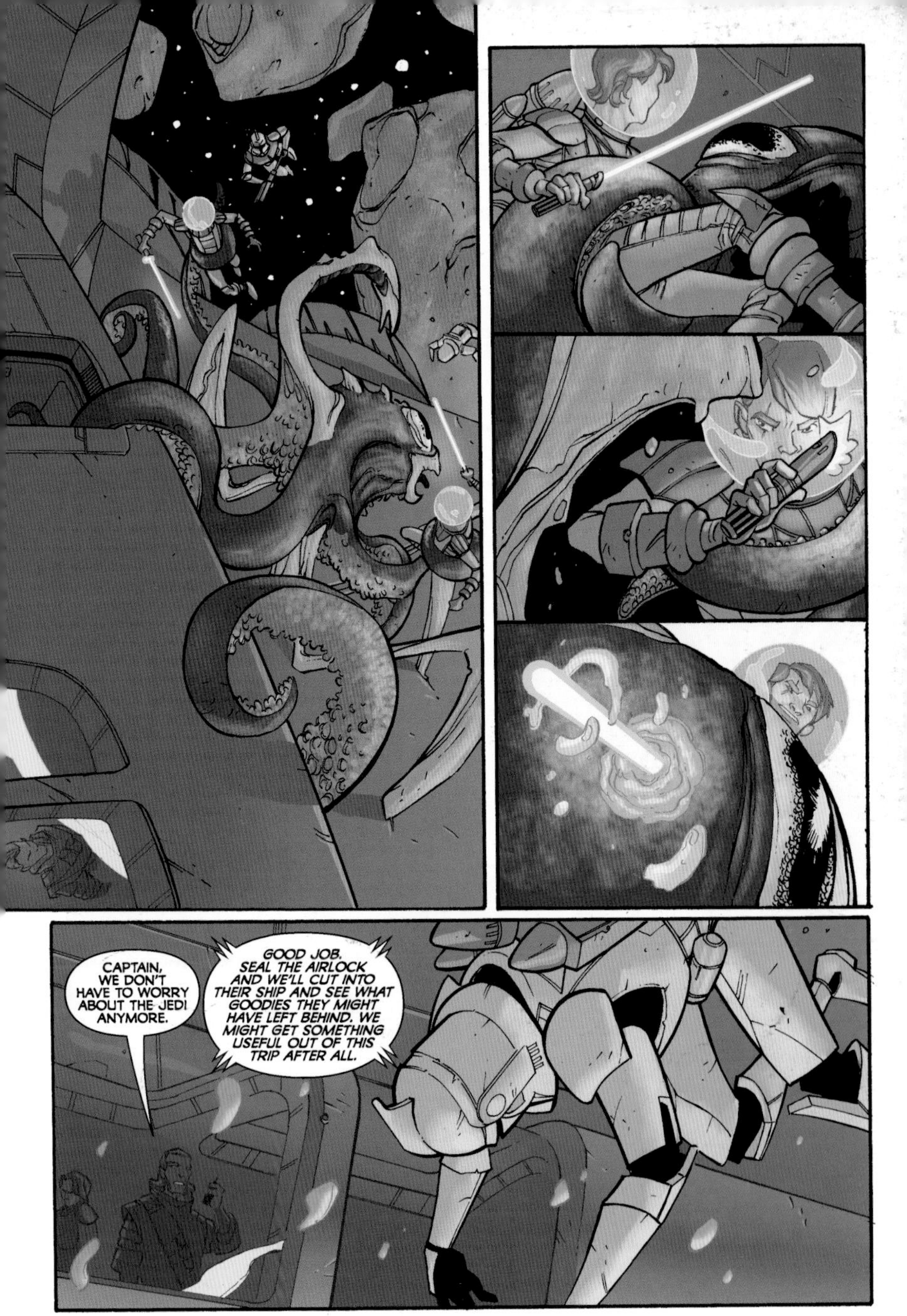
CAPTAIN, WE DON'T HAVE TO WORRY ABOUT THE JEDI ANYMORE.
GOOD JOB. SEAL THE AIRLOCK AND WE'LL CUT INTO THEIR SHIP AND SEE WHAT GOODIES THEY MIGHT HAVE LEFT BEHIND. WE MIGHT GET SOMETHING USEFUL OUT OF THIS TRIP AFTER ALL.

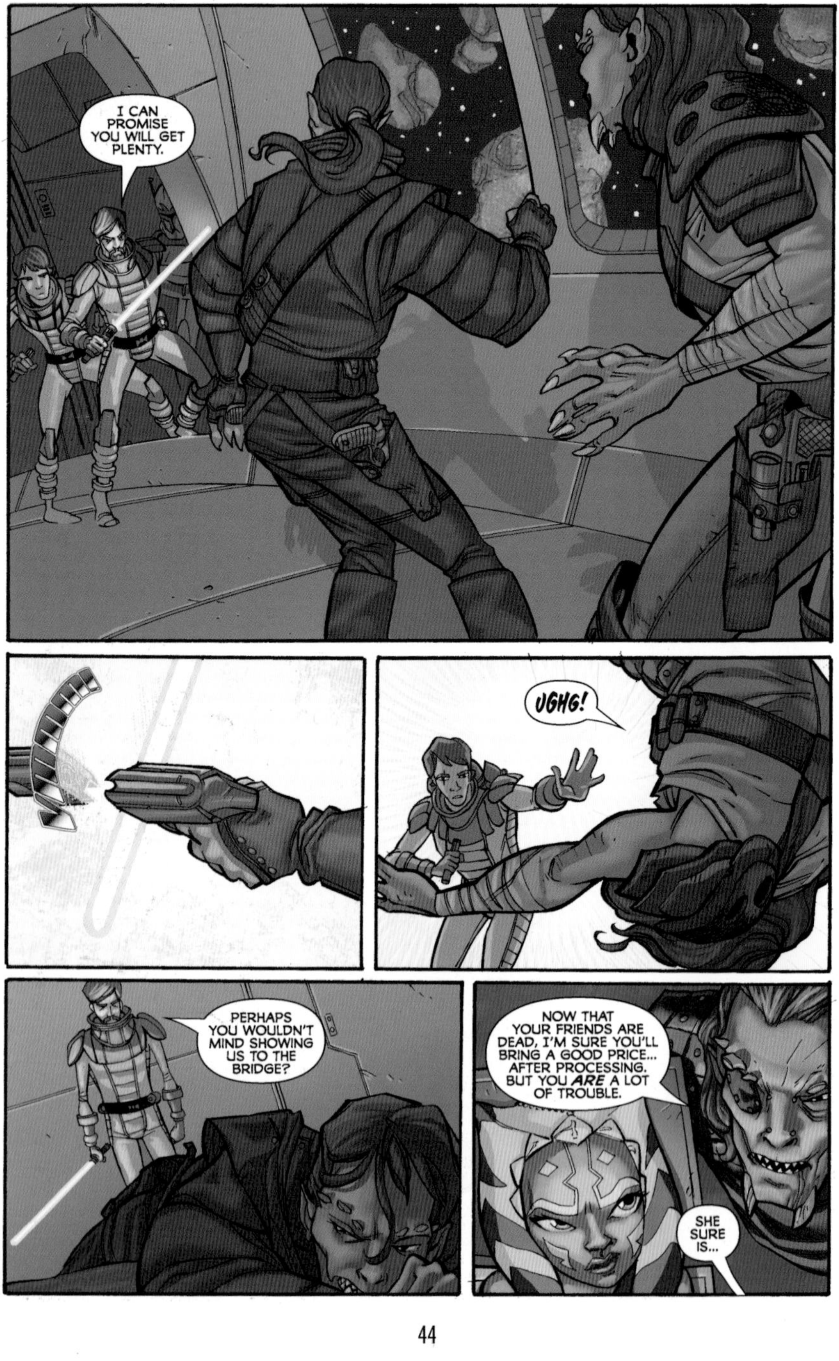
I CAN PROMISE YOU WILL GET PLENTY.
UGHG!
PERHAPS YOU WOULDN'T MIND SHOWING US TO THE BRIDGE?
NOW THAT YOUR FRIENDS ARE DEAD, I'M SURE YOU'LL BRING A GOOD PRICE... AFTER PROCESSING. BUT YOU ARE A LOT OF TROUBLE.
SHE SURE IS...

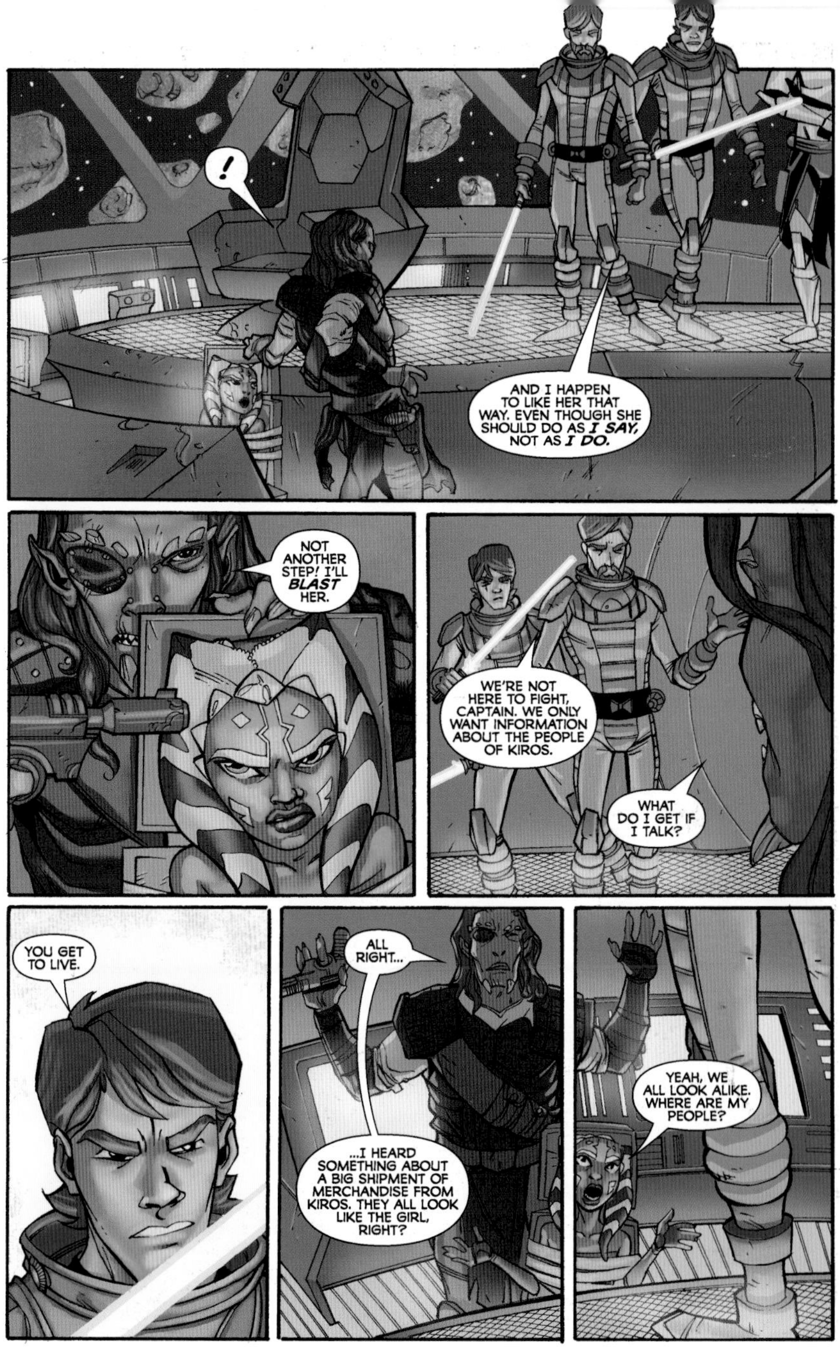
!
AND I HAPPEN TO LIKE HER THAT WAY. EVEN THOUGH SHE SHOULD DO AS I SAY, NOT AS I DO.
NOT ANOTHER STEP! I'LL BLAST HER.
WE'RE NOT HERE TO FIGHT, CAPTAIN. WE ONLY WANT INFORMATION ABOUT THE PEOPLE OF KIROS.
WHAT DO I GET IF I TALK?
YOU GET TO LIVE.
ALL RIGHT...
...I HEARD SOMETHING ABOUT A BIG SHIPMENT OF MERCHANDISE FROM KIROS. THEY ALL LOOK LIKE THE GIRL, RIGHT?
YEAH, WE ALL LOOK ALIKE. WHERE ARE MY PEOPLE?

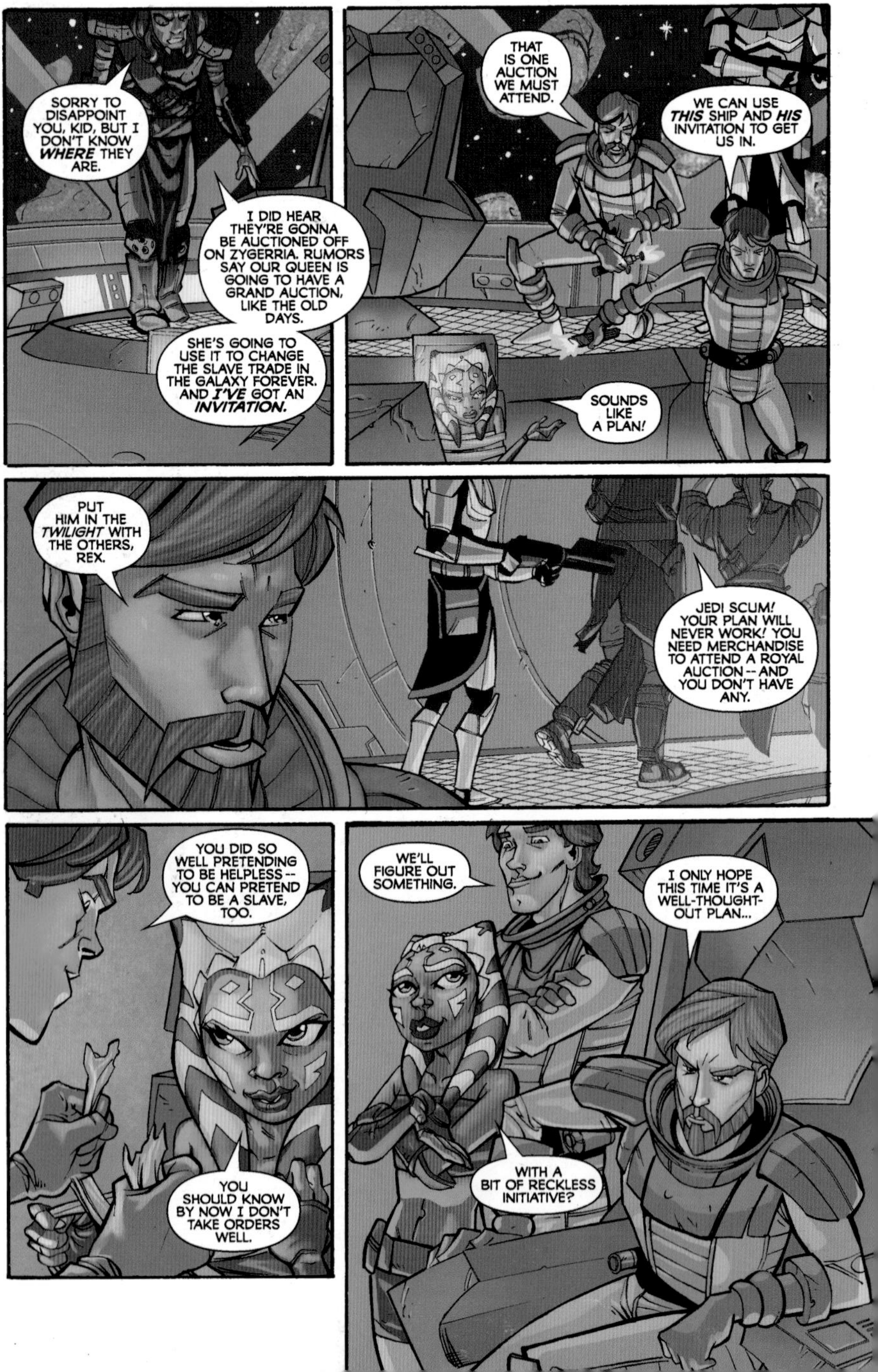
SORRY TO DISAPPOINT YOU, KID, BUT I DON'T KNOW *WHERE* THEY ARE.
I DID HEAR THEY'RE GONNA BE AUCTIONED OFF ON ZYGERRIA. RUMORS SAY OUR QUEEN IS GOING TO HAVE A GRAND AUCTION, LIKE THE OLD DAYS.
SHE'S GOING TO USE IT TO CHANGE THE SLAVE TRADE IN THE GALAXY FOREVER. AND *I'VE* GOT AN *INVITATION.*
THAT IS ONE AUCTION WE MUST ATTEND.
WE CAN USE *THIS* SHIP AND *HIS* INVITATION TO GET US IN.
SOUNDS LIKE A PLAN!
PUT HIM IN THE *TWILIGHT* WITH THE OTHERS, REX.
JEDI SCUM! YOUR PLAN WILL NEVER WORK! YOU NEED MERCHANDISE TO ATTEND A ROYAL AUCTION -- AND YOU DON'T HAVE ANY.
YOU DID SO WELL PRETENDING TO BE HELPLESS -- YOU CAN PRETEND TO BE A SLAVE, TOO.
YOU SHOULD KNOW BY NOW I DON'T TAKE ORDERS WELL.
WE'LL FIGURE OUT SOMETHING.
I ONLY HOPE THIS TIME IT'S A WELL-THOUGHT-OUT PLAN...
WITH A BIT OF RECKLESS INITIATIVE?

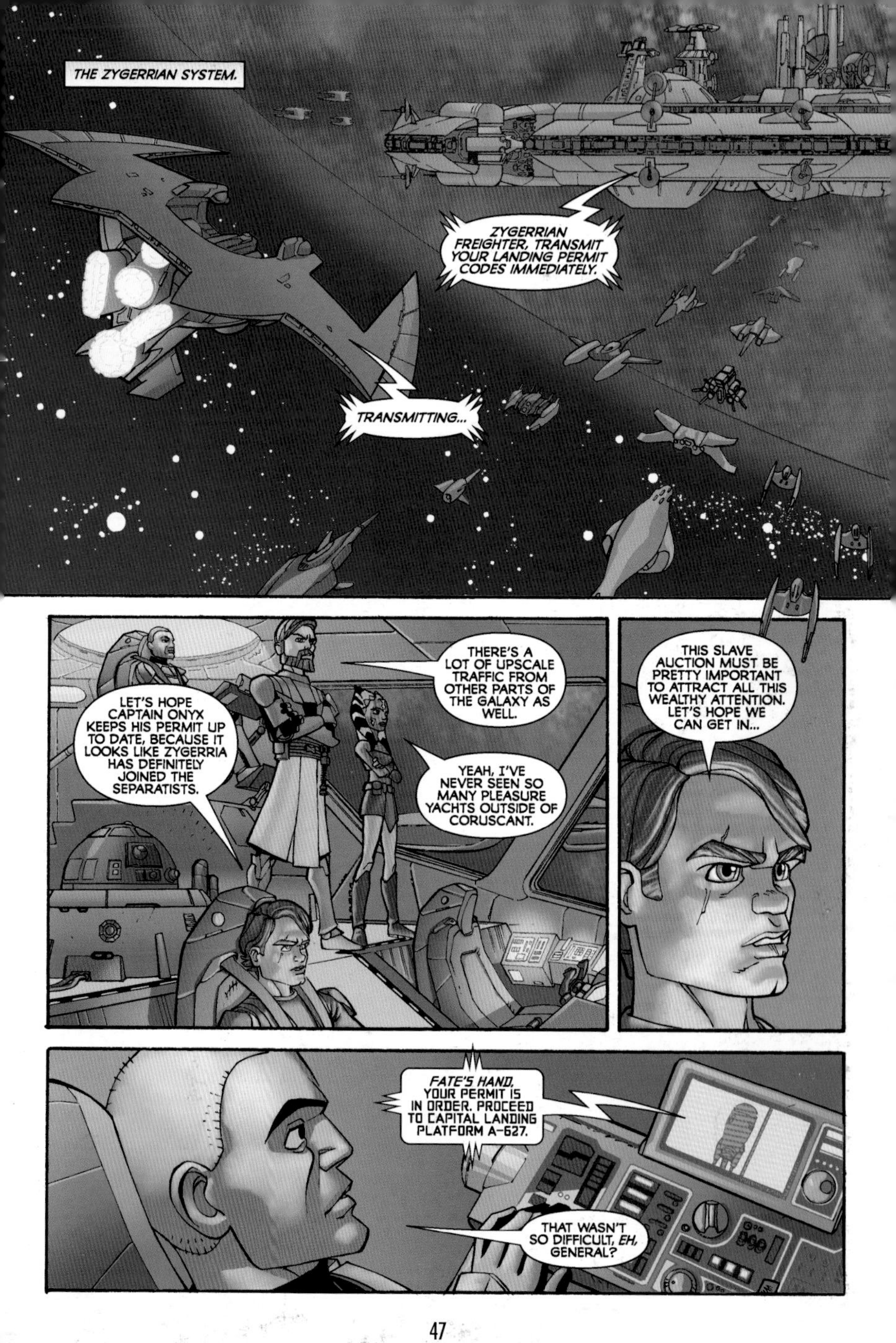
THE ZYGERRIAN SYSTEM.
ZYGERRIAN FREIGHTER, TRANSMIT YOUR LANDING PERMIT CODES IMMEDIATELY.
TRANSMITTING...
THERE'S A LOT OF UPSCALE TRAFFIC FROM OTHER PARTS OF THE GALAXY AS WELL.
LET'S HOPE CAPTAIN ONYX KEEPS HIS PERMIT UP TO DATE, BECAUSE IT LOOKS LIKE ZYGERRIA HAS DEFINITELY JOINED THE SEPARATISTS.
YEAH, I'VE NEVER SEEN SO MANY PLEASURE YACHTS OUTSIDE OF CORUSCANT.
THIS SLAVE AUCTION MUST BE PRETTY IMPORTANT TO ATTRACT ALL THIS WEALTHY ATTENTION. LET'S HOPE WE CAN GET IN...
FATE'S HAND, YOUR PERMIT IS IN ORDER. PROCEED TO CAPITAL LANDING PLATFORM A-627.
THAT WASN'T SO DIFFICULT, EH, GENERAL?

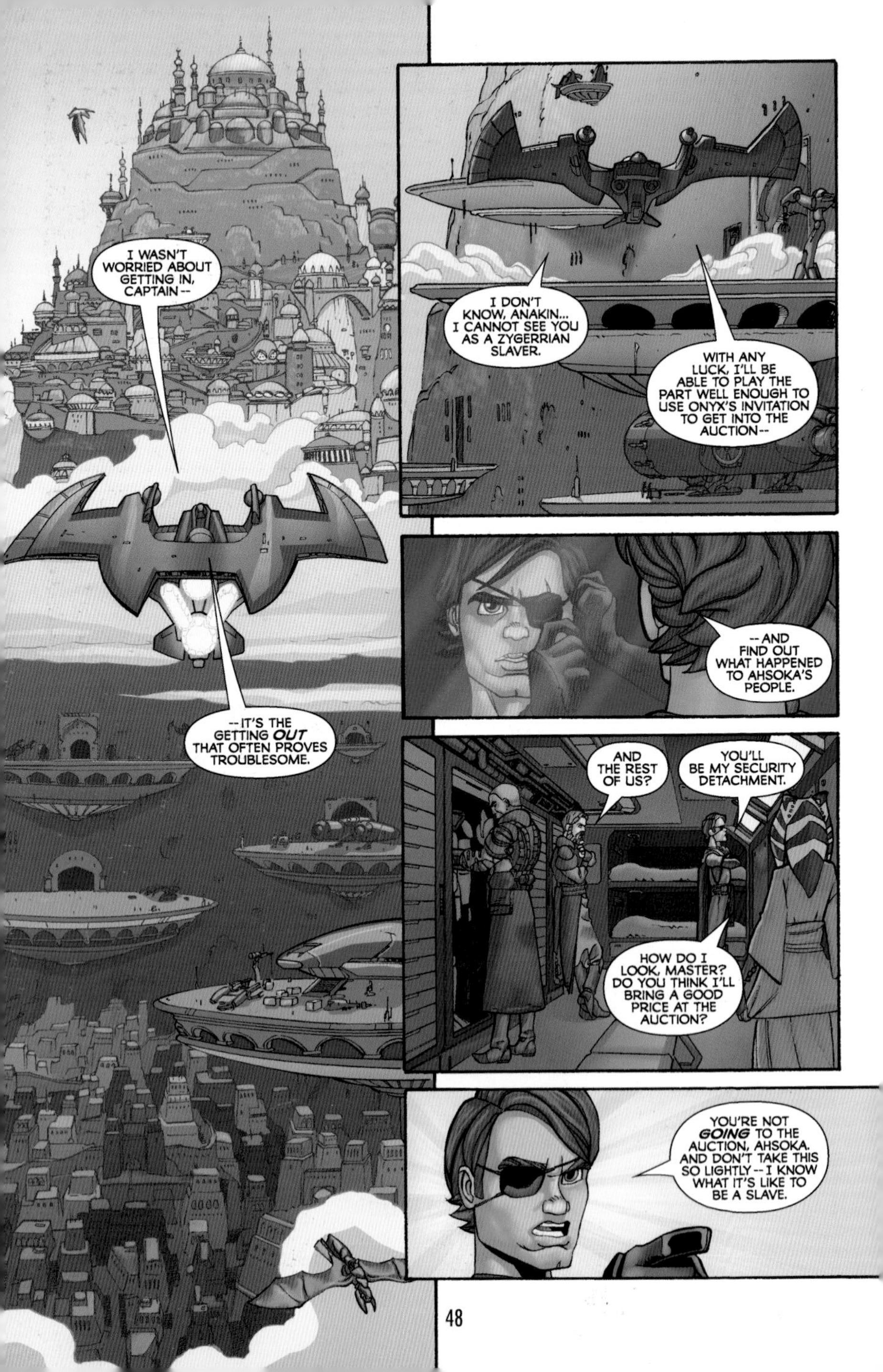

I WASN'T WORRIED ABOUT GETTING IN, CAPTAIN --
-- IT'S THE GETTING OUT THAT OFTEN PROVES TROUBLESOME.
I DON'T KNOW, ANAKIN... I CANNOT SEE YOU AS A ZYGERRIAN SLAVER.
WITH ANY LUCK, I'LL BE ABLE TO PLAY THE PART WELL ENOUGH TO USE ONYX'S INVITATION TO GET INTO THE AUCTION --
-- AND FIND OUT WHAT HAPPENED TO AHSOKA'S PEOPLE.
AND THE REST OF US?
YOU'LL BE MY SECURITY DETACHMENT.
HOW DO I LOOK, MASTER? DO YOU THINK I'LL BRING A GOOD PRICE AT THE AUCTION?
YOU'RE NOT GOING TO THE AUCTION, AHSOKA. AND DON'T TAKE THIS SO LIGHTLY -- I KNOW WHAT IT'S LIKE TO BE A SLAVE.

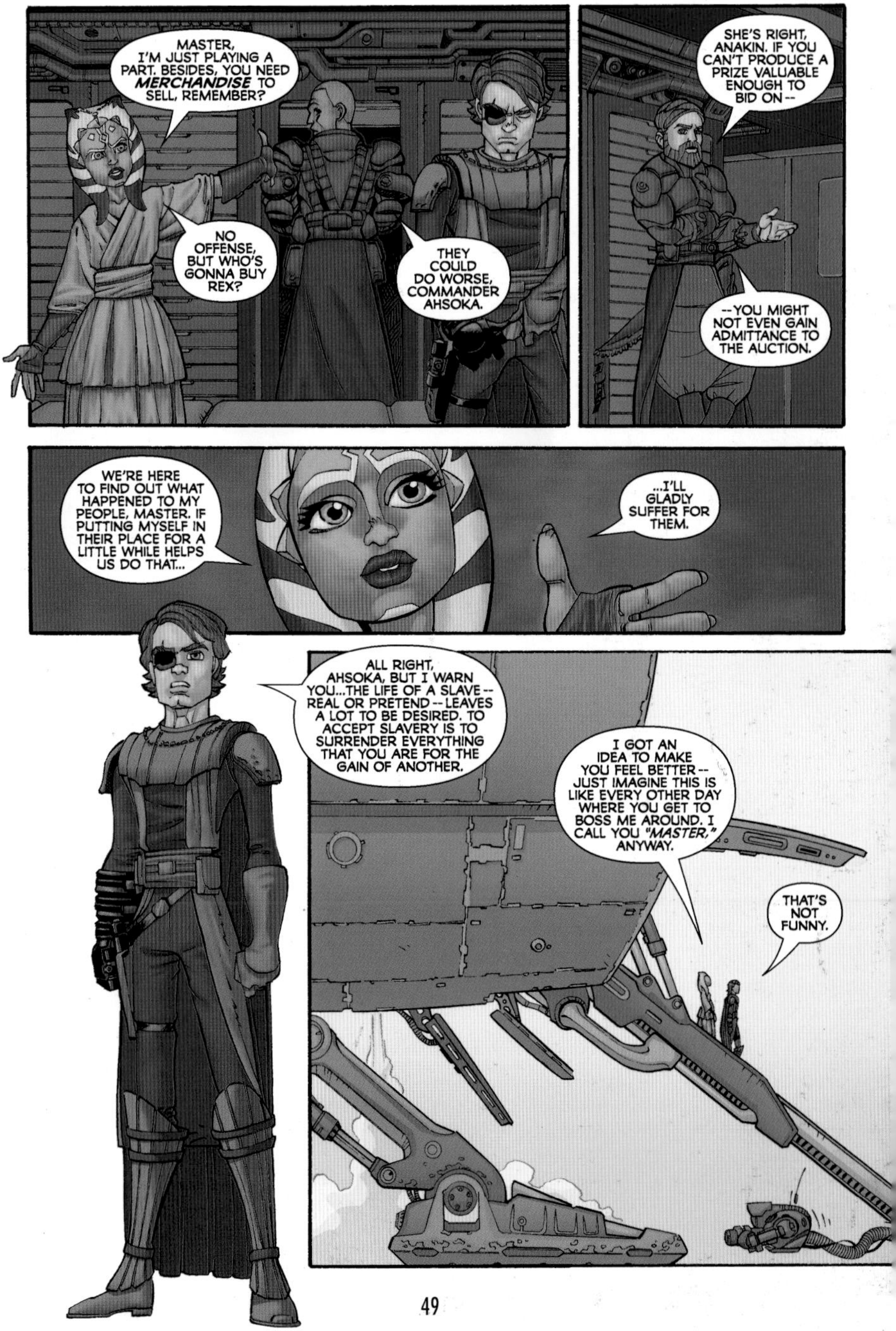
MASTER, I'M JUST PLAYING A PART. BESIDES, YOU NEED *MERCHANDISE* TO SELL, REMEMBER?
NO OFFENSE, BUT WHO'S GONNA BUY REX?
THEY COULD DO WORSE, COMMANDER AHSOKA.
SHE'S RIGHT, ANAKIN. IF YOU CAN'T PRODUCE A PRIZE VALUABLE ENOUGH TO BID ON--
--YOU MIGHT NOT EVEN GAIN ADMITTANCE TO THE AUCTION.
WE'RE HERE TO FIND OUT WHAT HAPPENED TO MY PEOPLE, MASTER. IF PUTTING MYSELF IN THEIR PLACE FOR A LITTLE WHILE HELPS US DO THAT...
...I'LL GLADLY SUFFER FOR THEM.
ALL RIGHT, AHSOKA, BUT I WARN YOU...THE LIFE OF A SLAVE--REAL OR PRETEND--LEAVES A LOT TO BE DESIRED. TO ACCEPT SLAVERY IS TO SURRENDER EVERYTHING THAT YOU ARE FOR THE GAIN OF ANOTHER.
I GOT AN IDEA TO MAKE YOU FEEL BETTER--JUST IMAGINE THIS IS LIKE EVERY OTHER DAY WHERE YOU GET TO BOSS ME AROUND. I CALL YOU *"MASTER,"* ANYWAY.
THAT'S NOT FUNNY.

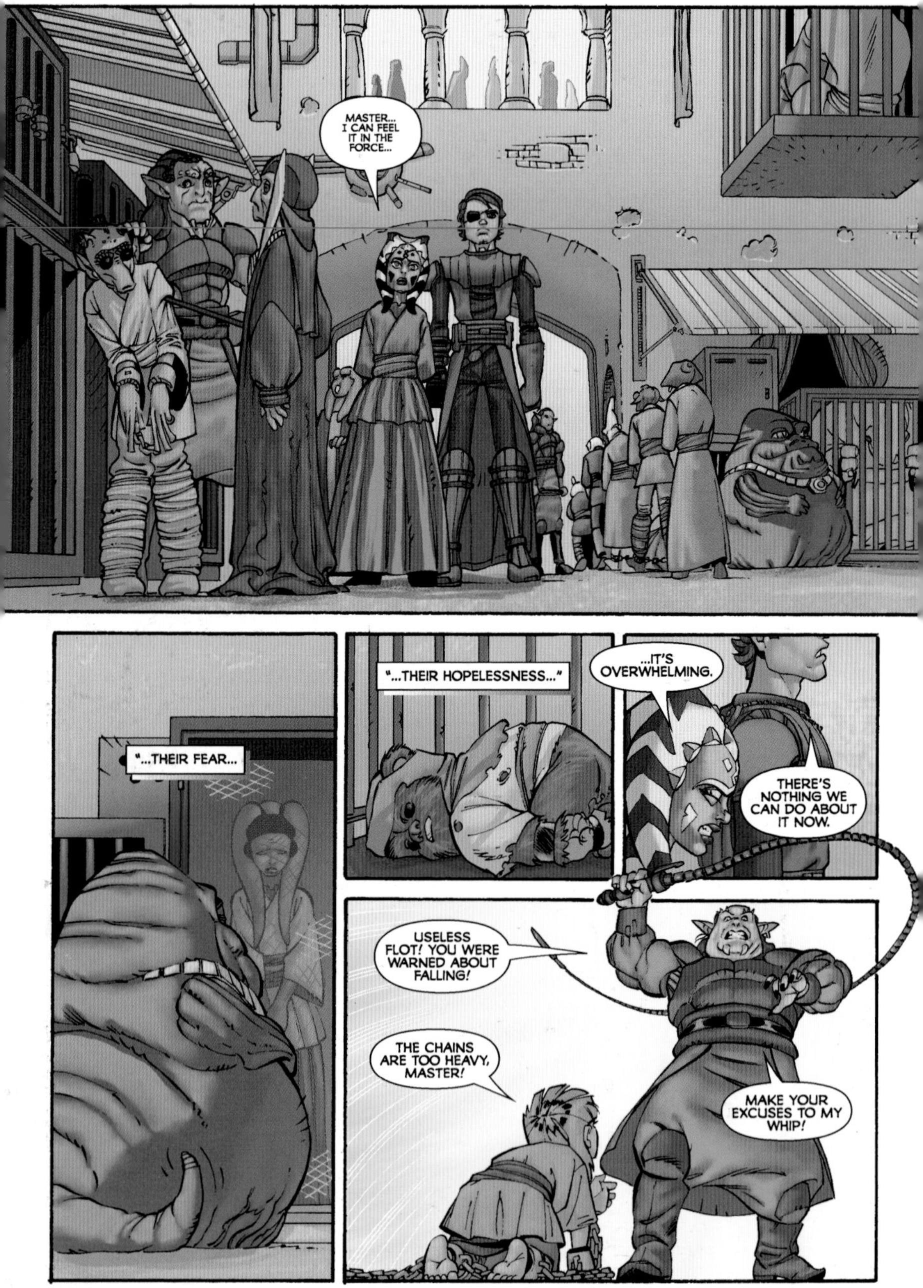
MASTER... I CAN FEEL IT IN THE FORCE...
"...THEIR FEAR...
"...THEIR HOPELESSNESS..."
...IT'S OVERWHELMING.
THERE'S NOTHING WE CAN DO ABOUT IT NOW.
USELESS FLOT! YOU WERE WARNED ABOUT FALLING!
THE CHAINS ARE TOO HEAVY, MASTER!
MAKE YOUR EXCUSES TO MY WHIP!

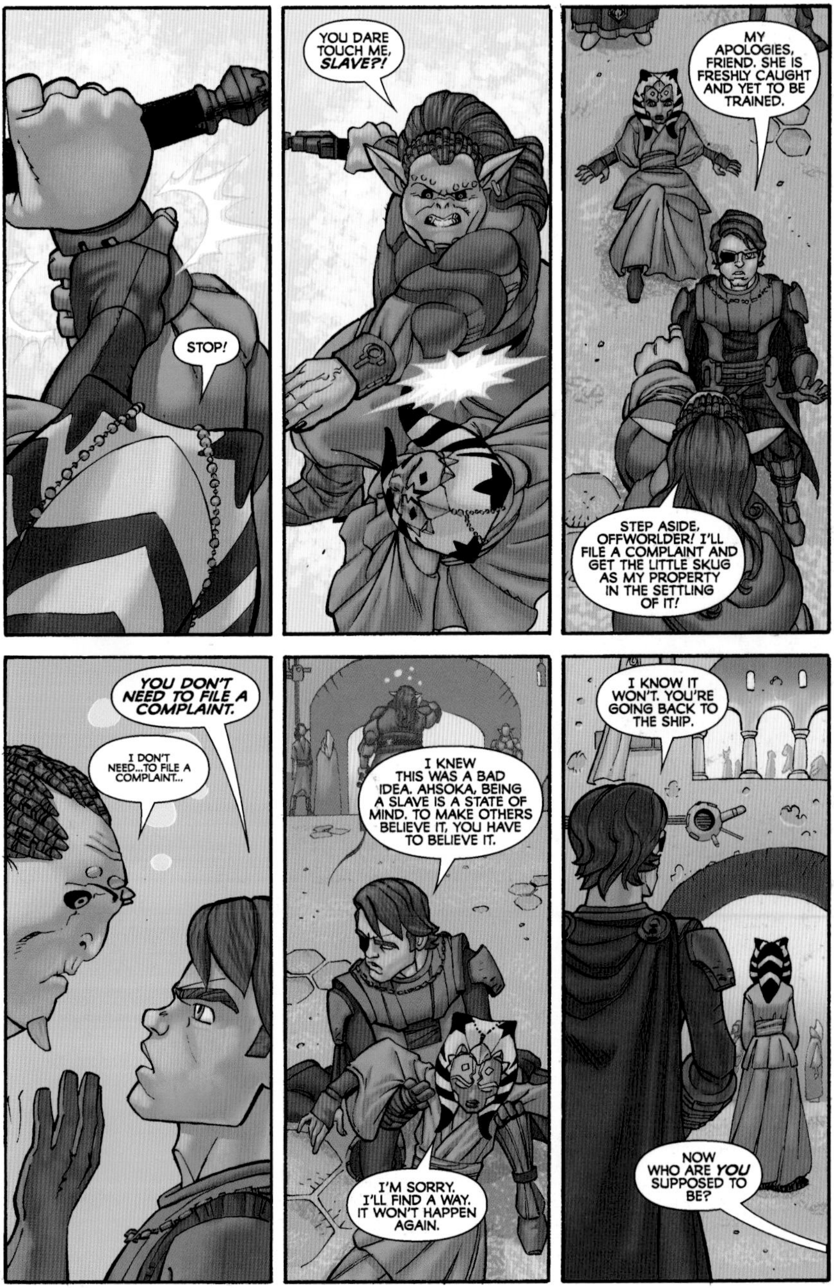
STOP!
YOU DARE TOUCH ME, *SLAVE?!*
MY APOLOGIES, FRIEND. SHE IS FRESHLY CAUGHT AND YET TO BE TRAINED.
STEP ASIDE, OFFWORLDER! I'LL FILE A COMPLAINT AND GET THE LITTLE SKUG AS MY PROPERTY IN THE SETTLING OF IT!
YOU DON'T NEED TO FILE A COMPLAINT.
I DON'T NEED...TO FILE A COMPLAINT...
I KNEW THIS WAS A BAD IDEA. AHSOKA, BEING A SLAVE IS A STATE OF MIND. TO MAKE OTHERS BELIEVE IT, YOU HAVE TO BELIEVE IT.
I'M SORRY. I'LL FIND A WAY. IT WON'T HAPPEN AGAIN.
I KNOW IT WON'T. YOU'RE GOING BACK TO THE SHIP.
NOW WHO ARE *YOU* SUPPOSED TO BE?

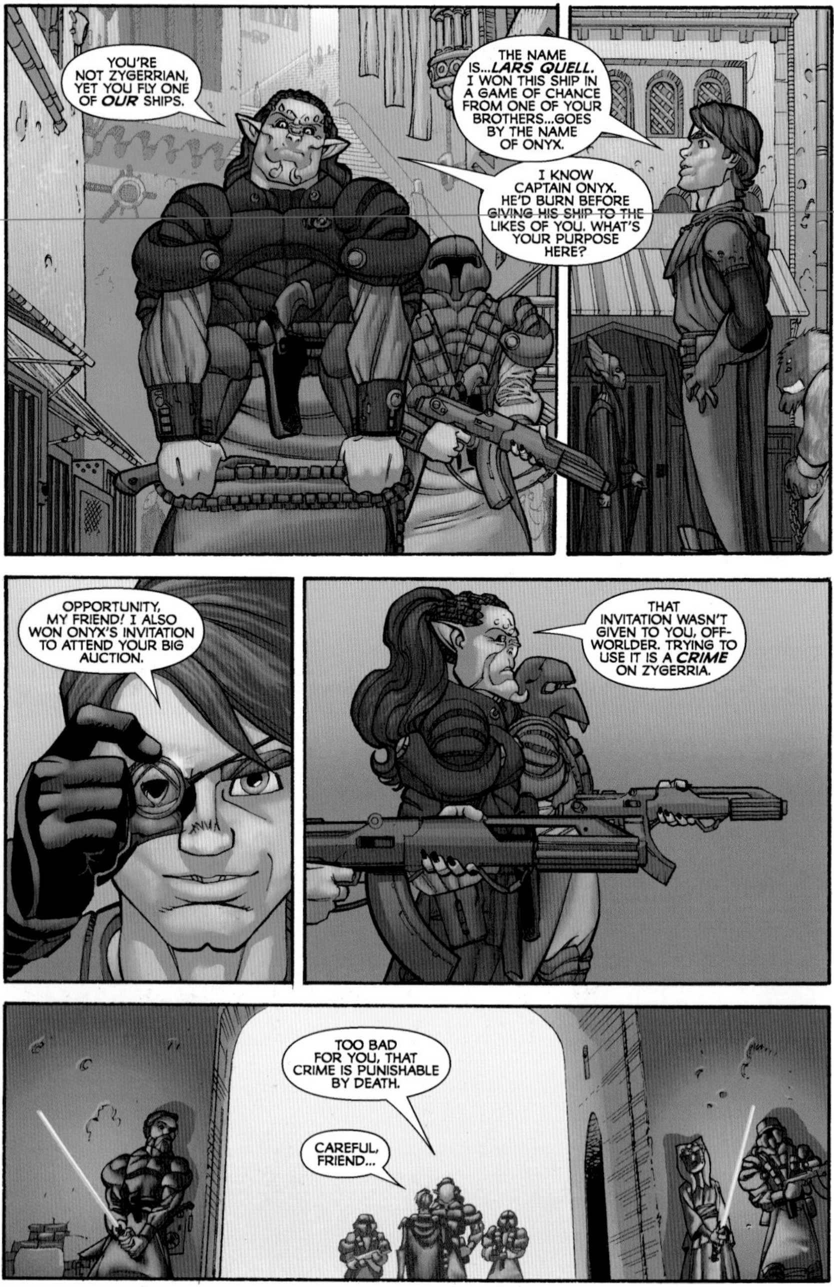
YOU'RE NOT ZYGERRIAN, YET YOU FLY ONE OF OUR SHIPS.
THE NAME IS...LARS QUELL. I WON THIS SHIP IN A GAME OF CHANCE FROM ONE OF YOUR BROTHERS...GOES BY THE NAME OF ONYX.
I KNOW CAPTAIN ONYX. HE'D BURN BEFORE GIVING HIS SHIP TO THE LIKES OF YOU. WHAT'S YOUR PURPOSE HERE?
OPPORTUNITY, MY FRIEND! I ALSO WON ONYX'S INVITATION TO ATTEND YOUR BIG AUCTION.
THAT INVITATION WASN'T GIVEN TO YOU, OFF-WORLDER. TRYING TO USE IT IS A CRIME ON ZYGERRIA.
TOO BAD FOR YOU, THAT CRIME IS PUNISHABLE BY DEATH.
CAREFUL, FRIEND...

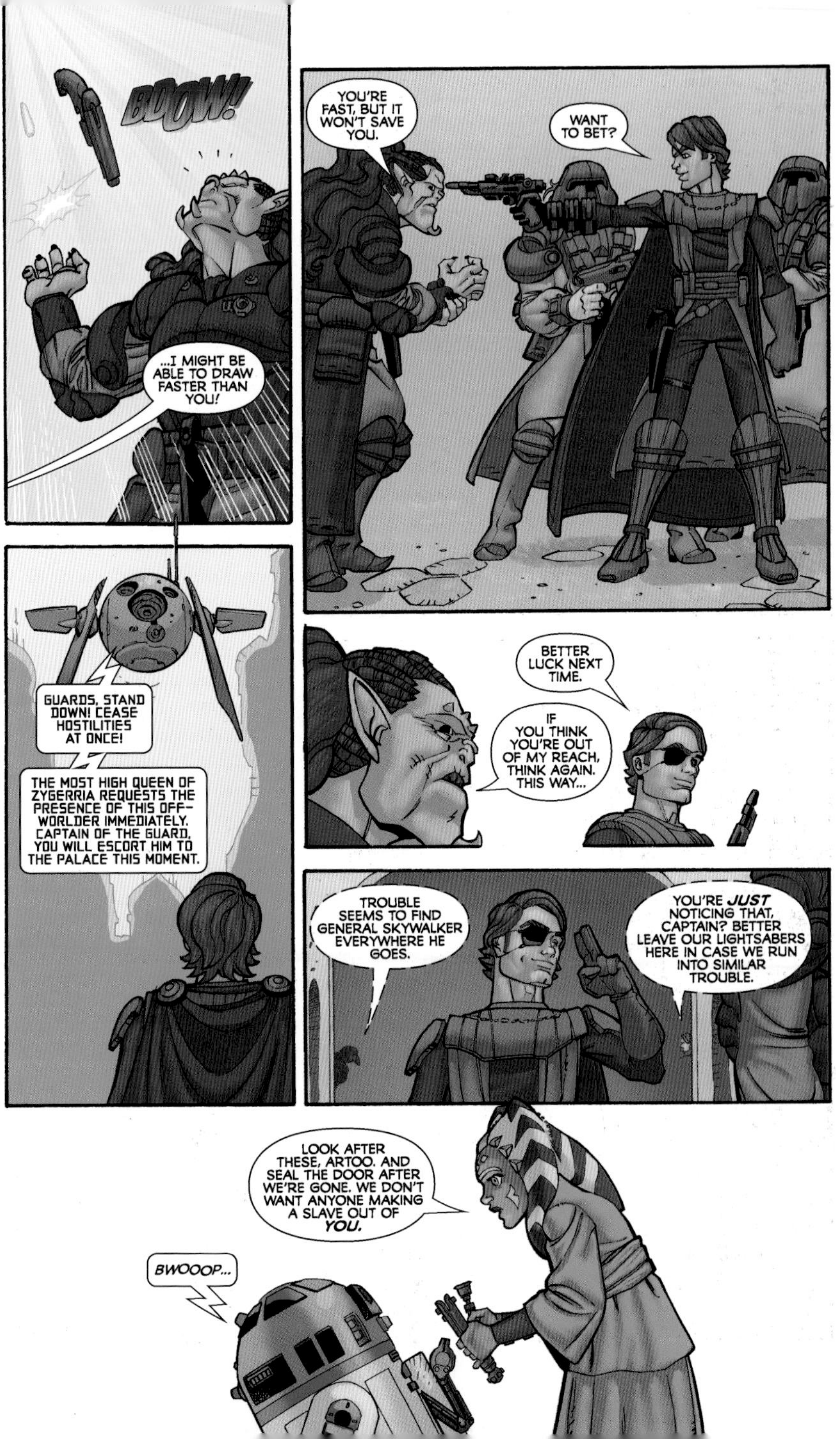
BDOW!
...I MIGHT BE ABLE TO DRAW FASTER THAN YOU!
YOU'RE FAST, BUT IT WON'T SAVE YOU.
WANT TO BET?
GUARDS, STAND DOWN! CEASE HOSTILITIES AT ONCE!
THE MOST HIGH QUEEN OF ZYGERRIA REQUESTS THE PRESENCE OF THIS OFF-WORLDER IMMEDIATELY. CAPTAIN OF THE GUARD, YOU WILL ESCORT HIM TO THE PALACE THIS MOMENT.
BETTER LUCK NEXT TIME.
IF YOU THINK YOU'RE OUT OF MY REACH, THINK AGAIN. THIS WAY...
TROUBLE SEEMS TO FIND GENERAL SKYWALKER EVERYWHERE HE GOES.
YOU'RE *JUST* NOTICING THAT, CAPTAIN? BETTER LEAVE OUR LIGHTSABERS HERE IN CASE WE RUN INTO SIMILAR TROUBLE.
LOOK AFTER THESE, ARTOO. AND SEAL THE DOOR AFTER WE'RE GONE. WE DON'T WANT ANYONE MAKING A SLAVE OUT OF ***YOU.***
BWOOOP...

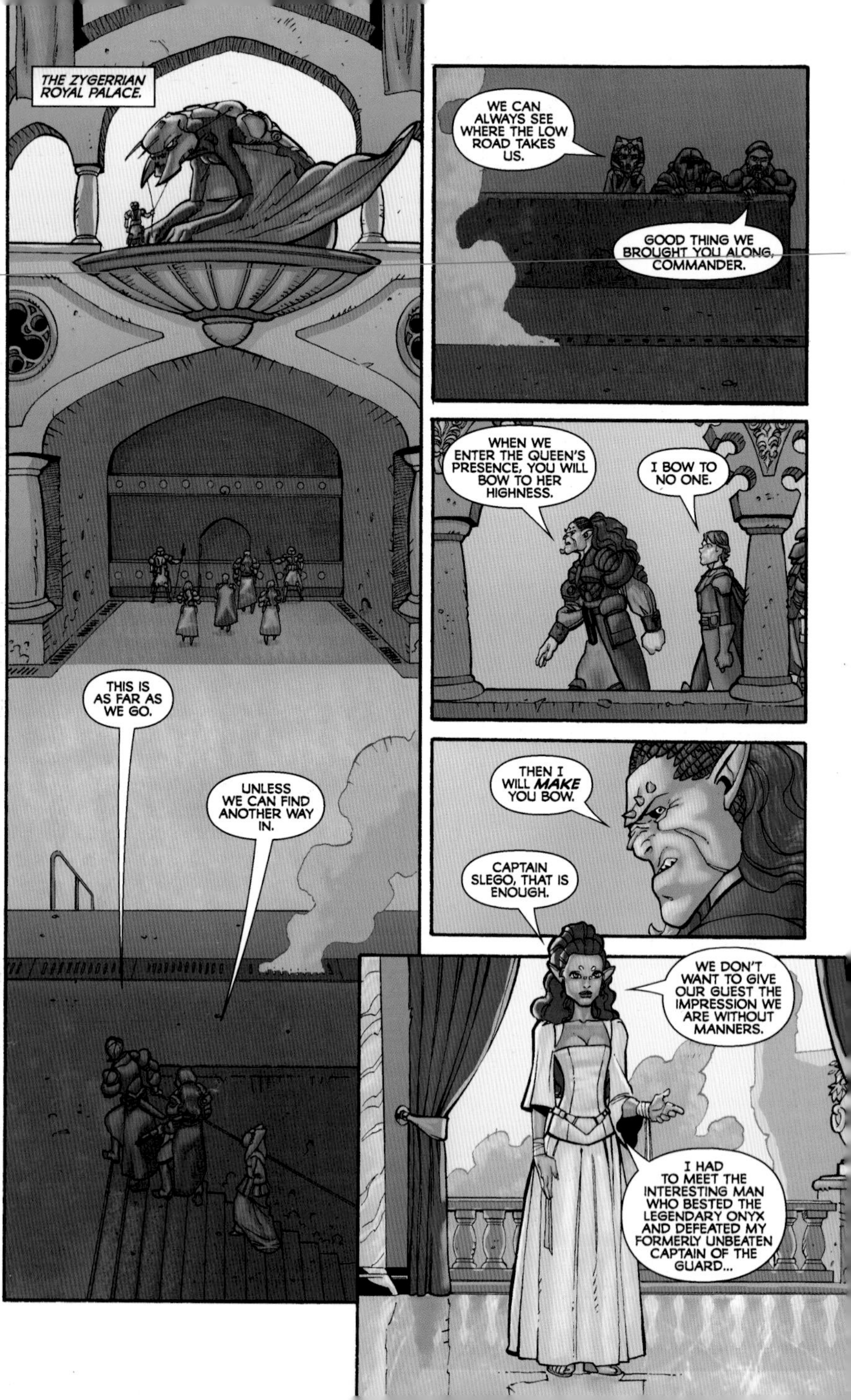
THE ZYGERRIAN ROYAL PALACE.
THIS IS AS FAR AS WE GO.
UNLESS WE CAN FIND ANOTHER WAY IN.
WE CAN ALWAYS SEE WHERE THE LOW ROAD TAKES US.
GOOD THING WE BROUGHT YOU ALONG, COMMANDER.
WHEN WE ENTER THE QUEEN'S PRESENCE, YOU WILL BOW TO HER HIGHNESS.
I BOW TO NO ONE.
THEN I WILL MAKE YOU BOW.
CAPTAIN SLEGO, THAT IS ENOUGH.
WE DON'T WANT TO GIVE OUR GUEST THE IMPRESSION WE ARE WITHOUT MANNERS.
I HAD TO MEET THE INTERESTING MAN WHO BESTED THE LEGENDARY ONYX AND DEFEATED MY FORMERLY UNBEATEN CAPTAIN OF THE GUARD...

...AND WHO IS SO BOLD HE WILL NOT BOW TO ME.

I MEAN NO DISRESPECT, BUT YOU ARE NOT *MY* QUEEN.

NOT *YET*, PERHAPS. LEAVE US, CAPTAIN.

AS YOU WISH.

TELL ME HOW YOU CAME TO MY WORLD, QUELL, IS IT?

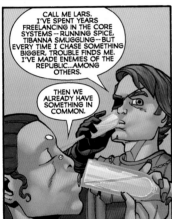

CALL ME LARS. I'VE SPENT YEARS FREELANCING IN THE CORE SYSTEMS -- RUNNING SPICE, TIBANNA SMUGGLING -- BUT EVERY TIME I CHASE SOMETHING BIGGER, TROUBLE FINDS ME. I'VE MADE ENEMIES OF THE REPUBLIC...AMONG OTHERS.

THEN WE ALREADY HAVE SOMETHING IN COMMON.

WE SEEK A BETTER LIFE...

...AND THERE ARE MANY WHO WOULD STOP US FROM TAKING IT.

WALK WITH ME, LARS QUELL... I LIKE THAT NAME. IT SOUNDS LIKE A NAME THAT I CAN TRUST.

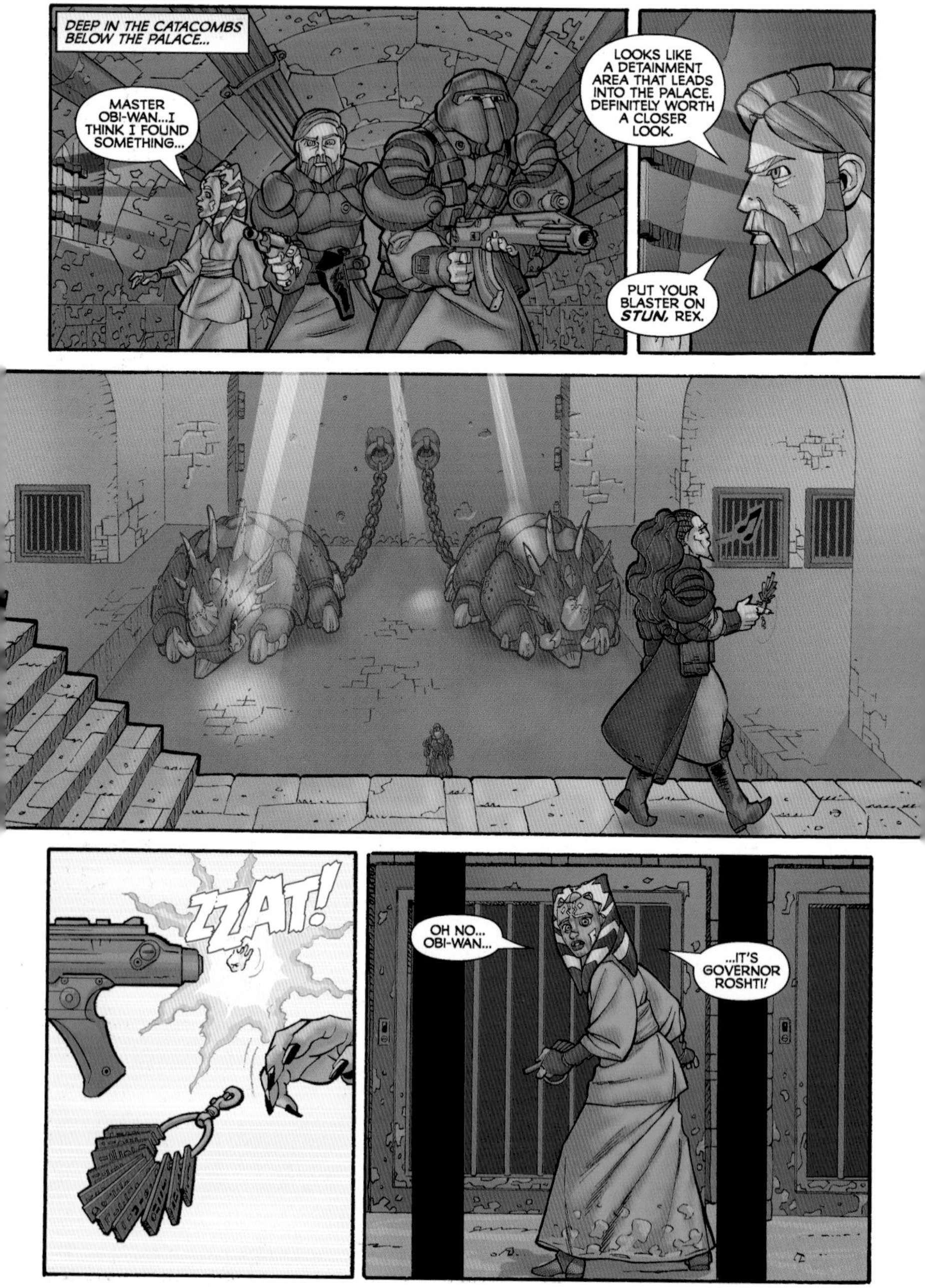
DEEP IN THE CATACOMBS BELOW THE PALACE...
MASTER OBI-WAN...I THINK I FOUND SOMETHING...
LOOKS LIKE A DETAINMENT AREA THAT LEADS INTO THE PALACE. DEFINITELY WORTH A CLOSER LOOK.
PUT YOUR BLASTER ON STUN, REX.
ZZAT!
OH NO... OBI-WAN...
...IT'S GOVERNOR ROSHTI!

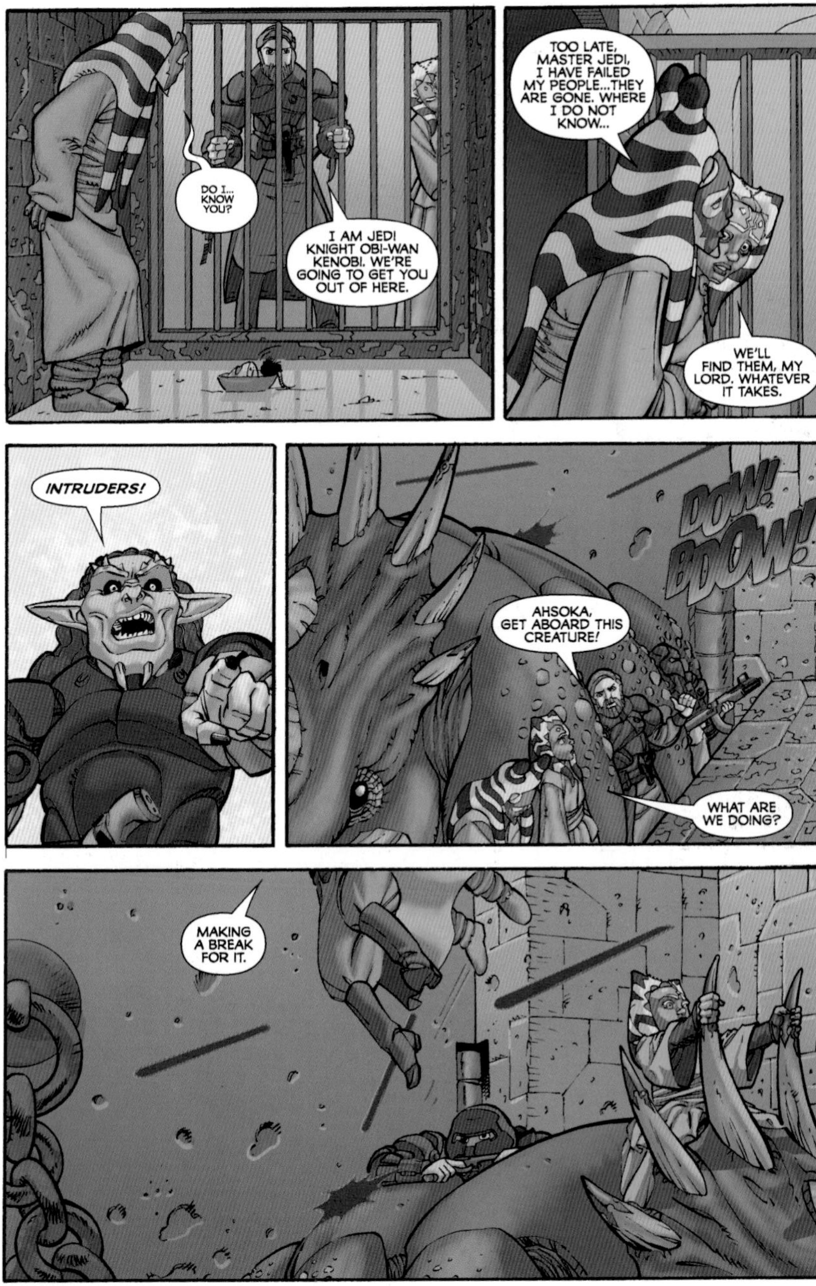
DO I... KNOW YOU?
I AM JEDI KNIGHT OBI-WAN KENOBI. WE'RE GOING TO GET YOU OUT OF HERE.
TOO LATE, MASTER JEDI, I HAVE FAILED MY PEOPLE...THEY ARE GONE. WHERE I DO NOT KNOW...
WE'LL FIND THEM, MY LORD. WHATEVER IT TAKES.
INTRUDERS!
DOW! BDOW!
AHSOKA, GET ABOARD THIS CREATURE!
WHAT ARE WE DOING?
MAKING A BREAK FOR IT.

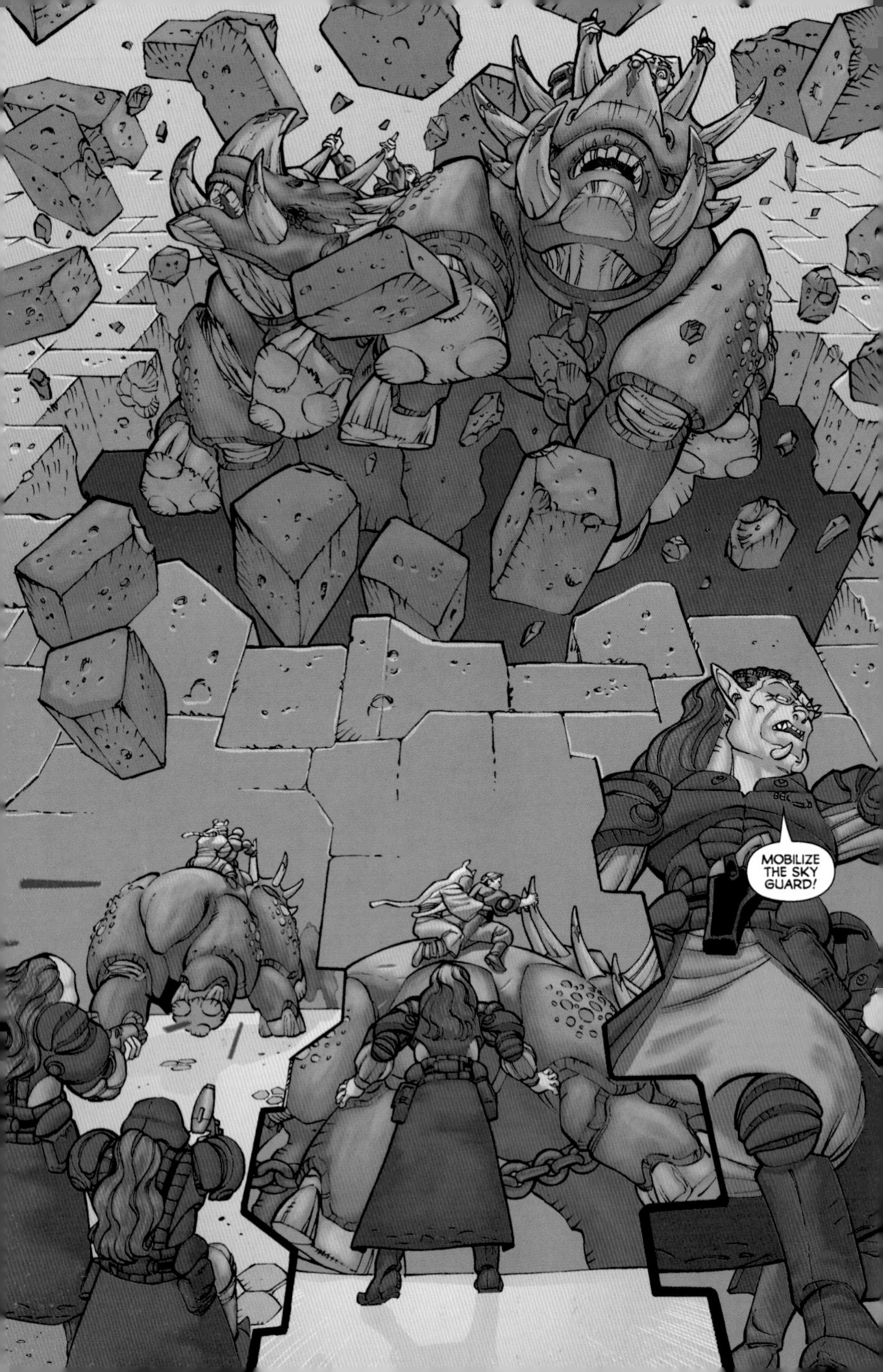
MOBILIZE THE SKY GUARD!

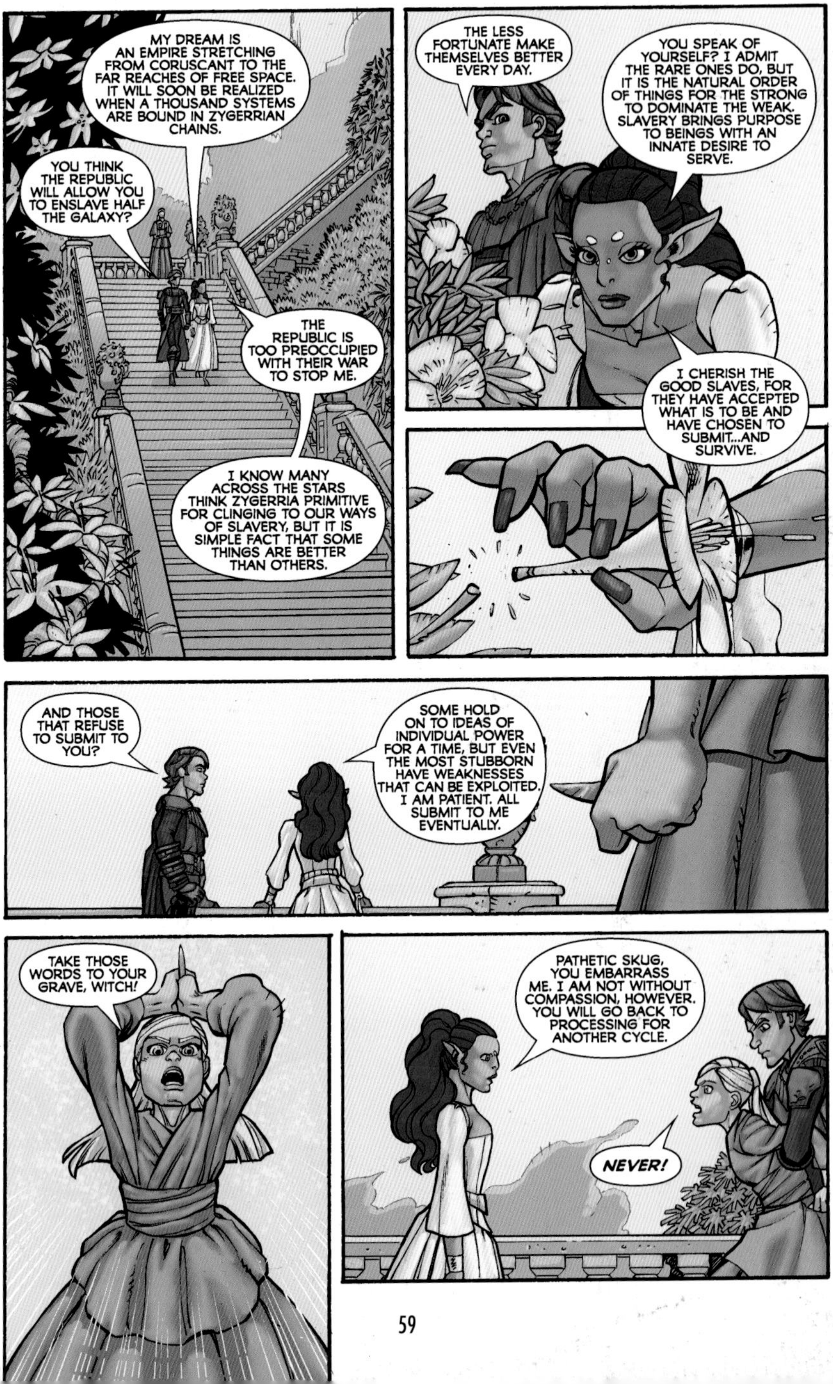
MY DREAM IS AN EMPIRE STRETCHING FROM CORUSCANT TO THE FAR REACHES OF FREE SPACE. IT WILL SOON BE REALIZED WHEN A THOUSAND SYSTEMS ARE BOUND IN ZYGERRIAN CHAINS.
YOU THINK THE REPUBLIC WILL ALLOW YOU TO ENSLAVE HALF THE GALAXY?
THE REPUBLIC IS TOO PREOCCUPIED WITH THEIR WAR TO STOP ME.
I KNOW MANY ACROSS THE STARS THINK ZYGERRIA PRIMITIVE FOR CLINGING TO OUR WAYS OF SLAVERY, BUT IT IS SIMPLE FACT THAT SOME THINGS ARE BETTER THAN OTHERS.
THE LESS FORTUNATE MAKE THEMSELVES BETTER EVERY DAY.
YOU SPEAK OF YOURSELF? I ADMIT THE RARE ONES DO, BUT IT IS THE NATURAL ORDER OF THINGS FOR THE STRONG TO DOMINATE THE WEAK. SLAVERY BRINGS PURPOSE TO BEINGS WITH AN INNATE DESIRE TO SERVE.
I CHERISH THE GOOD SLAVES, FOR THEY HAVE ACCEPTED WHAT IS TO BE AND HAVE CHOSEN TO SUBMIT...AND SURVIVE.
AND THOSE THAT REFUSE TO SUBMIT TO YOU?
SOME HOLD ON TO IDEAS OF INDIVIDUAL POWER FOR A TIME, BUT EVEN THE MOST STUBBORN HAVE WEAKNESSES THAT CAN BE EXPLOITED. I AM PATIENT. ALL SUBMIT TO ME EVENTUALLY.
TAKE THOSE WORDS TO YOUR GRAVE, WITCH!
PATHETIC SKUG, YOU EMBARRASS ME. I AM NOT WITHOUT COMPASSION, HOWEVER. YOU WILL GO BACK TO PROCESSING FOR ANOTHER CYCLE.
NEVER!

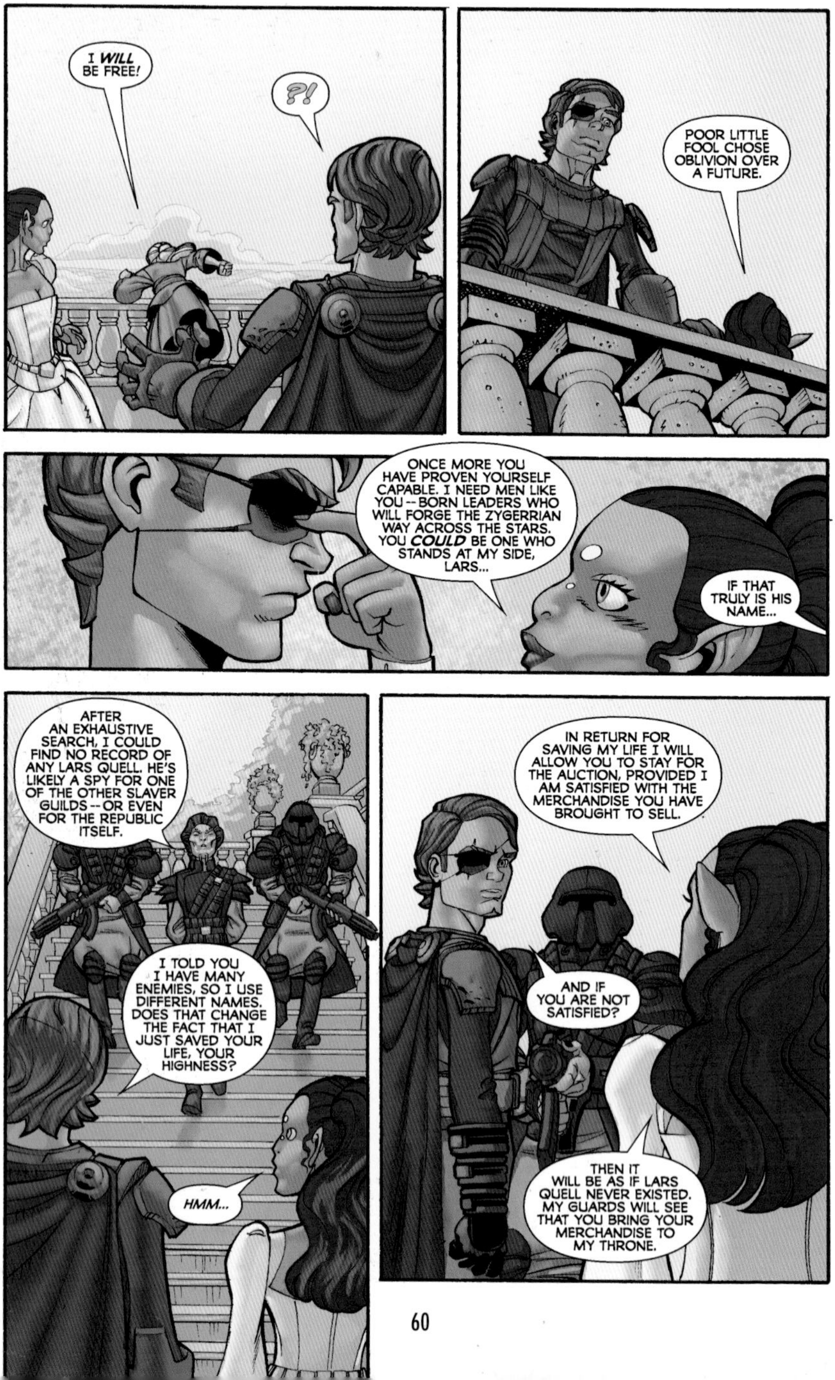
I WILL BE FREE!
?!
POOR LITTLE FOOL CHOSE OBLIVION OVER A FUTURE.
ONCE MORE YOU HAVE PROVEN YOURSELF CAPABLE. I NEED MEN LIKE YOU -- BORN LEADERS WHO WILL FORGE THE ZYGERRIAN WAY ACROSS THE STARS. YOU COULD BE ONE WHO STANDS AT MY SIDE, LARS...
IF THAT TRULY IS HIS NAME...
AFTER AN EXHAUSTIVE SEARCH, I COULD FIND NO RECORD OF ANY LARS QUELL. HE'S LIKELY A SPY FOR ONE OF THE OTHER SLAVER GUILDS -- OR EVEN FOR THE REPUBLIC ITSELF.
I TOLD YOU I HAVE MANY ENEMIES, SO I USE DIFFERENT NAMES. DOES THAT CHANGE THE FACT THAT I JUST SAVED YOUR LIFE, YOUR HIGHNESS?
HMM...
IN RETURN FOR SAVING MY LIFE I WILL ALLOW YOU TO STAY FOR THE AUCTION, PROVIDED I AM SATISFIED WITH THE MERCHANDISE YOU HAVE BROUGHT TO SELL.
AND IF YOU ARE NOT SATISFIED?
THEN IT WILL BE AS IF LARS QUELL NEVER EXISTED. MY GUARDS WILL SEE THAT YOU BRING YOUR MERCHANDISE TO MY THRONE.

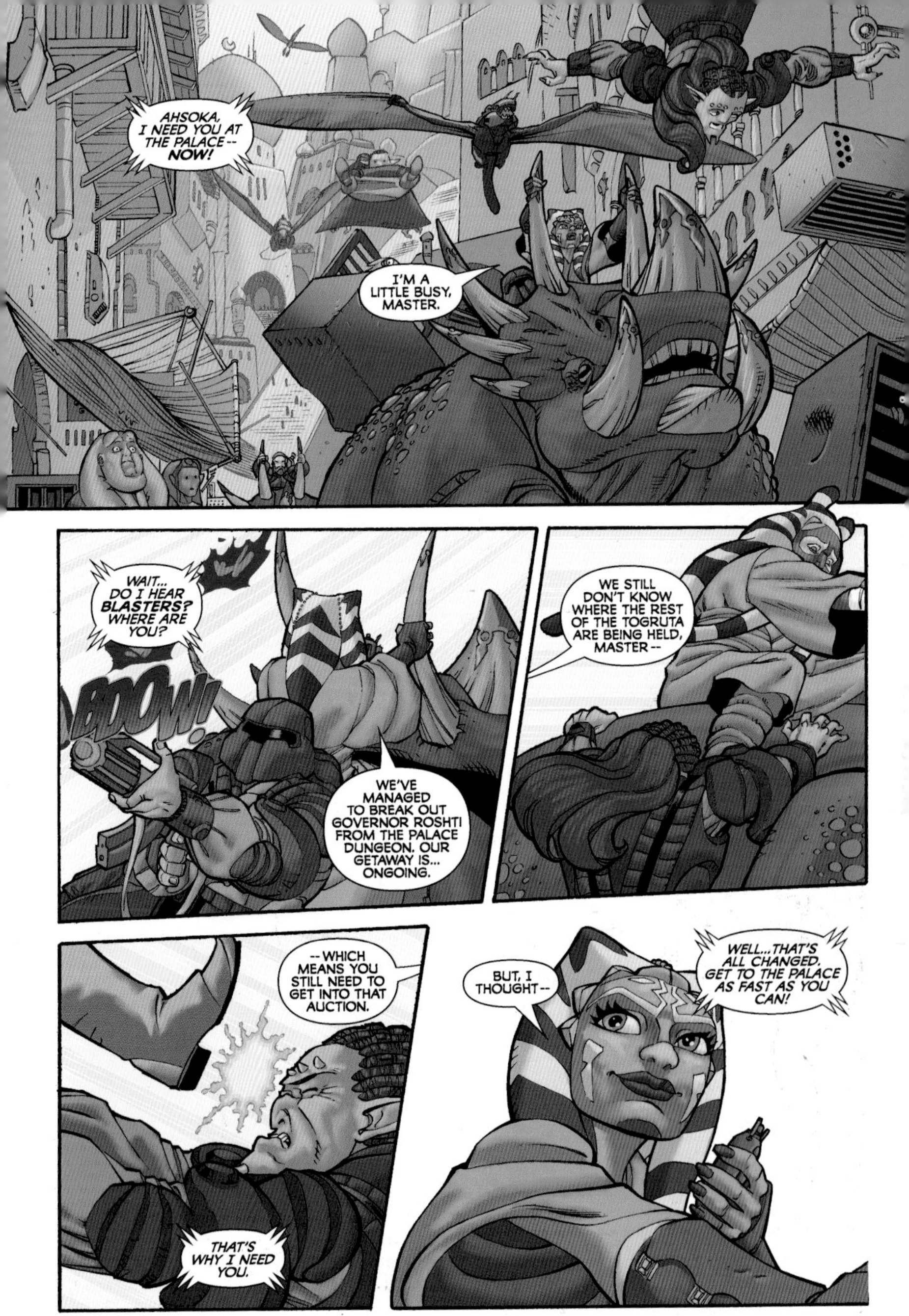
AHSOKA, I NEED YOU AT THE PALACE -- NOW!
I'M A LITTLE BUSY, MASTER.
WAIT... DO I HEAR BLASTERS? WHERE ARE YOU?
BDOW!
WE'VE MANAGED TO BREAK OUT GOVERNOR ROSHTI FROM THE PALACE DUNGEON. OUR GETAWAY IS... ONGOING.
WE STILL DON'T KNOW WHERE THE REST OF THE TOGRUTA ARE BEING HELD, MASTER --
-- WHICH MEANS YOU STILL NEED TO GET INTO THAT AUCTION.
THAT'S WHY I NEED YOU.
BUT, I THOUGHT --
WELL...THAT'S ALL CHANGED. GET TO THE PALACE AS FAST AS YOU CAN!

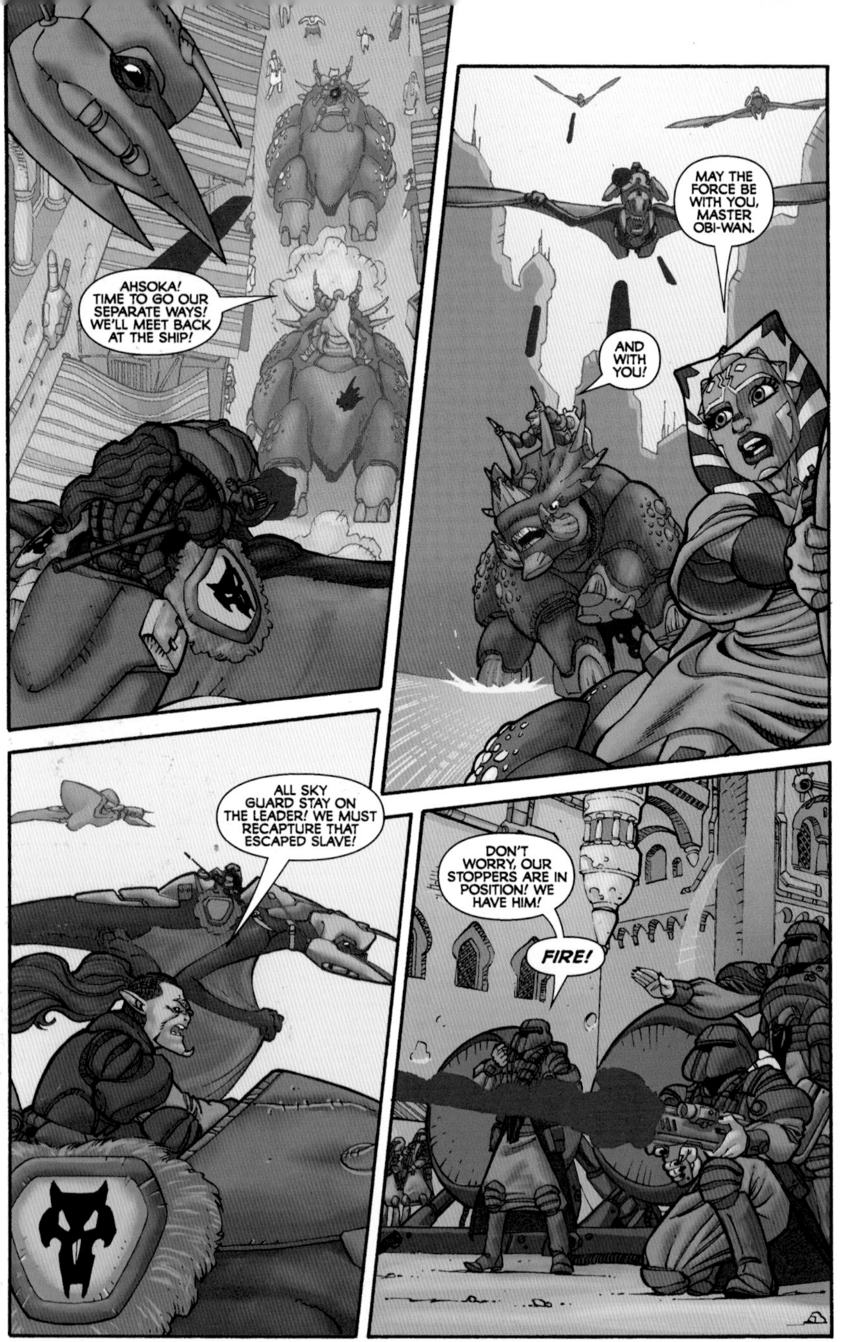
AHSOKA! TIME TO GO OUR SEPARATE WAYS! WE'LL MEET BACK AT THE SHIP!
MAY THE FORCE BE WITH YOU, MASTER OBI-WAN.
AND WITH YOU!
ALL SKY GUARD STAY ON THE LEADER! WE MUST RECAPTURE THAT ESCAPED SLAVE!
DON'T WORRY, OUR STOPPERS ARE IN POSITION! WE HAVE HIM!
FIRE!

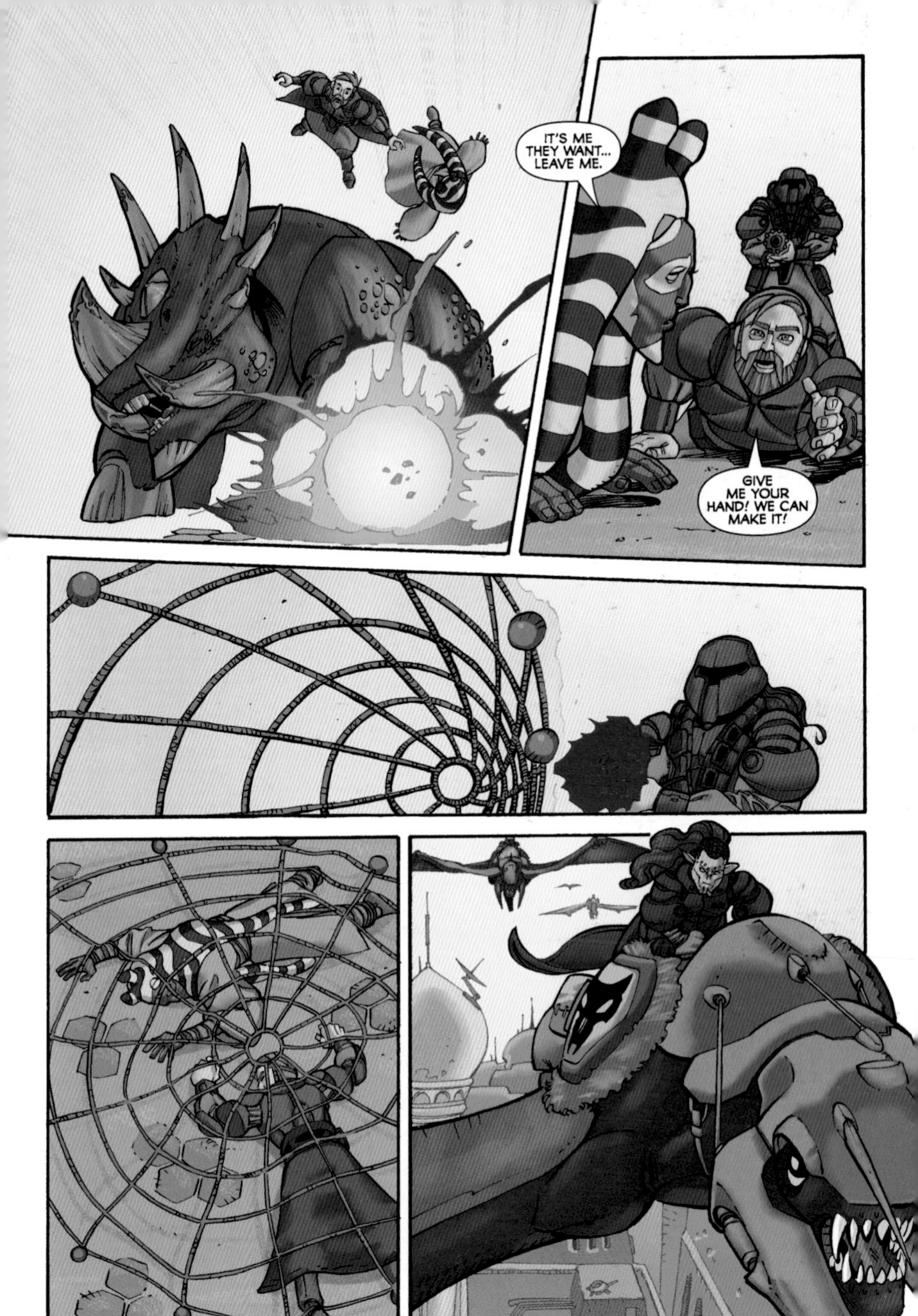
IT'S ME THEY WANT... LEAVE ME.
GIVE ME YOUR HAND! WE CAN MAKE IT!

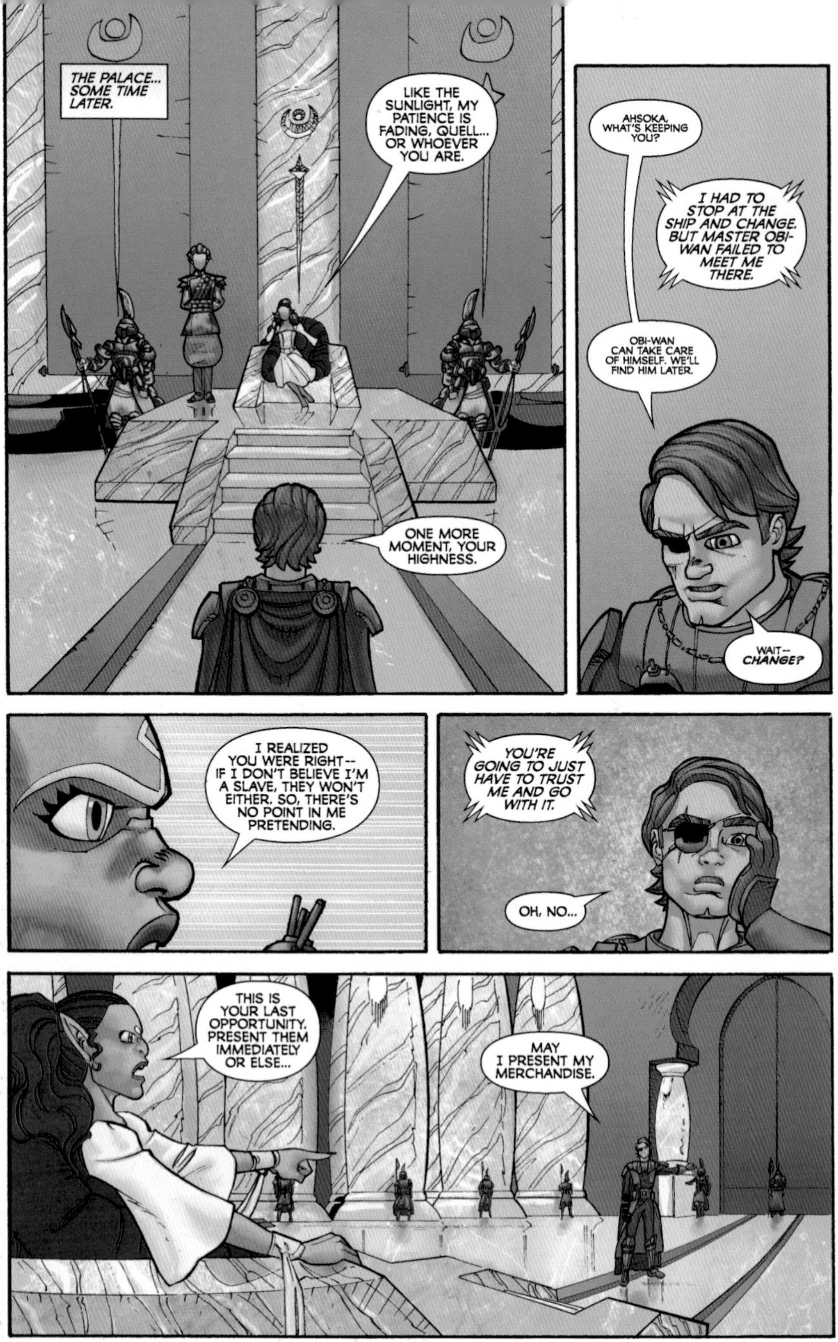
THE PALACE... SOME TIME LATER.
LIKE THE SUNLIGHT, MY PATIENCE IS FADING, QUELL... OR WHOEVER YOU ARE.
ONE MORE MOMENT, YOUR HIGHNESS.
AHSOKA, WHAT'S KEEPING YOU?
I HAD TO STOP AT THE SHIP AND CHANGE. BUT MASTER OBI-WAN FAILED TO MEET ME THERE.
OBI-WAN CAN TAKE CARE OF HIMSELF. WE'LL FIND HIM LATER.
WAIT-- CHANGE?
I REALIZED YOU WERE RIGHT-- IF I DON'T BELIEVE I'M A SLAVE, THEY WON'T EITHER. SO, THERE'S NO POINT IN ME PRETENDING.
YOU'RE GOING TO JUST HAVE TO TRUST ME AND GO WITH IT.
OH, NO...
THIS IS YOUR LAST OPPORTUNITY. PRESENT THEM IMMEDIATELY OR ELSE...
MAY I PRESENT MY MERCHANDISE.

YOU WILL, PAY FOR THIS, *BRIGAND!* WHEN MY FATHER LEARNS OF THIS, HIS ROYAL GUARD WILL HUNT YOU DOWN AND BURN YOU!

DO YOU NOT RECOGNIZE ROYALTY? I AM PRINCESS ZAA VASHEE, *HEIRESS* TO THE THRONE OF SHILI.

OH. I HAVE HEARD OF YOUR HIGHNESS...

AND I AM AWARE SHE IS RARELY ALLOWED OFF HER HOMEWORLD.

IT WAS *I* WHO DECIDED THE TIME HAD COME FOR ME TO SEE THE GALAXY! MY TRIP WAS WITHOUT INCIDENT -- UNTIL THIS INSOLENT WRETCH *ABDUCTED* ME!

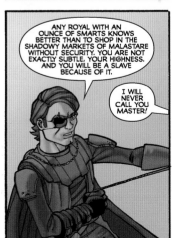

ANY ROYAL WITH AN OUNCE OF SMARTS KNOWS BETTER THAN TO SHOP IN THE SHADOWY MARKETS OF MALASTARE WITHOUT SECURITY. YOU ARE NOT EXACTLY SUBTLE, YOUR HIGHNESS. AND YOU WILL BE A SLAVE BECAUSE OF IT.

I WILL NEVER CALL YOU MASTER!

WE'LL SEE ABOUT THAT!

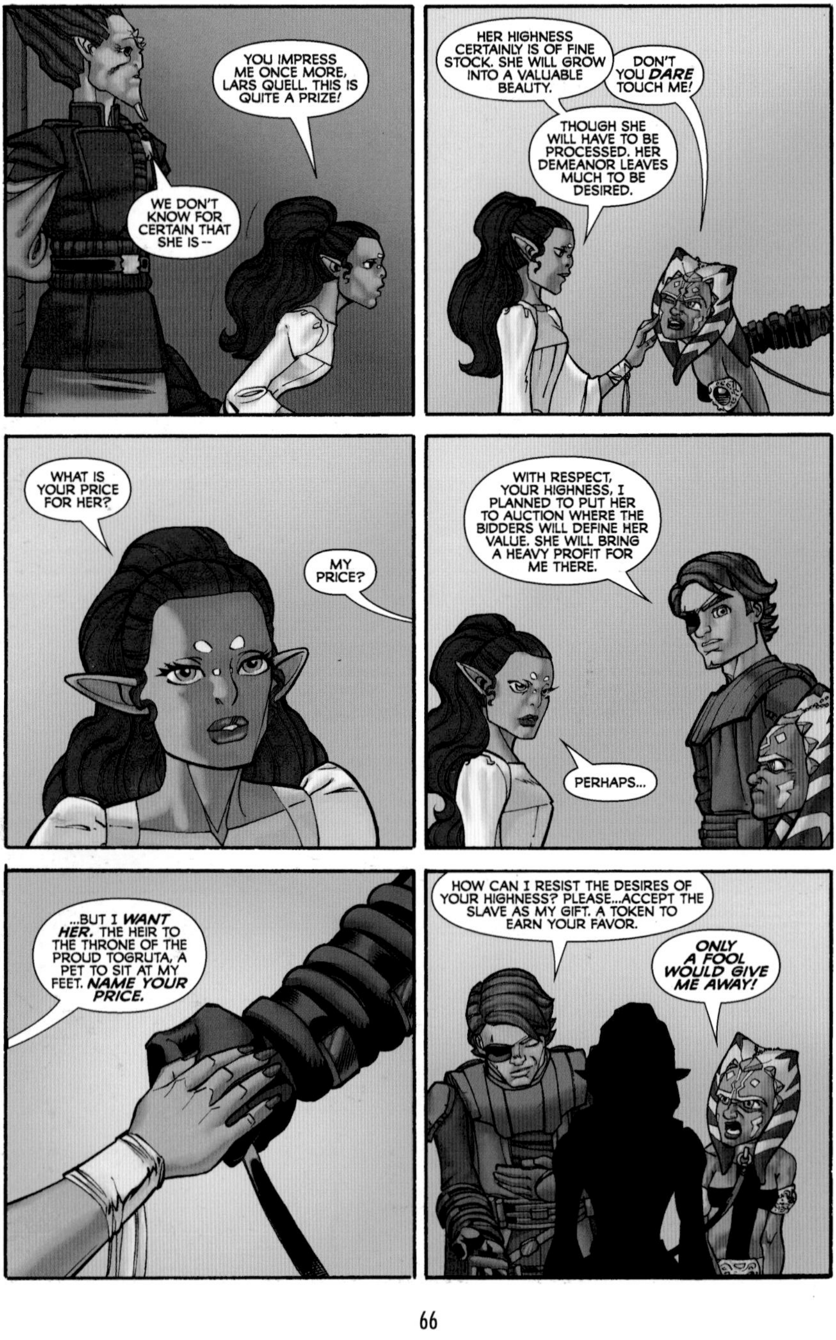
YOU IMPRESS ME ONCE MORE, LARS QUELL. THIS IS QUITE A PRIZE!
WE DON'T KNOW FOR CERTAIN THAT SHE IS --
HER HIGHNESS CERTAINLY IS OF FINE STOCK. SHE WILL GROW INTO A VALUABLE BEAUTY.
THOUGH SHE WILL HAVE TO BE PROCESSED. HER DEMEANOR LEAVES MUCH TO BE DESIRED.
DON'T YOU *DARE* TOUCH ME!
WHAT IS YOUR PRICE FOR HER?
MY PRICE?
WITH RESPECT, YOUR HIGHNESS, I PLANNED TO PUT HER TO AUCTION WHERE THE BIDDERS WILL DEFINE HER VALUE. SHE WILL BRING A HEAVY PROFIT FOR ME THERE.
PERHAPS...
...BUT I *WANT HER.* THE HEIR TO THE THRONE OF THE PROUD TOGRUTA, A PET TO SIT AT MY FEET. *NAME YOUR PRICE.*
HOW CAN I RESIST THE DESIRES OF YOUR HIGHNESS? PLEASE...ACCEPT THE SLAVE AS MY GIFT. A TOKEN TO EARN YOUR FAVOR.
ONLY A FOOL WOULD GIVE ME AWAY!

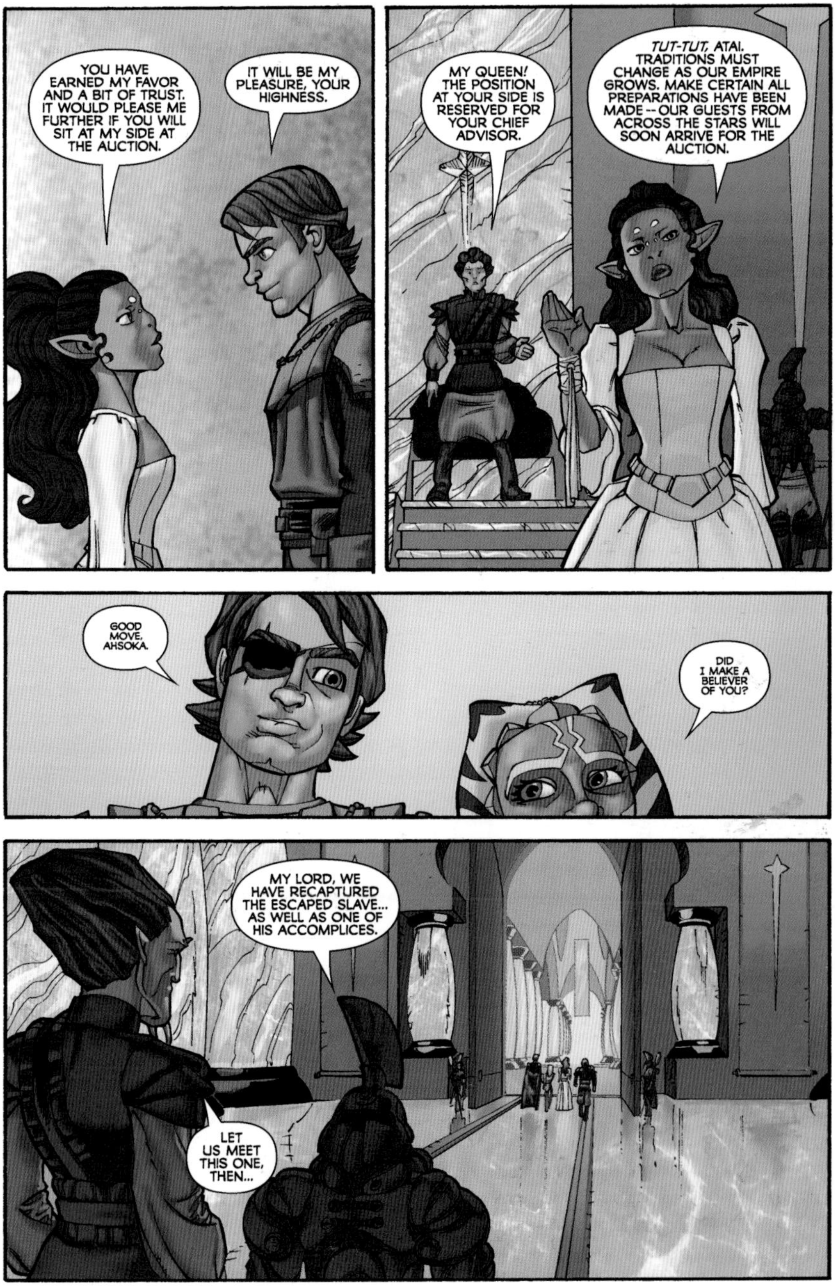
YOU HAVE EARNED MY FAVOR AND A BIT OF TRUST. IT WOULD PLEASE ME FURTHER IF YOU WILL SIT AT MY SIDE AT THE AUCTION.
IT WILL BE MY PLEASURE, YOUR HIGHNESS.
MY QUEEN! THE POSITION AT YOUR SIDE IS RESERVED FOR YOUR CHIEF ADVISOR.
TUT-TUT, ATAI. TRADITIONS MUST CHANGE AS OUR EMPIRE GROWS. MAKE CERTAIN ALL PREPARATIONS HAVE BEEN MADE -- OUR GUESTS FROM ACROSS THE STARS WILL SOON ARRIVE FOR THE AUCTION.
GOOD MOVE, AHSOKA.
DID I MAKE A BELIEVER OF YOU?
MY LORD, WE HAVE RECAPTURED THE ESCAPED SLAVE... AS WELL AS ONE OF HIS ACCOMPLICES.
LET US MEET THIS ONE, THEN...

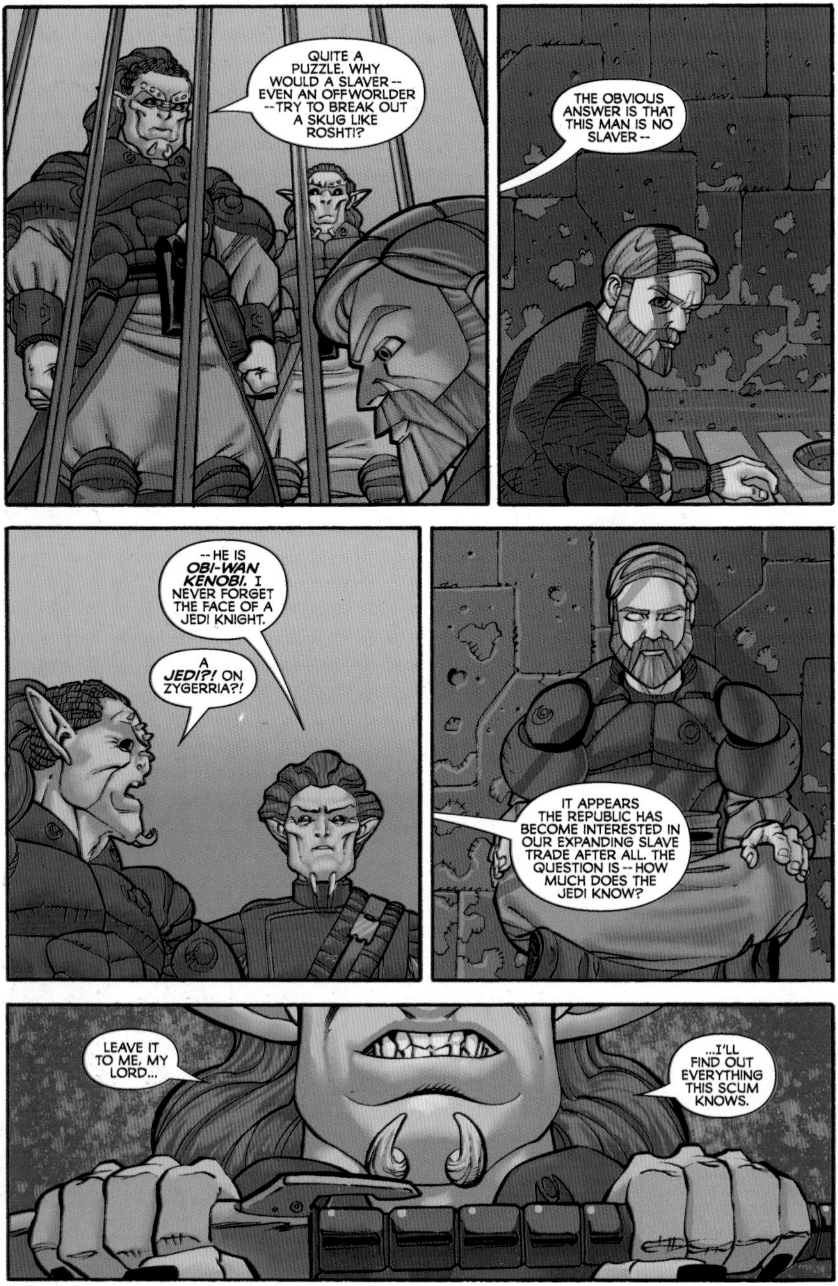
QUITE A PUZZLE. WHY WOULD A SLAVER -- EVEN AN OFFWORLDER --TRY TO BREAK OUT A SKUG LIKE ROSHTI?
THE OBVIOUS ANSWER IS THAT THIS MAN IS NO SLAVER --
--HE IS OBI-WAN KENOBI. I NEVER FORGET THE FACE OF A JEDI KNIGHT.
A JEDI?! ON ZYGERRIA?!
IT APPEARS THE REPUBLIC HAS BECOME INTERESTED IN OUR EXPANDING SLAVE TRADE AFTER ALL. THE QUESTION IS --HOW MUCH DOES THE JEDI KNOW?
LEAVE IT TO ME, MY LORD...
...I'LL FIND OUT EVERYTHING THIS SCUM KNOWS.

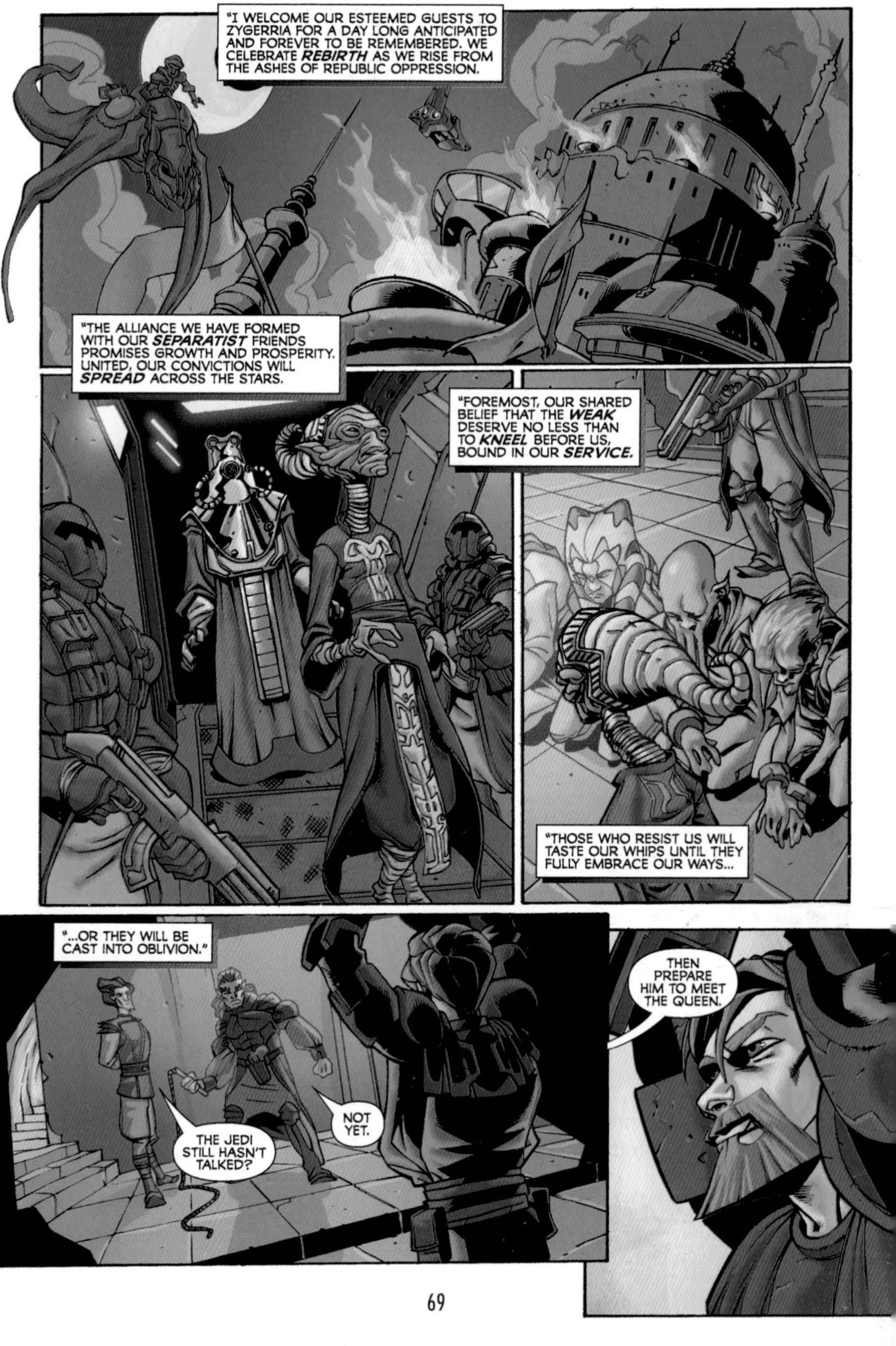
"I WELCOME OUR ESTEEMED GUESTS TO ZYGERRIA FOR A DAY LONG ANTICIPATED AND FOREVER TO BE REMEMBERED. WE CELEBRATE **REBIRTH** AS WE RISE FROM THE ASHES OF REPUBLIC OPPRESSION.
"THE ALLIANCE WE HAVE FORMED WITH OUR **SEPARATIST** FRIENDS PROMISES GROWTH AND PROSPERITY. UNITED, OUR CONVICTIONS WILL **SPREAD** ACROSS THE STARS.
"FOREMOST, OUR SHARED BELIEF THAT THE **WEAK** DESERVE NO LESS THAN TO **KNEEL** BEFORE US, BOUND IN OUR **SERVICE.**
"THOSE WHO RESIST US WILL TASTE OUR WHIPS UNTIL THEY FULLY EMBRACE OUR WAYS...
"...OR THEY WILL BE CAST INTO OBLIVION."
THE JEDI STILL HASN'T TALKED?
NOT YET.
THEN PREPARE HIM TO MEET THE QUEEN.

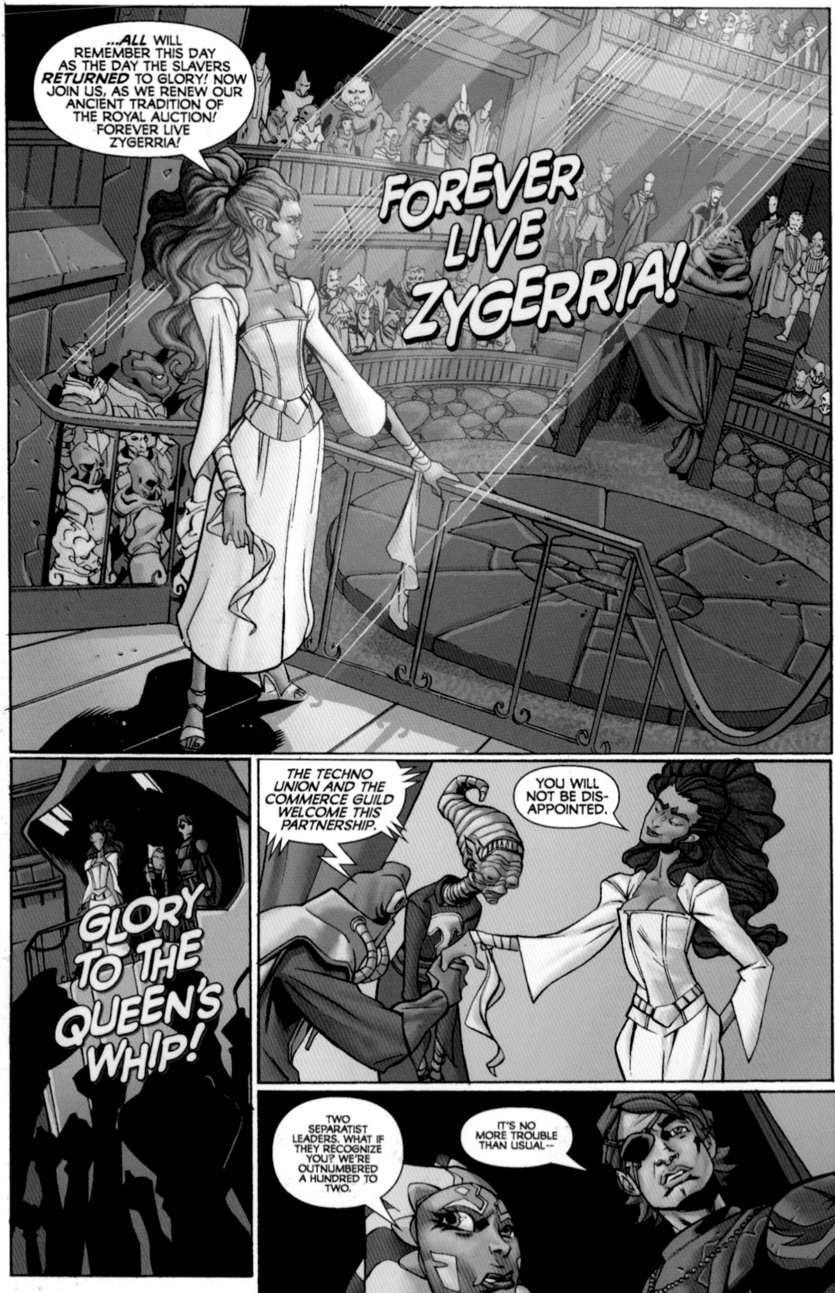
...ALL WILL REMEMBER THIS DAY AS THE DAY THE SLAVERS RETURNED TO GLORY! NOW JOIN US, AS WE RENEW OUR ANCIENT TRADITION OF THE ROYAL AUCTION! FOREVER LIVE ZYGERRIA!
FOREVER LIVE ZYGERRIA!
GLORY TO THE QUEEN'S WHIP!
THE TECHNO UNION AND THE COMMERCE GUILD WELCOME THIS PARTNERSHIP.
YOU WILL NOT BE DIS-APPOINTED.
TWO SEPARATIST LEADERS. WHAT IF THEY RECOGNIZE YOU? WE'RE OUTNUMBERED A HUNDRED TO TWO.
IT'S NO MORE TROUBLE THAN USUAL--

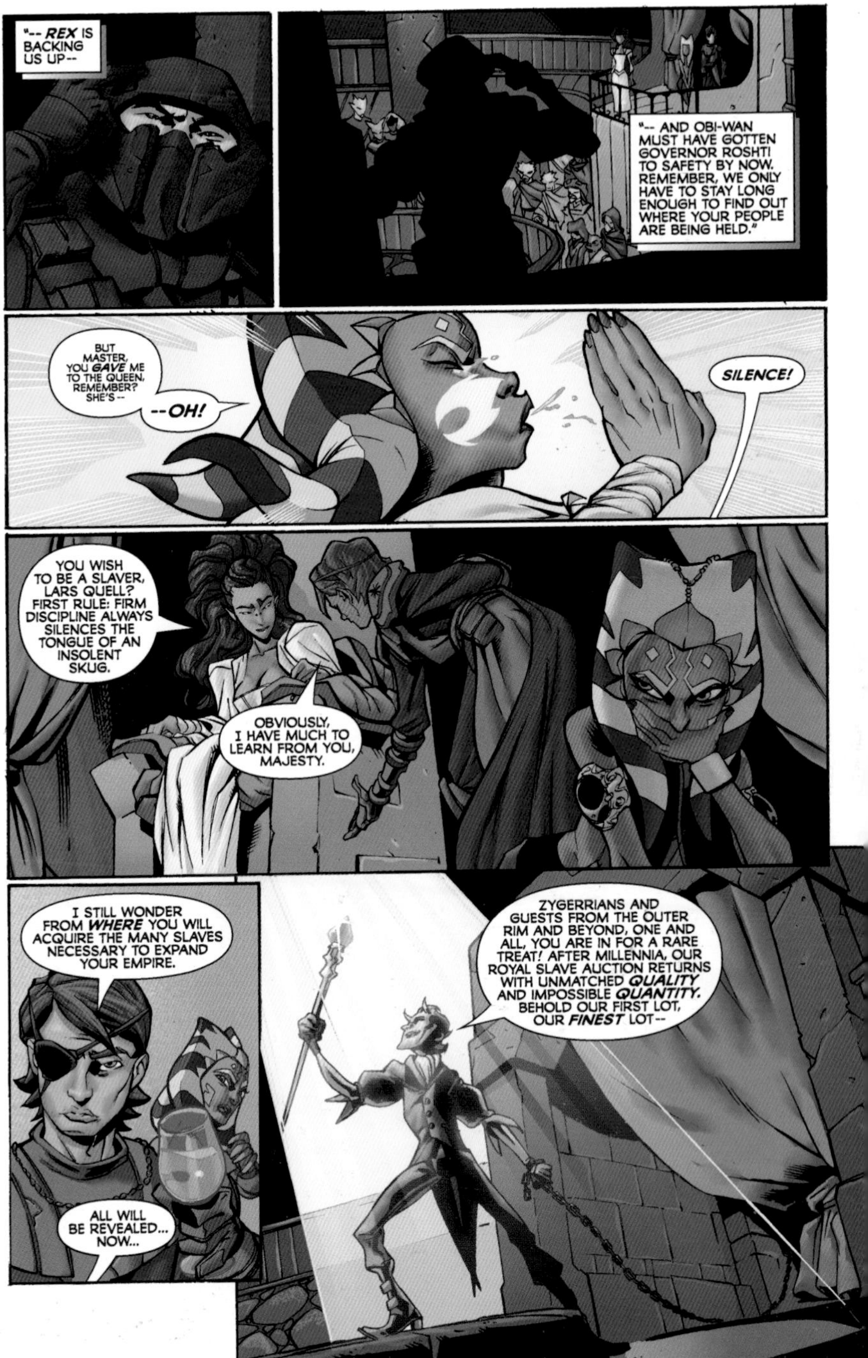
"-- *REX* IS BACKING US UP--
"-- AND OBI-WAN MUST HAVE GOTTEN GOVERNOR ROSHTI TO SAFETY BY NOW. REMEMBER, WE ONLY HAVE TO STAY LONG ENOUGH TO FIND OUT WHERE YOUR PEOPLE ARE BEING HELD."
BUT MASTER, YOU *GAVE* ME TO THE QUEEN, REMEMBER? SHE'S --
--OH!
SILENCE!
YOU WISH TO BE A SLAVER, LARS QUELL? FIRST RULE: FIRM DISCIPLINE ALWAYS SILENCES THE TONGUE OF AN INSOLENT SKUG.
OBVIOUSLY, I HAVE MUCH TO LEARN FROM YOU, MAJESTY.
I STILL WONDER FROM *WHERE* YOU WILL ACQUIRE THE MANY SLAVES NECESSARY TO EXPAND YOUR EMPIRE.
ALL WILL BE REVEALED... NOW...
ZYGERRIANS AND GUESTS FROM THE OUTER RIM AND BEYOND, ONE AND ALL, YOU ARE IN FOR A RARE TREAT! AFTER MILLENNIA, OUR ROYAL SLAVE AUCTION RETURNS WITH UNMATCHED *QUALITY* AND IMPOSSIBLE *QUANTITY.* BEHOLD OUR FIRST LOT, OUR *FINEST* LOT--

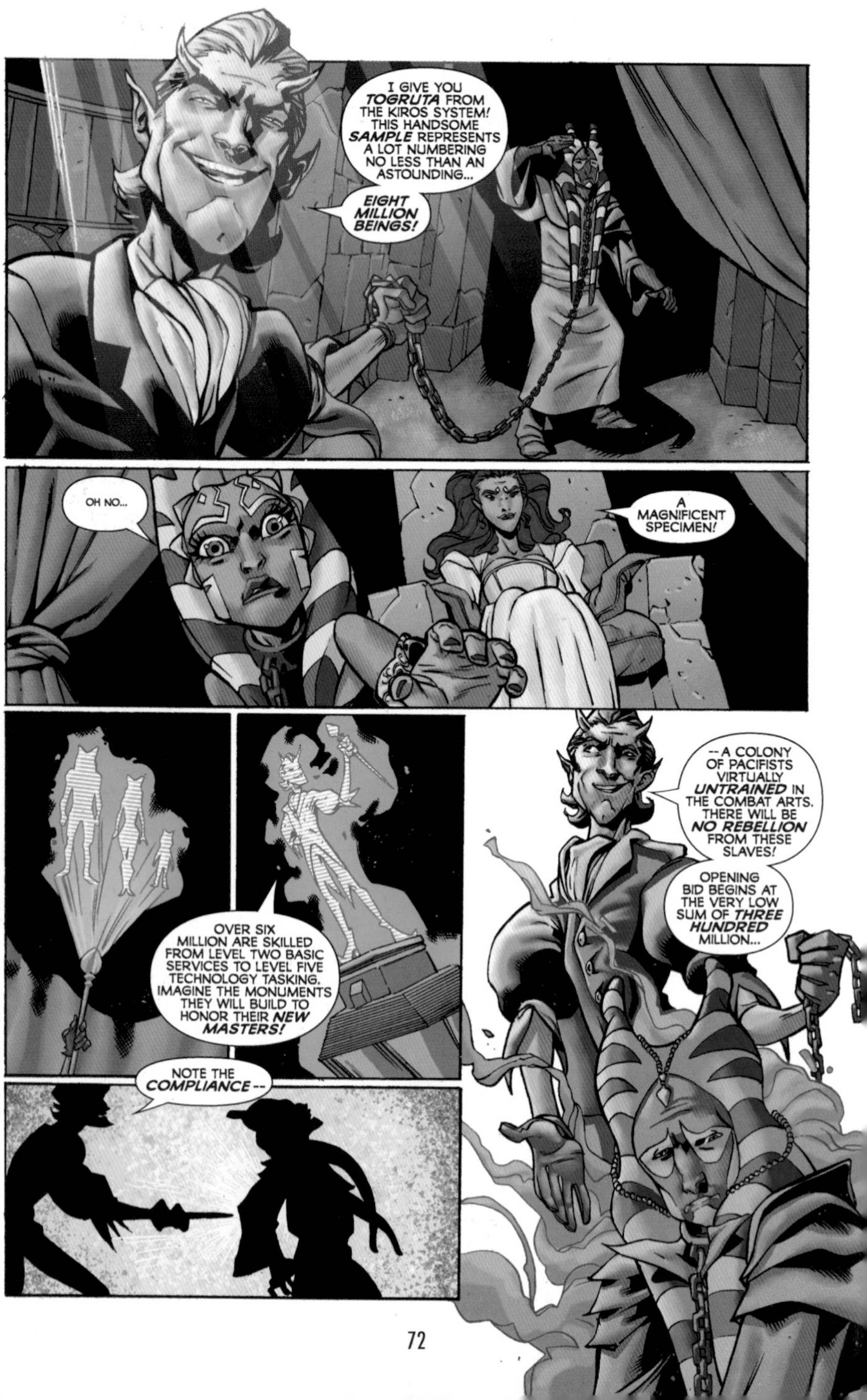
I GIVE YOU *TOGRUTA* FROM THE KIROS SYSTEM! THIS HANDSOME *SAMPLE* REPRESENTS A LOT NUMBERING NO LESS THAN AN ASTOUNDING...
EIGHT MILLION BEINGS!
OH NO...
A MAGNIFICENT SPECIMEN!
OVER SIX MILLION ARE SKILLED FROM LEVEL TWO BASIC SERVICES TO LEVEL FIVE TECHNOLOGY TASKING. IMAGINE THE MONUMENTS THEY WILL BUILD TO HONOR THEIR *NEW MASTERS!*
NOTE THE *COMPLIANCE* --
-- A COLONY OF PACIFISTS VIRTUALLY *UNTRAINED* IN THE COMBAT ARTS. THERE WILL BE *NO REBELLION* FROM THESE SLAVES!
OPENING BID BEGINS AT THE VERY LOW SUM OF *THREE HUNDRED* MILLION...

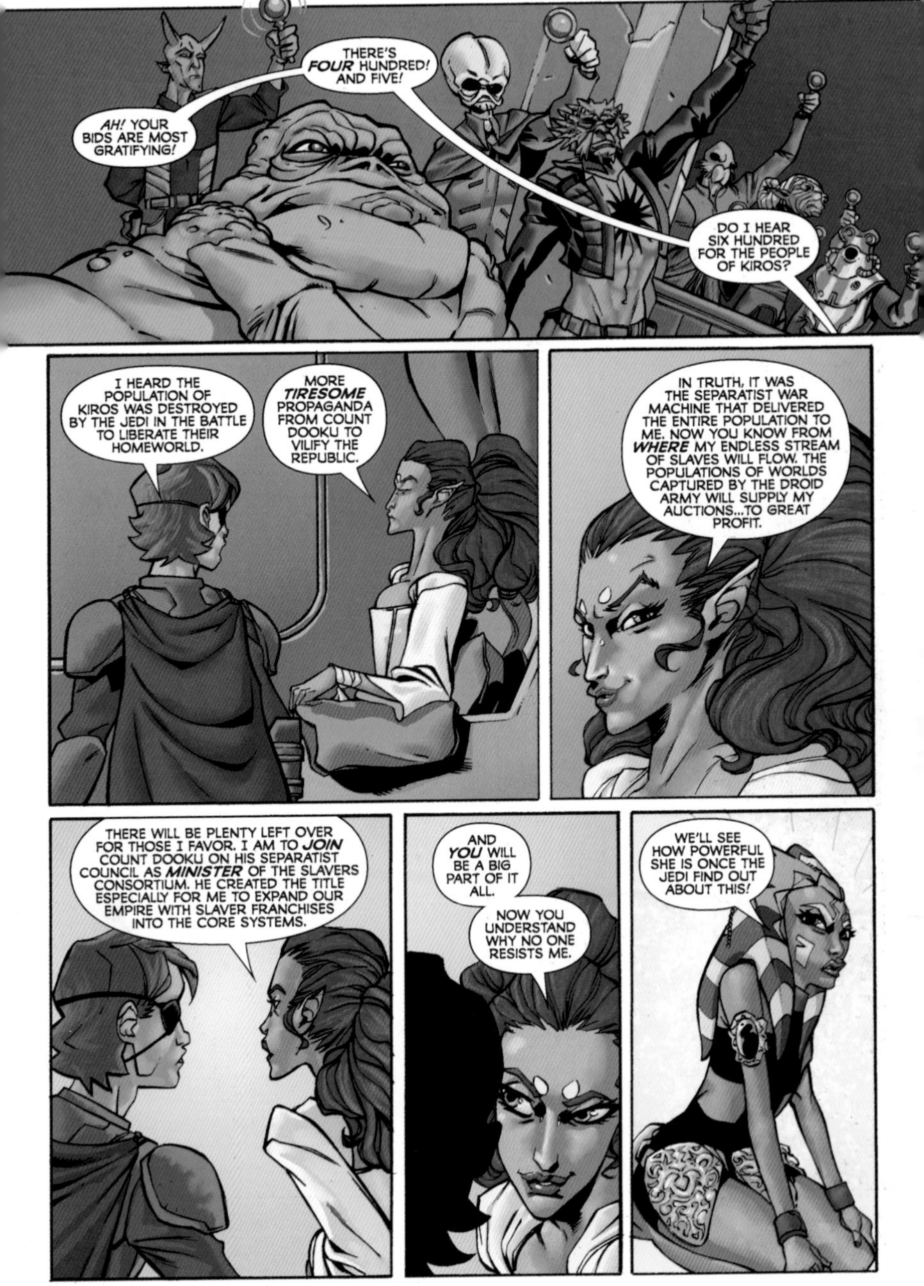

THERE'S *FOUR* HUNDRED! AND FIVE!
AH! YOUR BIDS ARE MOST GRATIFYING!
DO I HEAR SIX HUNDRED FOR THE PEOPLE OF KIROS?
I HEARD THE POPULATION OF KIROS WAS DESTROYED BY THE JEDI IN THE BATTLE TO LIBERATE THEIR HOMEWORLD.
MORE *TIRESOME* PROPAGANDA FROM COUNT DOOKU TO VILIFY THE REPUBLIC.
IN TRUTH, IT WAS THE SEPARATIST WAR MACHINE THAT DELIVERED THE ENTIRE POPULATION TO ME. NOW YOU KNOW FROM *WHERE* MY ENDLESS STREAM OF SLAVES WILL FLOW. THE POPULATIONS OF WORLDS CAPTURED BY THE DROID ARMY WILL SUPPLY MY AUCTIONS...TO GREAT PROFIT.
THERE WILL BE PLENTY LEFT OVER FOR THOSE I FAVOR. I AM TO *JOIN* COUNT DOOKU ON HIS SEPARATIST COUNCIL AS *MINISTER* OF THE SLAVERS CONSORTIUM. HE CREATED THE TITLE ESPECIALLY FOR ME TO EXPAND OUR EMPIRE WITH SLAVER FRANCHISES INTO THE CORE SYSTEMS.
AND *YOU* WILL BE A BIG PART OF IT ALL.
NOW YOU UNDERSTAND WHY NO ONE RESISTS ME.
WE'LL SEE HOW POWERFUL SHE IS ONCE THE JEDI FIND OUT ABOUT THIS!

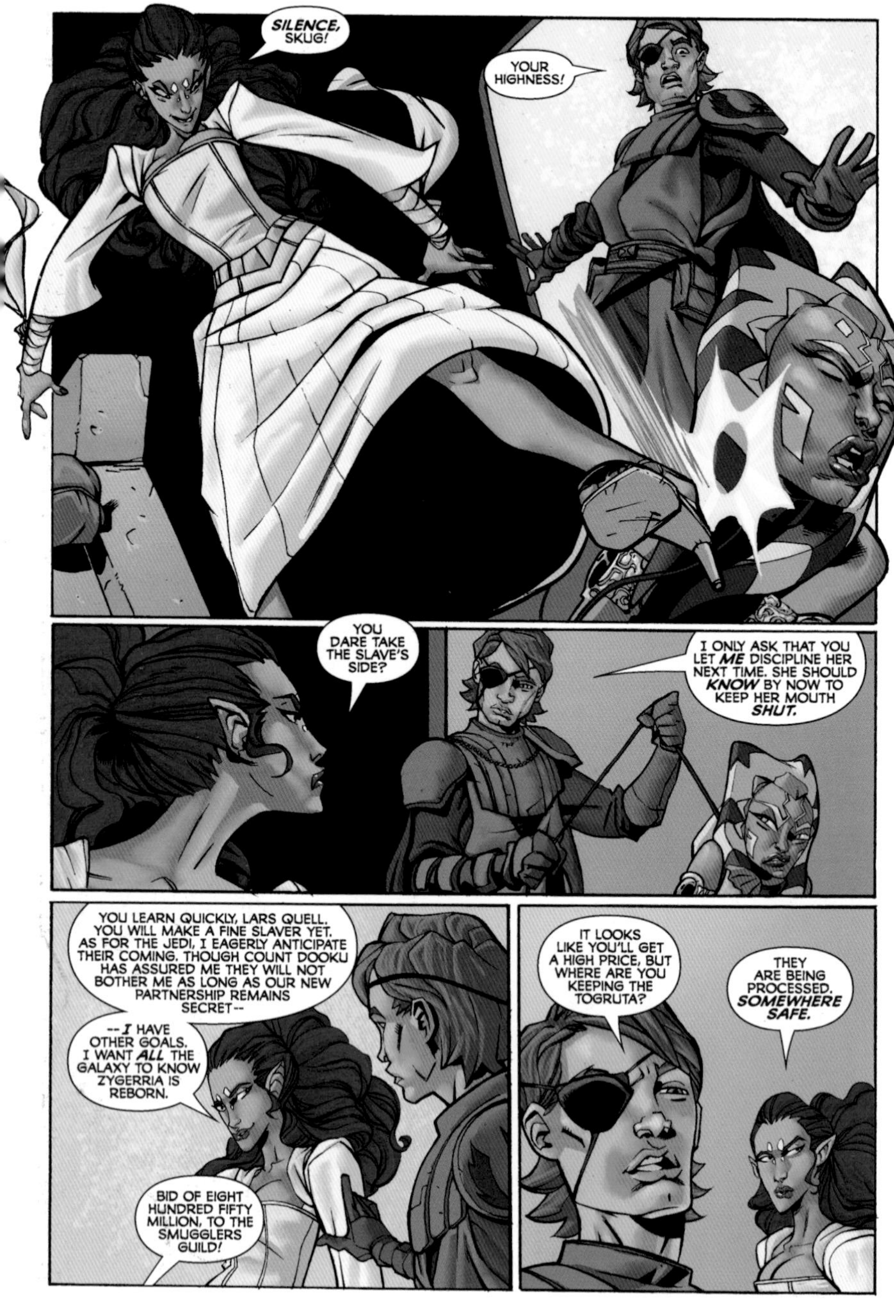

SILENCE, SKUG!
YOUR HIGHNESS!
YOU DARE TAKE THE SLAVE'S SIDE?
I ONLY ASK THAT YOU LET ME DISCIPLINE HER NEXT TIME. SHE SHOULD KNOW BY NOW TO KEEP HER MOUTH SHUT.
YOU LEARN QUICKLY, LARS QUELL. YOU WILL MAKE A FINE SLAVER YET. AS FOR THE JEDI, I EAGERLY ANTICIPATE THEIR COMING. THOUGH COUNT DOOKU HAS ASSURED ME THEY WILL NOT BOTHER ME AS LONG AS OUR NEW PARTNERSHIP REMAINS SECRET--
--I HAVE OTHER GOALS. I WANT ALL THE GALAXY TO KNOW ZYGERRIA IS REBORN.
BID OF EIGHT HUNDRED FIFTY MILLION, TO THE SMUGGLERS GUILD!
IT LOOKS LIKE YOU'LL GET A HIGH PRICE, BUT WHERE ARE YOU KEEPING THE TOGRUTA?
THEY ARE BEING PROCESSED. SOMEWHERE SAFE.

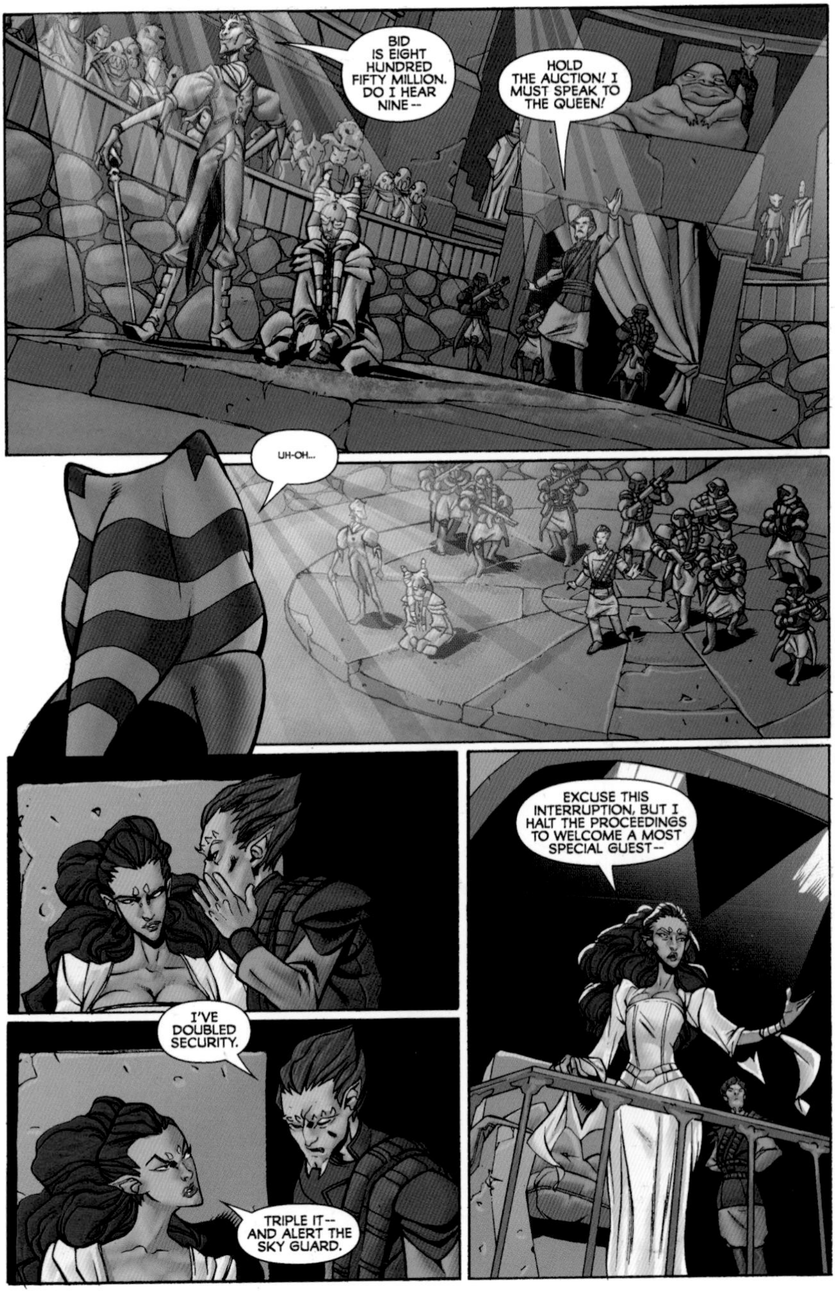
BID IS EIGHT HUNDRED FIFTY MILLION. DO I HEAR NINE--
HOLD THE AUCTION! I MUST SPEAK TO THE QUEEN!
UH-OH...
I'VE DOUBLED SECURITY.
TRIPLE IT-- AND ALERT THE SKY GUARD.
EXCUSE THIS INTERRUPTION, BUT I HALT THE PROCEEDINGS TO WELCOME A MOST SPECIAL GUEST--

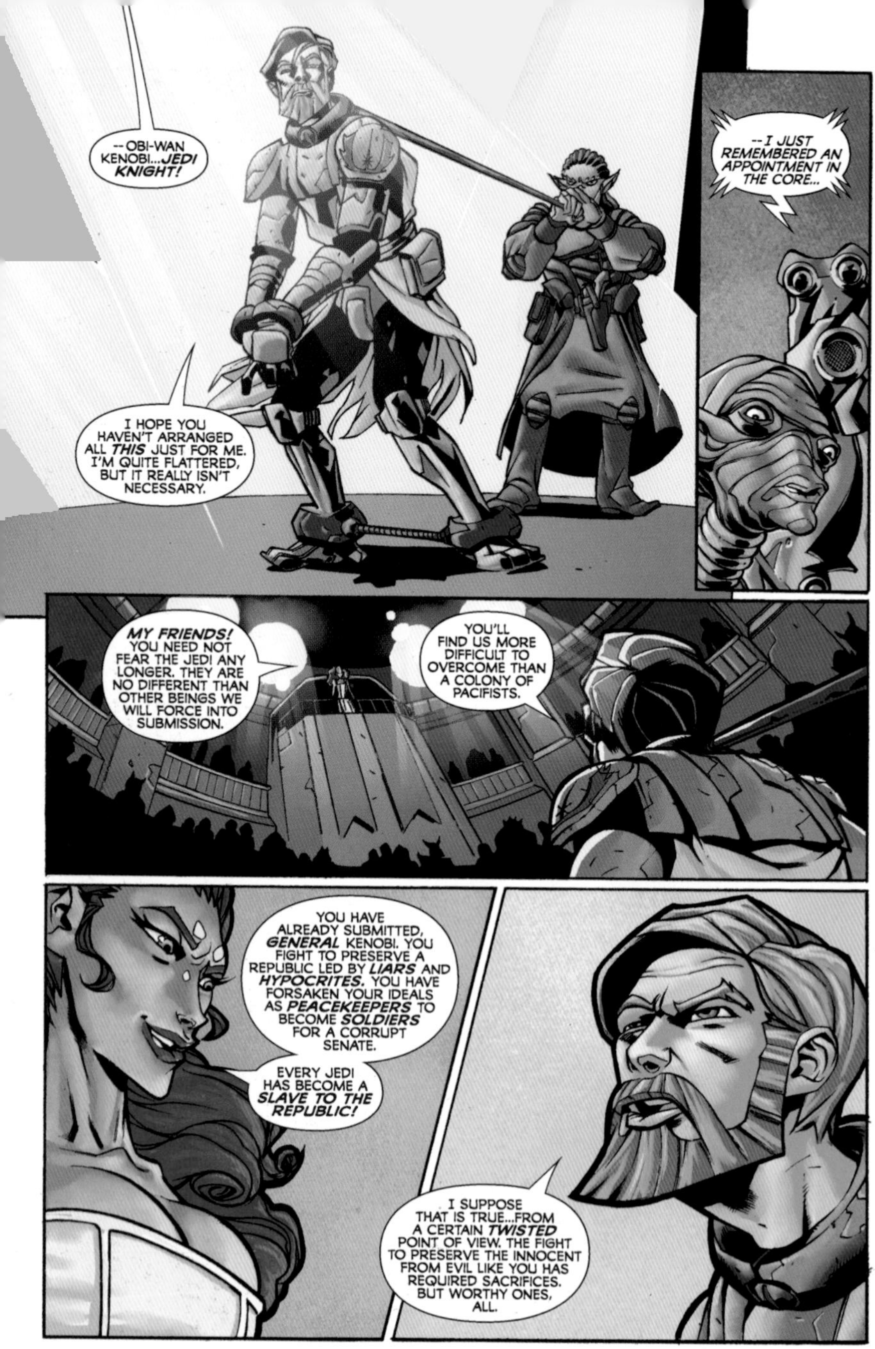
-- OBI-WAN KENOBI... JEDI KNIGHT!
--I JUST REMEMBERED AN APPOINTMENT IN THE CORE...
I HOPE YOU HAVEN'T ARRANGED ALL THIS JUST FOR ME. I'M QUITE FLATTERED, BUT IT REALLY ISN'T NECESSARY.
MY FRIENDS! YOU NEED NOT FEAR THE JEDI ANY LONGER. THEY ARE NO DIFFERENT THAN OTHER BEINGS WE WILL FORCE INTO SUBMISSION.
YOU'LL FIND US MORE DIFFICULT TO OVERCOME THAN A COLONY OF PACIFISTS.
YOU HAVE ALREADY SUBMITTED, GENERAL KENOBI. YOU FIGHT TO PRESERVE A REPUBLIC LED BY LIARS AND HYPOCRITES. YOU HAVE FORSAKEN YOUR IDEALS AS PEACEKEEPERS TO BECOME SOLDIERS FOR A CORRUPT SENATE.
EVERY JEDI HAS BECOME A SLAVE TO THE REPUBLIC!
I SUPPOSE THAT IS TRUE...FROM A CERTAIN TWISTED POINT OF VIEW. THE FIGHT TO PRESERVE THE INNOCENT FROM EVIL LIKE YOU HAS REQUIRED SACRIFICES. BUT WORTHY ONES, ALL.

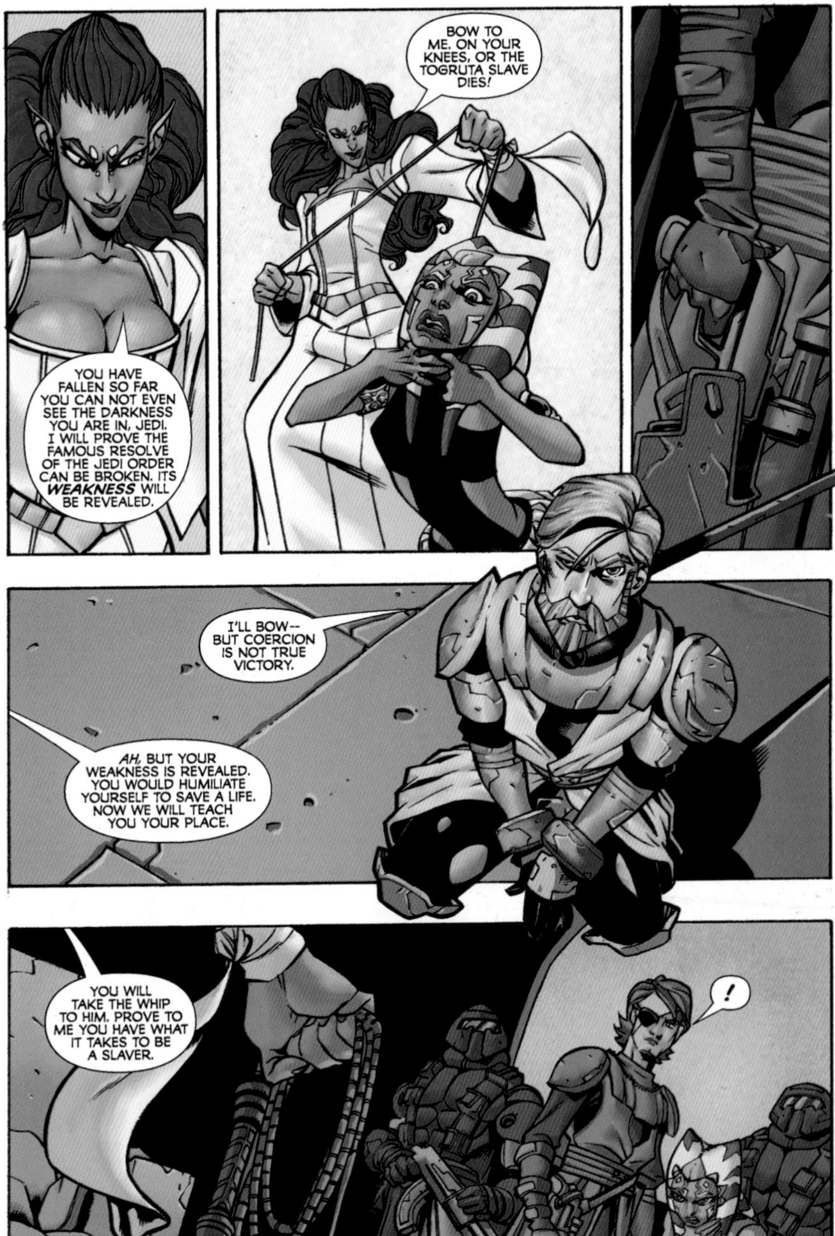
YOU HAVE FALLEN SO FAR YOU CAN NOT EVEN SEE THE DARKNESS YOU ARE IN, JEDI. I WILL PROVE THE FAMOUS RESOLVE OF THE JEDI ORDER CAN BE BROKEN. ITS *WEAKNESS* WILL BE REVEALED.
BOW TO ME. ON YOUR KNEES, OR THE TOGRUTA SLAVE DIES!
I'LL BOW-- BUT COERCION IS NOT TRUE VICTORY.
AH, BUT YOUR WEAKNESS IS REVEALED. YOU WOULD HUMILIATE YOURSELF TO SAVE A LIFE. NOW WE WILL TEACH YOU YOUR PLACE.
YOU WILL TAKE THE WHIP TO HIM. PROVE TO ME YOU HAVE WHAT IT TAKES TO BE A SLAVER.
!

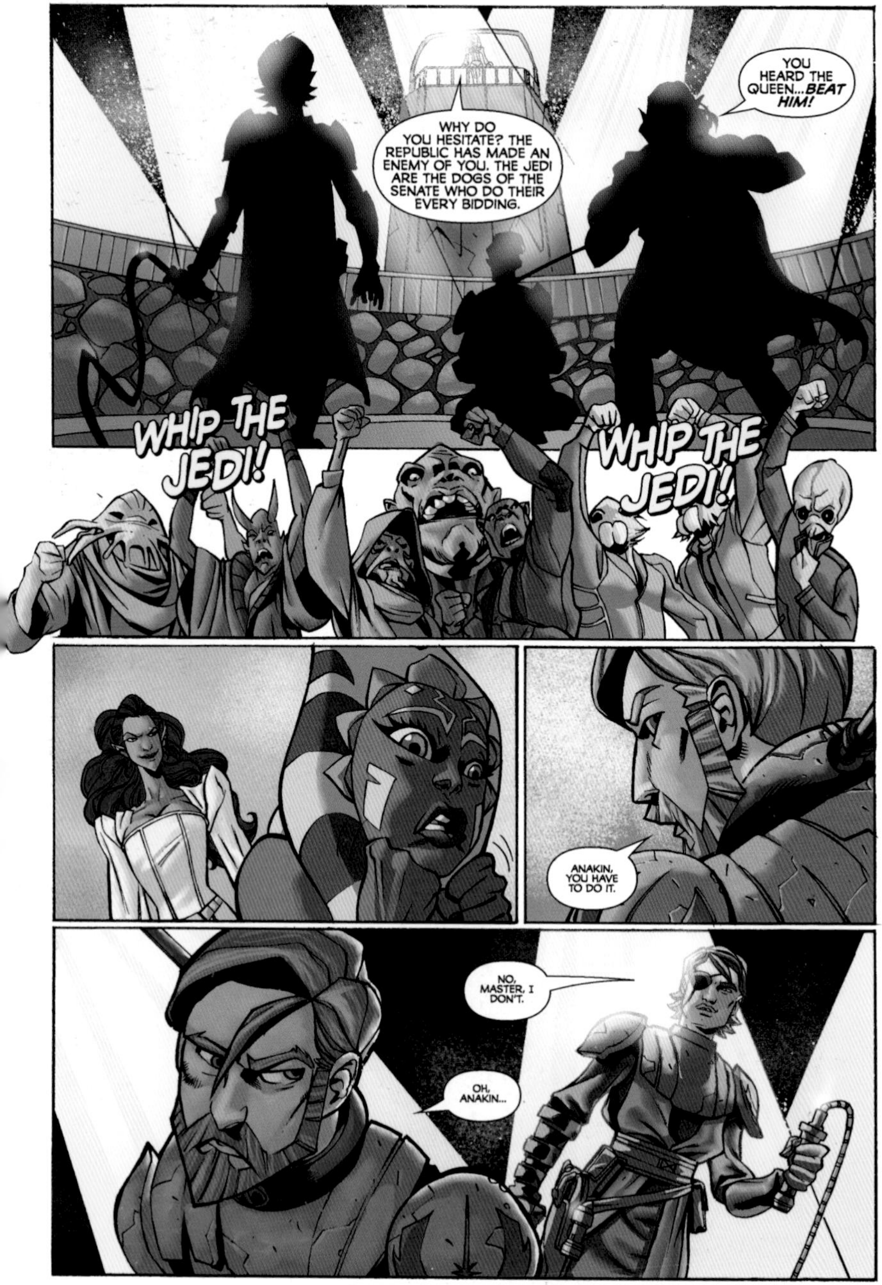
WHY DO YOU HESITATE? THE REPUBLIC HAS MADE AN ENEMY OF YOU. THE JEDI ARE THE DOGS OF THE SENATE WHO DO THEIR EVERY BIDDING.
YOU HEARD THE QUEEN...BEAT HIM!
WHIP THE JEDI!
WHIP THE JEDI!
ANAKIN, YOU HAVE TO DO IT.
NO, MASTER, I DON'T.
OH, ANAKIN...

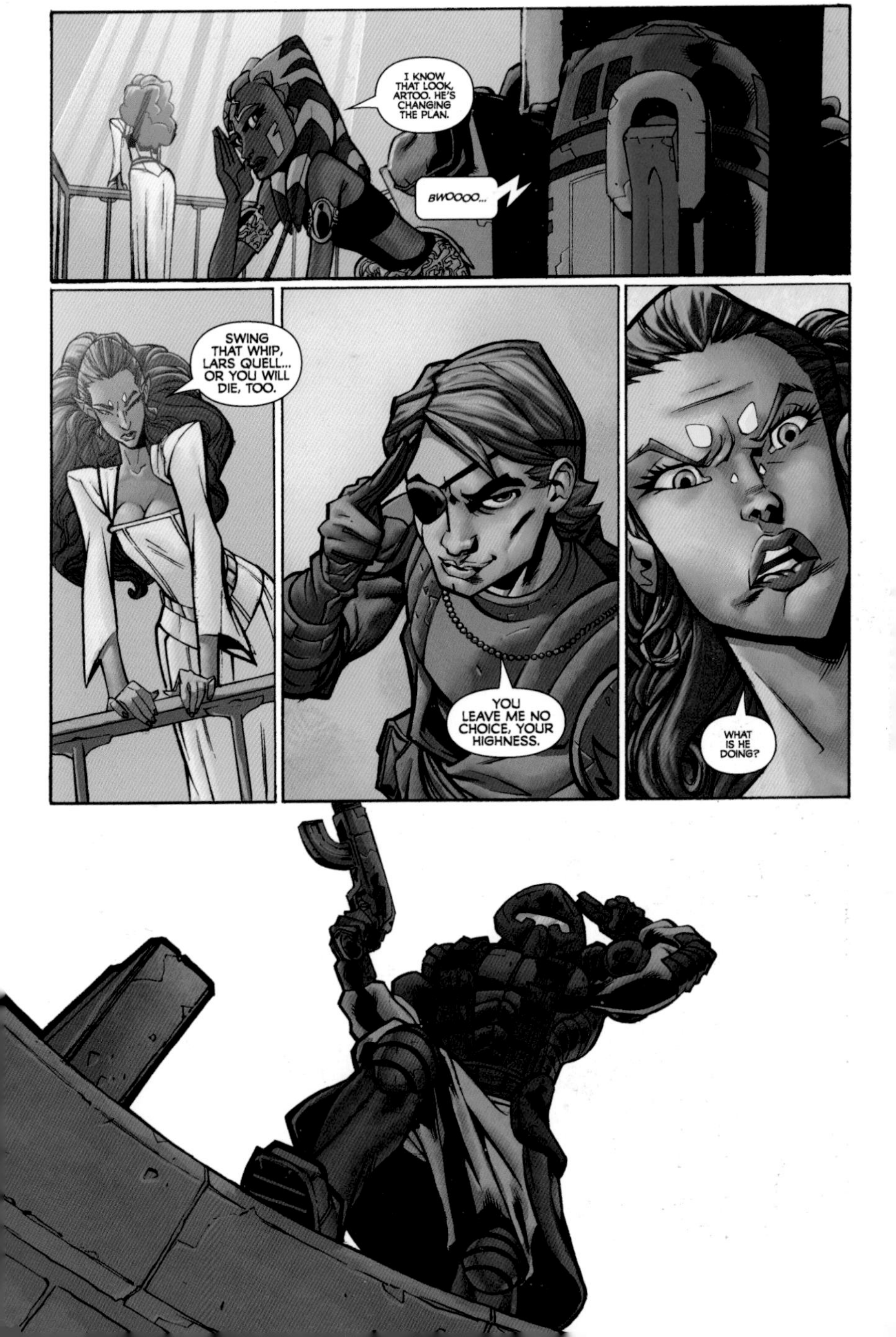
I KNOW THAT LOOK, ARTOO. HE'S CHANGING THE PLAN.
BWOOOO...
SWING THAT WHIP, LARS QUELL... OR YOU WILL DIE, TOO.
YOU LEAVE ME NO CHOICE, YOUR HIGHNESS.
WHAT IS HE DOING?

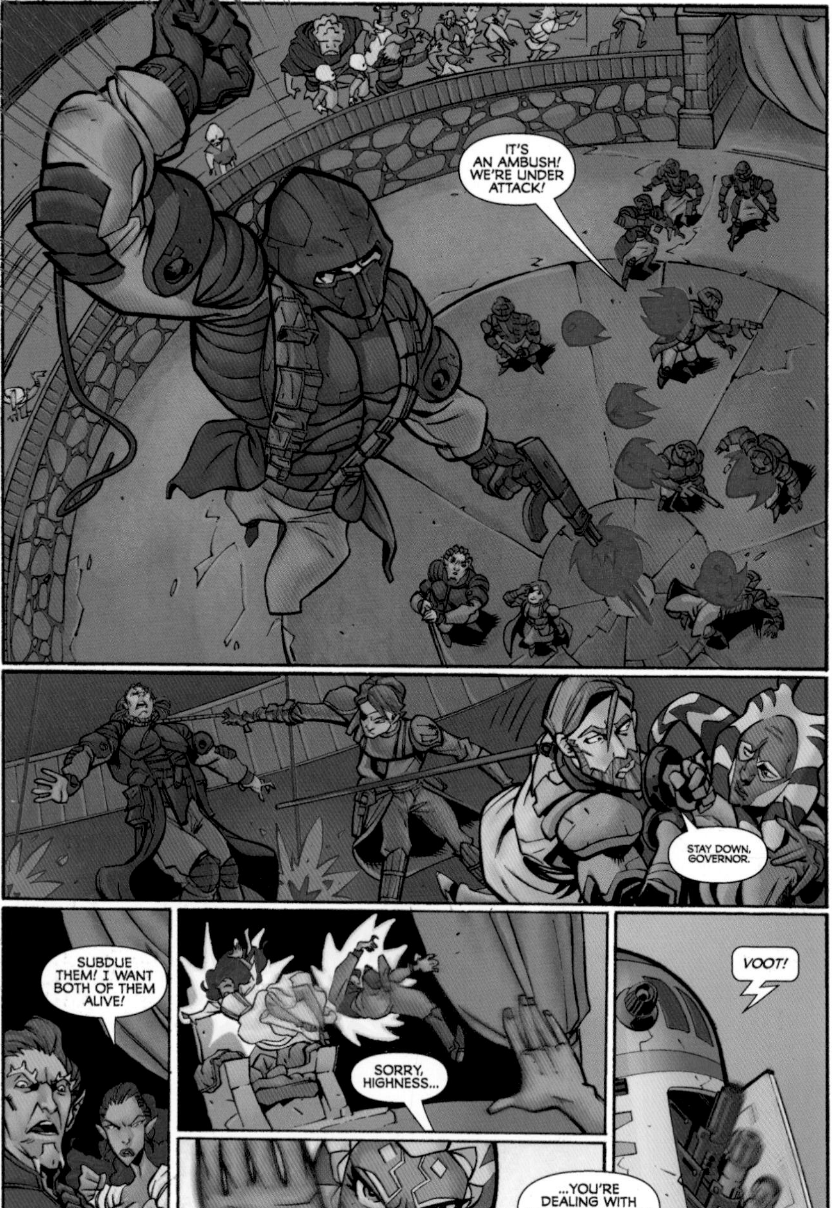
IT'S AN AMBUSH! WE'RE UNDER ATTACK!
STAY DOWN, GOVERNOR.
SUBDUE THEM! I WANT BOTH OF THEM ALIVE!
SORRY, HIGHNESS...
...YOU'RE DEALING WITH MORE THAN TWO JEDI TODAY.
VOOT!

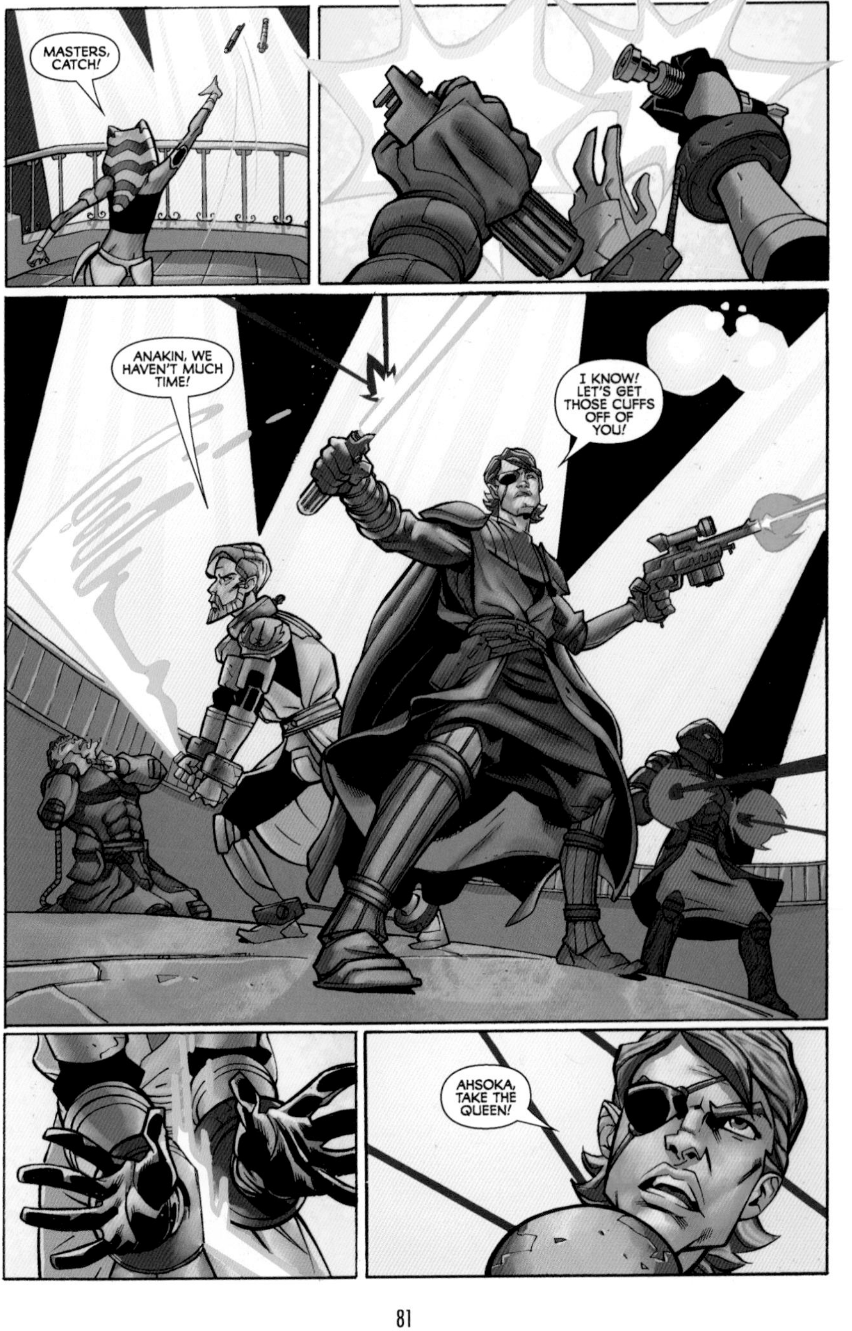
MASTERS, CATCH!
ANAKIN, WE HAVEN'T MUCH TIME!
I KNOW! LET'S GET THOSE CUFFS OFF OF YOU!
AHSOKA, TAKE THE QUEEN!

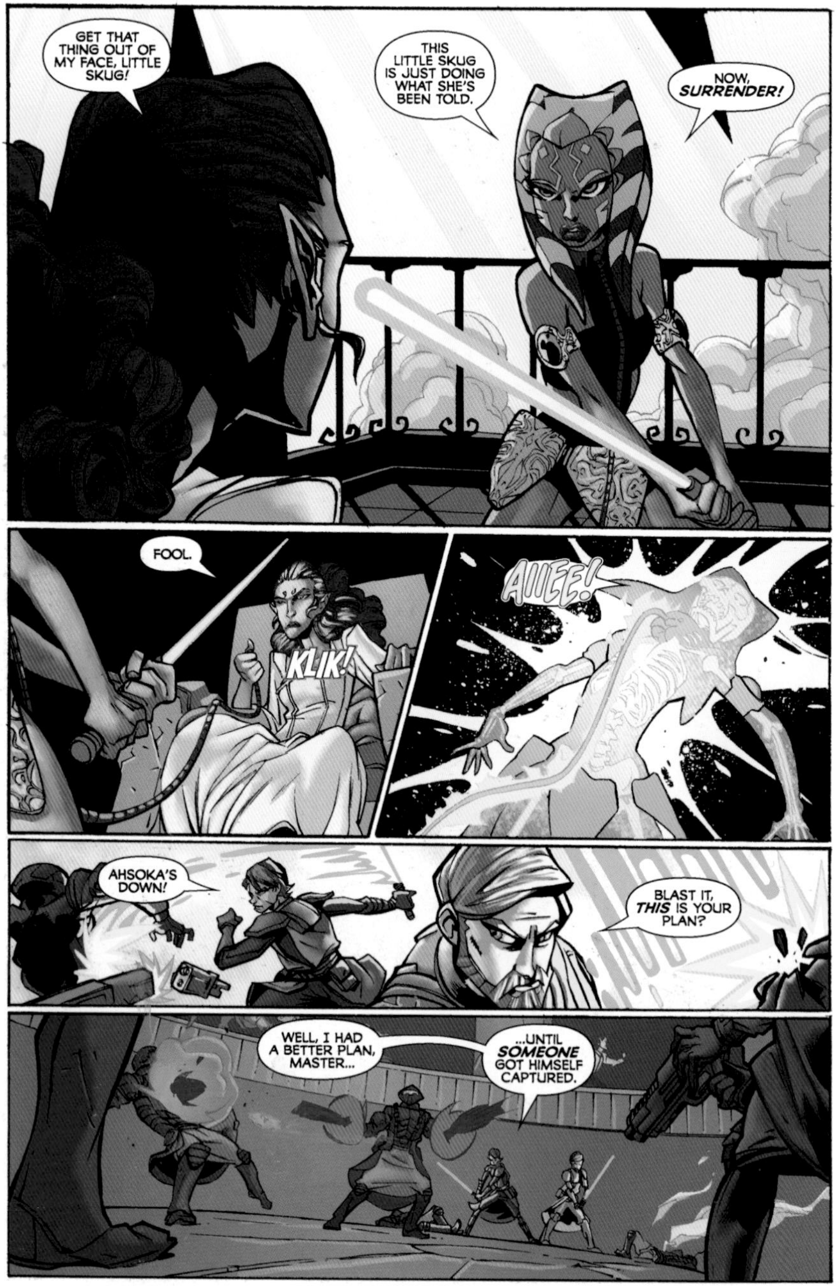
GET THAT THING OUT OF MY FACE, LITTLE SKUG!
THIS LITTLE SKUG IS JUST DOING WHAT SHE'S BEEN TOLD.
NOW, SURRENDER!
FOOL.
KLIK!
AIIEE!
AHSOKA'S DOWN!
BLAST IT, THIS IS YOUR PLAN?
WELL, I HAD A BETTER PLAN, MASTER...
...UNTIL SOMEONE GOT HIMSELF CAPTURED.

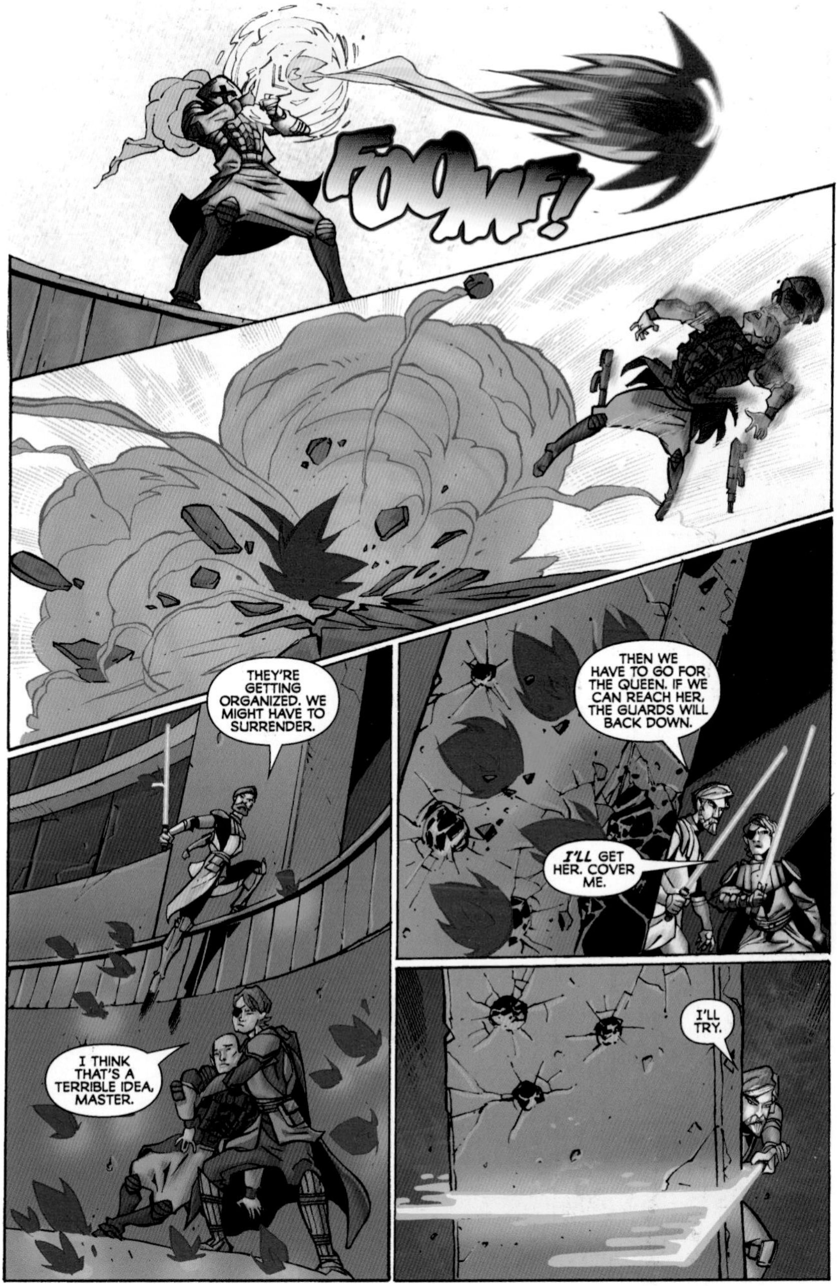
FOOMF!
THEY'RE GETTING ORGANIZED. WE MIGHT HAVE TO SURRENDER.
THEN WE HAVE TO GO FOR THE QUEEN. IF WE CAN REACH HER, THE GUARDS WILL BACK DOWN.
I'LL GET HER. COVER ME.
I THINK THAT'S A TERRIBLE IDEA, MASTER.
I'LL TRY.

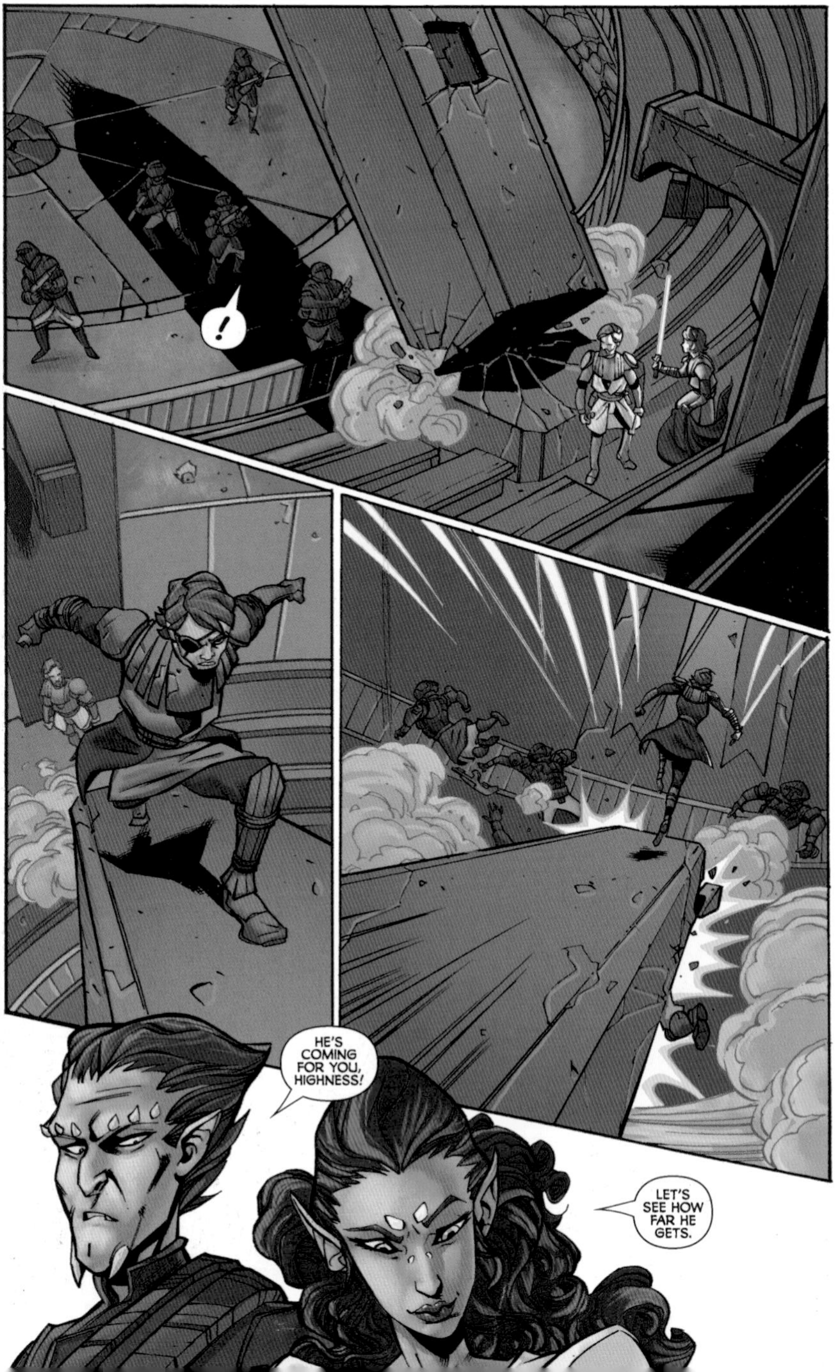
!
HE'S COMING FOR YOU, HIGHNESS!
LET'S SEE HOW FAR HE GETS.

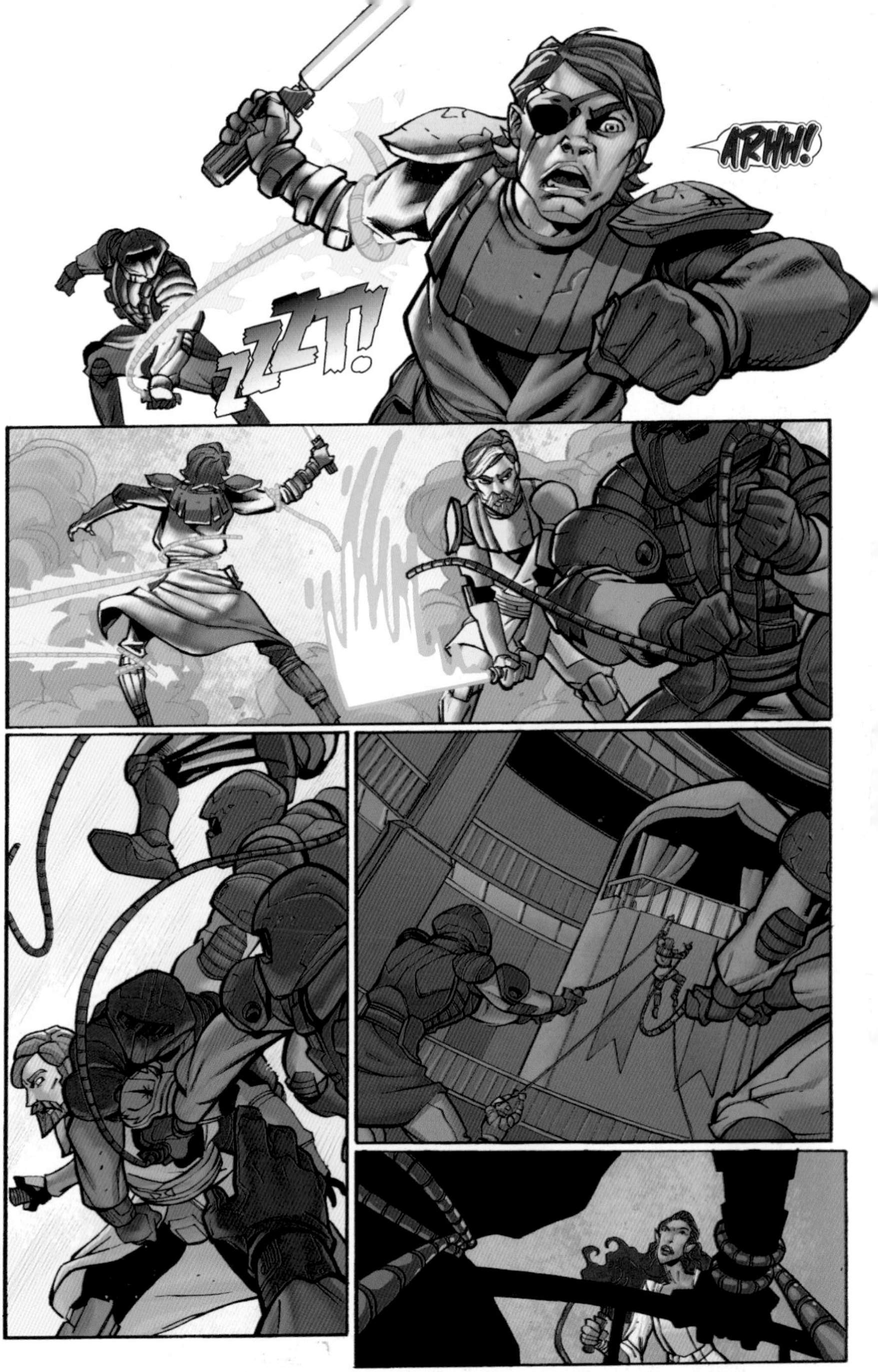
ARHH!
ZZZT!

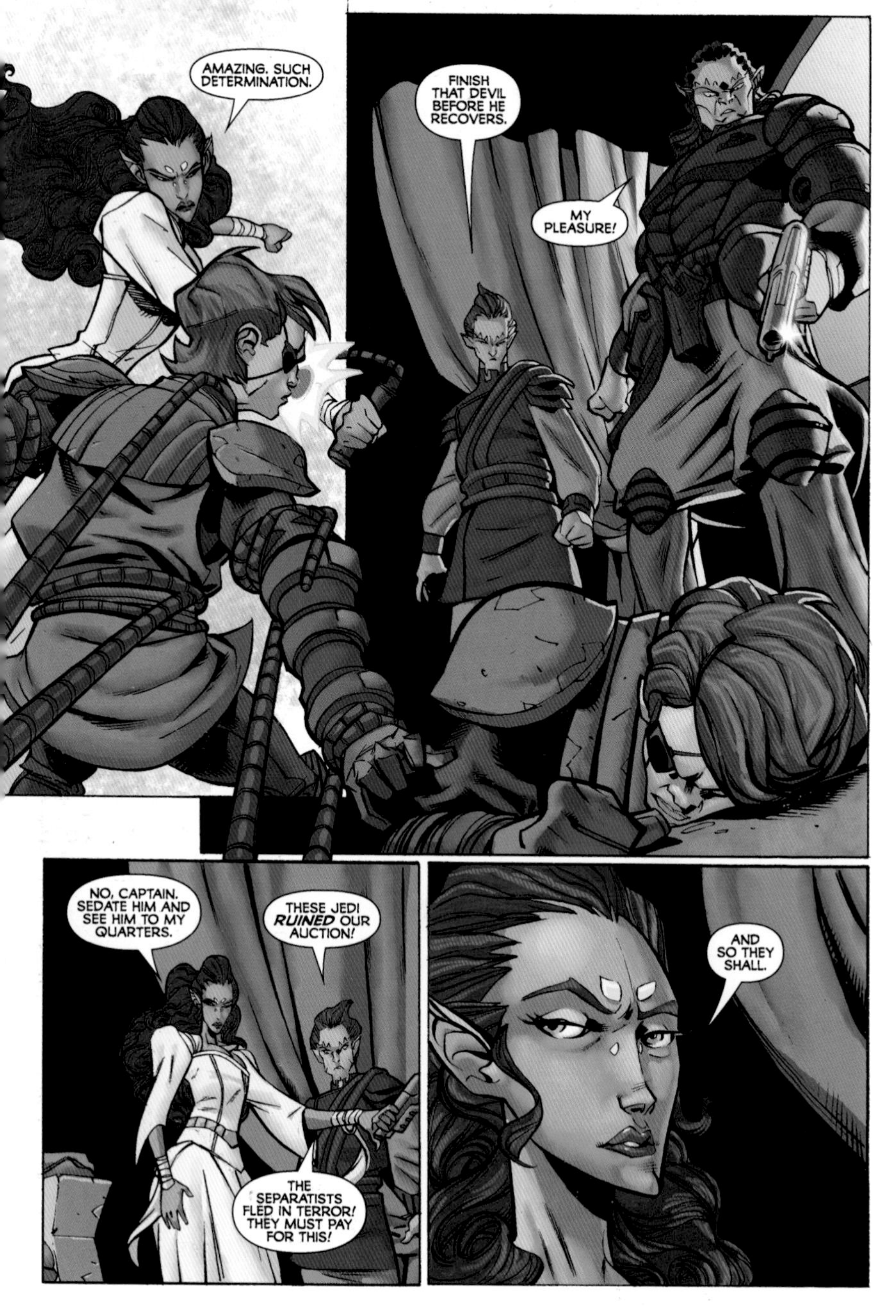
AMAZING. SUCH DETERMINATION.
FINISH THAT DEVIL BEFORE HE RECOVERS.
MY PLEASURE!
NO, CAPTAIN. SEDATE HIM AND SEE HIM TO MY QUARTERS.
THESE JEDI *RUINED* OUR AUCTION!
THE SEPARATISTS FLED IN TERROR! THEY MUST PAY FOR THIS!
AND SO THEY SHALL.

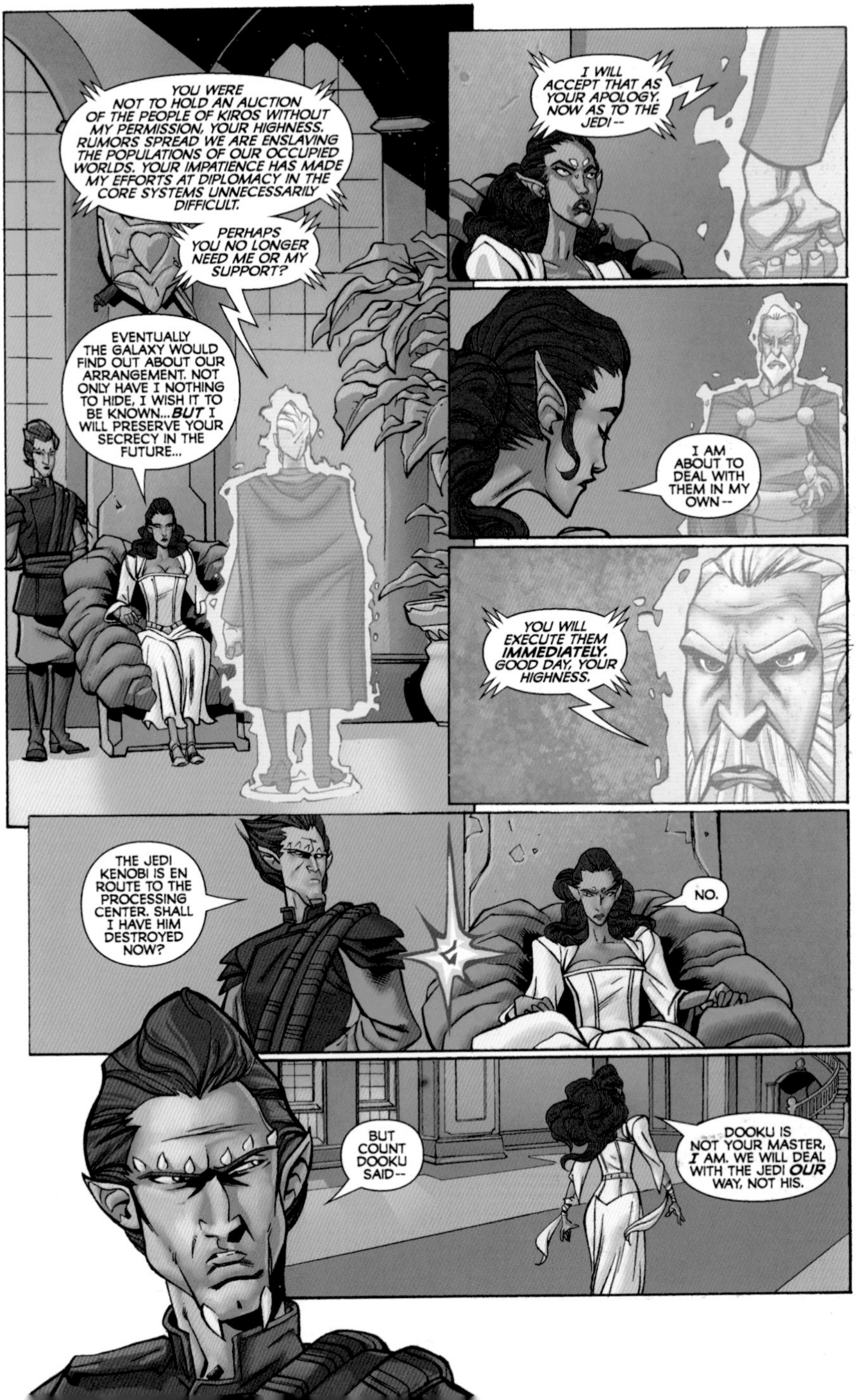
YOU WERE NOT TO HOLD AN AUCTION OF THE PEOPLE OF KIROS WITHOUT MY PERMISSION, YOUR HIGHNESS. RUMORS SPREAD WE ARE ENSLAVING THE POPULATIONS OF OUR OCCUPIED WORLDS. YOUR IMPATIENCE HAS MADE MY EFFORTS AT DIPLOMACY IN THE CORE SYSTEMS UNNECESSARILY DIFFICULT.
PERHAPS YOU NO LONGER NEED ME OR MY SUPPORT?
EVENTUALLY THE GALAXY WOULD FIND OUT ABOUT OUR ARRANGEMENT. NOT ONLY HAVE I NOTHING TO HIDE, I WISH IT TO BE KNOWN...*BUT* I WILL PRESERVE YOUR SECRECY IN THE FUTURE...
I WILL ACCEPT THAT AS YOUR APOLOGY. NOW AS TO THE JEDI--
I AM ABOUT TO DEAL WITH THEM IN MY OWN--
YOU WILL EXECUTE THEM *IMMEDIATELY.* GOOD DAY, YOUR HIGHNESS.
THE JEDI KENOBI IS EN ROUTE TO THE PROCESSING CENTER. SHALL I HAVE HIM DESTROYED NOW?
NO.
BUT COUNT DOOKU SAID--
DOOKU IS NOT YOUR MASTER, *I* AM. WE WILL DEAL WITH THE JEDI *OUR* WAY, NOT HIS.

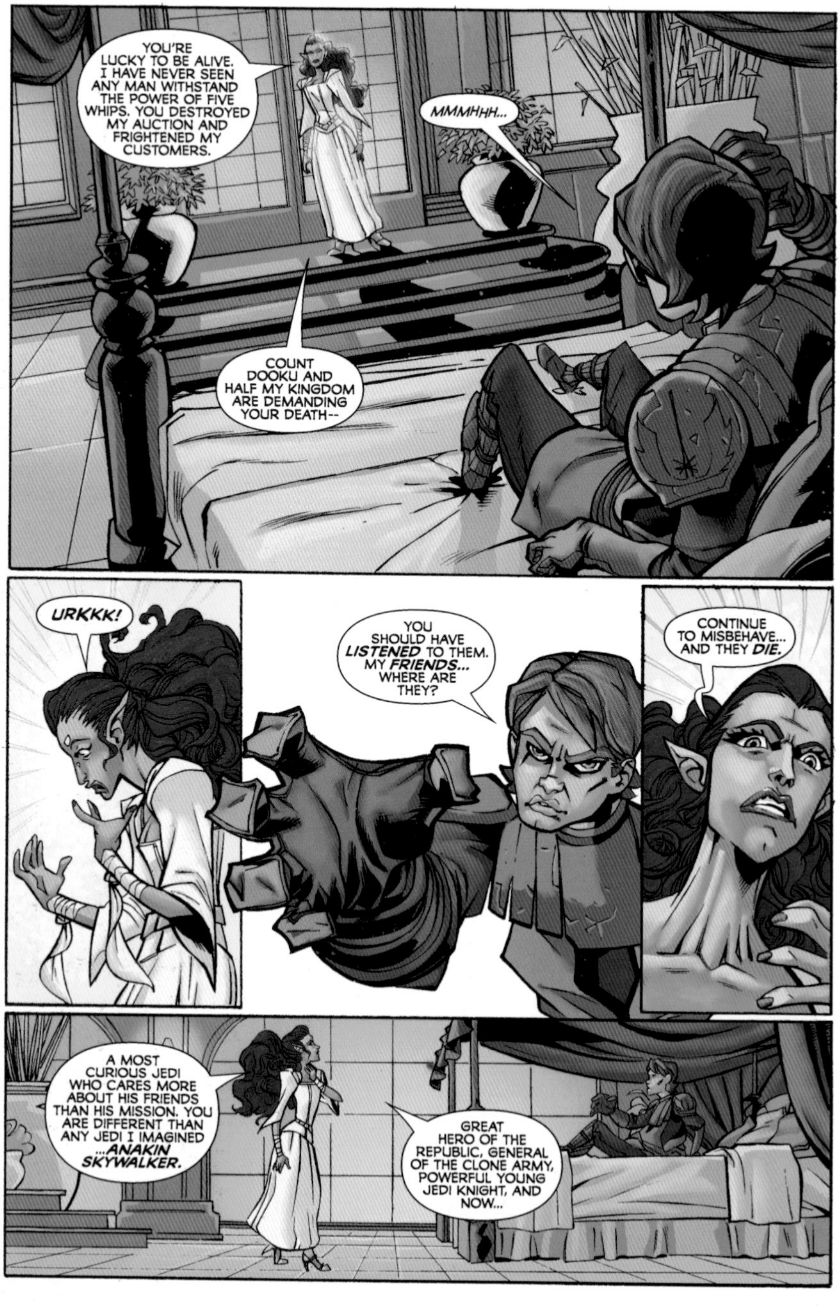
YOU'RE LUCKY TO BE ALIVE. I HAVE NEVER SEEN ANY MAN WITHSTAND THE POWER OF FIVE WHIPS. YOU DESTROYED MY AUCTION AND FRIGHTENED MY CUSTOMERS.
MMMHHH...
COUNT DOOKU AND HALF MY KINGDOM ARE DEMANDING YOUR DEATH--
URKKK!
YOU SHOULD HAVE LISTENED TO THEM. MY FRIENDS... WHERE ARE THEY?
CONTINUE TO MISBEHAVE... AND THEY DIE.
A MOST CURIOUS JEDI WHO CARES MORE ABOUT HIS FRIENDS THAN HIS MISSION. YOU ARE DIFFERENT THAN ANY JEDI I IMAGINED ...ANAKIN SKYWALKER.
GREAT HERO OF THE REPUBLIC, GENERAL OF THE CLONE ARMY, POWERFUL YOUNG JEDI KNIGHT, AND NOW...

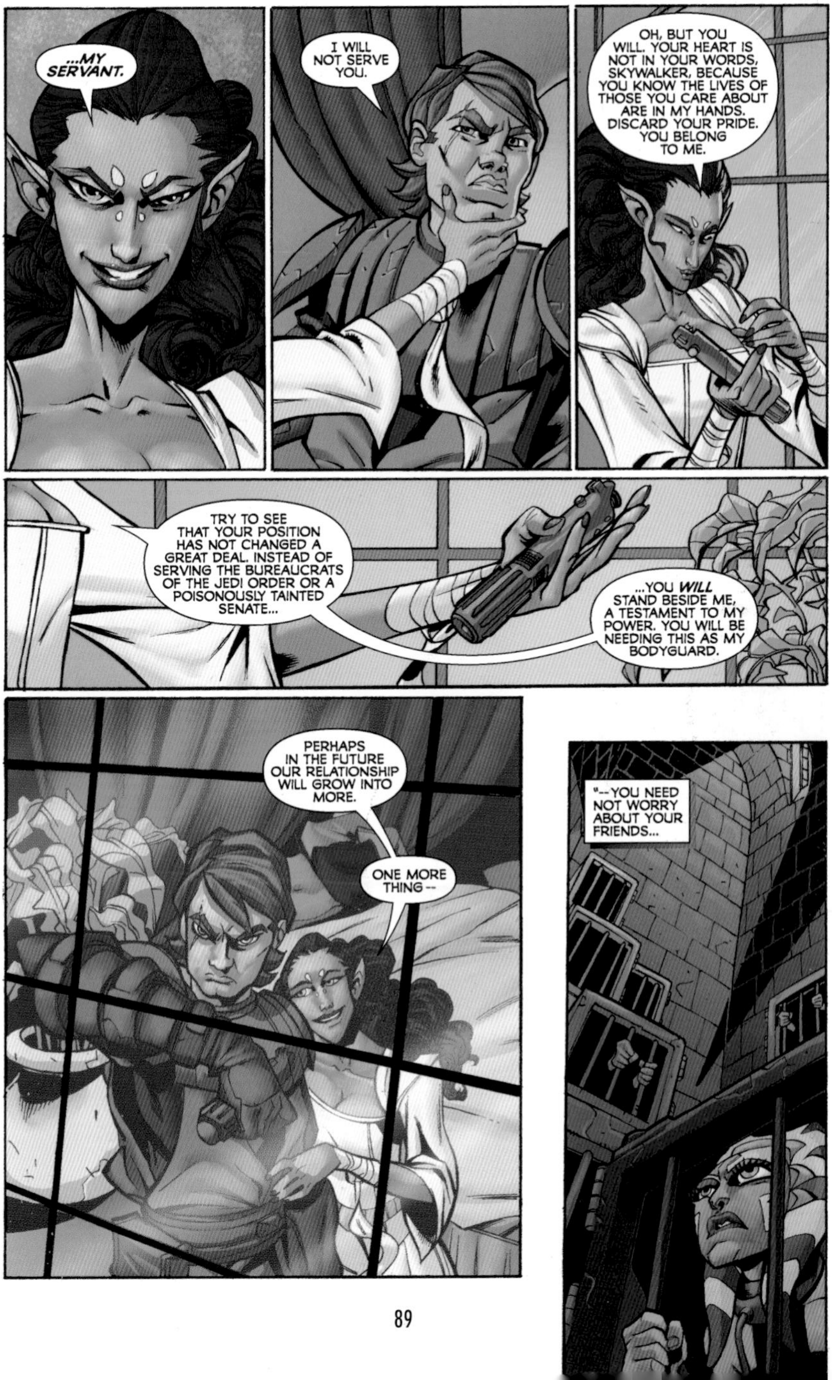
...MY SERVANT.
I WILL NOT SERVE YOU.
OH, BUT YOU WILL. YOUR HEART IS NOT IN YOUR WORDS, SKYWALKER, BECAUSE YOU KNOW THE LIVES OF THOSE YOU CARE ABOUT ARE IN MY HANDS. DISCARD YOUR PRIDE. YOU BELONG TO ME.
TRY TO SEE THAT YOUR POSITION HAS NOT CHANGED A GREAT DEAL. INSTEAD OF SERVING THE BUREAUCRATS OF THE JEDI ORDER OR A POISONOUSLY TAINTED SENATE...
...YOU *WILL* STAND BESIDE ME, A TESTAMENT TO MY POWER. YOU WILL BE NEEDING THIS AS MY BODYGUARD.
PERHAPS IN THE FUTURE OUR RELATIONSHIP WILL GROW INTO MORE.
ONE MORE THING --
"--YOU NEED NOT WORRY ABOUT YOUR FRIENDS...

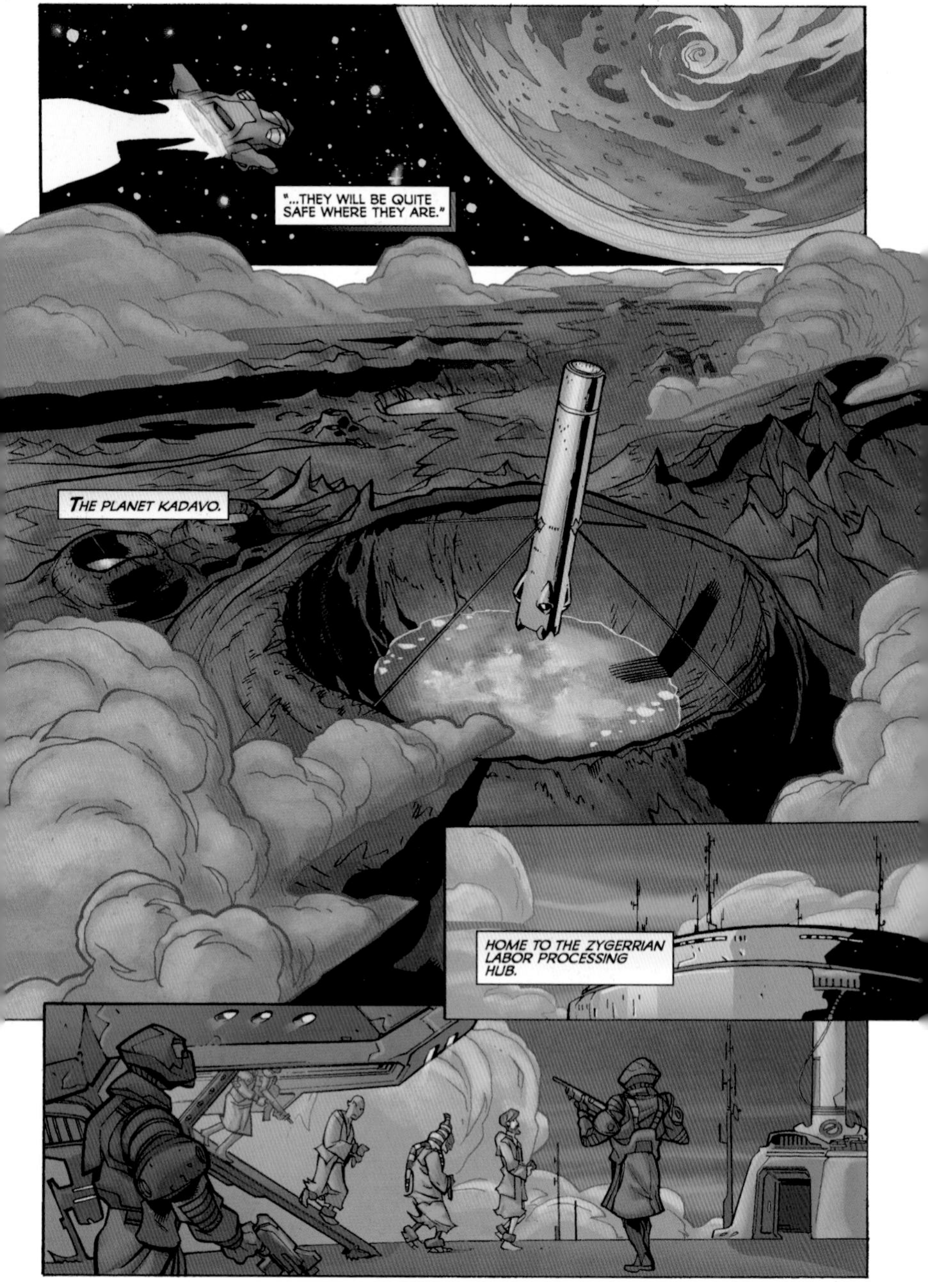
"...THEY WILL BE QUITE SAFE WHERE THEY ARE."
THE PLANET KADAVO.
HOME TO THE ZYGERRIAN LABOR PROCESSING HUB.

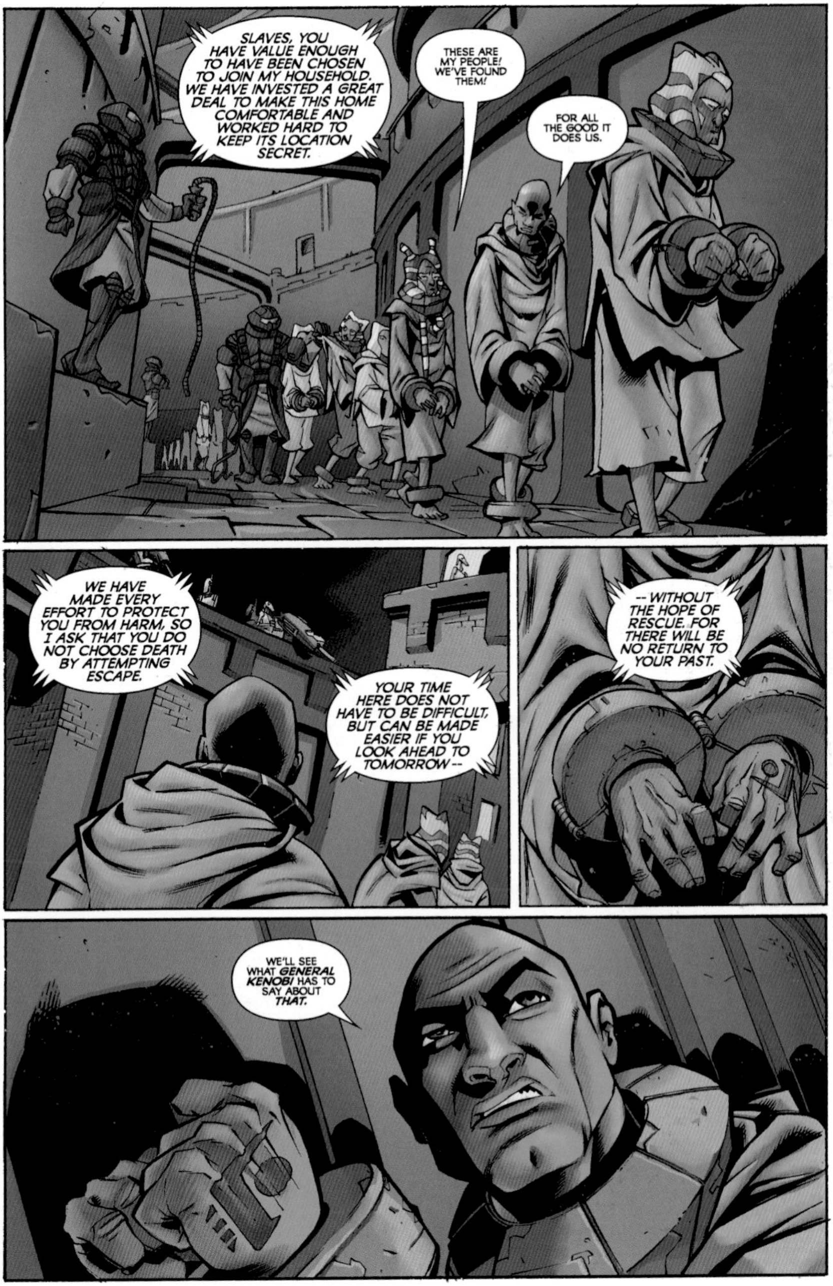
SLAVES, YOU HAVE VALUE ENOUGH TO HAVE BEEN CHOSEN TO JOIN MY HOUSEHOLD. WE HAVE INVESTED A GREAT DEAL TO MAKE THIS HOME COMFORTABLE AND WORKED HARD TO KEEP ITS LOCATION SECRET.
THESE ARE MY PEOPLE! WE'VE FOUND THEM!
FOR ALL THE GOOD IT DOES US.
WE HAVE MADE EVERY EFFORT TO PROTECT YOU FROM HARM, SO I ASK THAT YOU DO NOT CHOOSE DEATH BY ATTEMPTING ESCAPE.
YOUR TIME HERE DOES NOT HAVE TO BE DIFFICULT, BUT CAN BE MADE EASIER IF YOU LOOK AHEAD TO TOMORROW--
--WITHOUT THE HOPE OF RESCUE. FOR THERE WILL BE NO RETURN TO YOUR PAST.
WE'LL SEE WHAT GENERAL KENOBI HAS TO SAY ABOUT THAT.

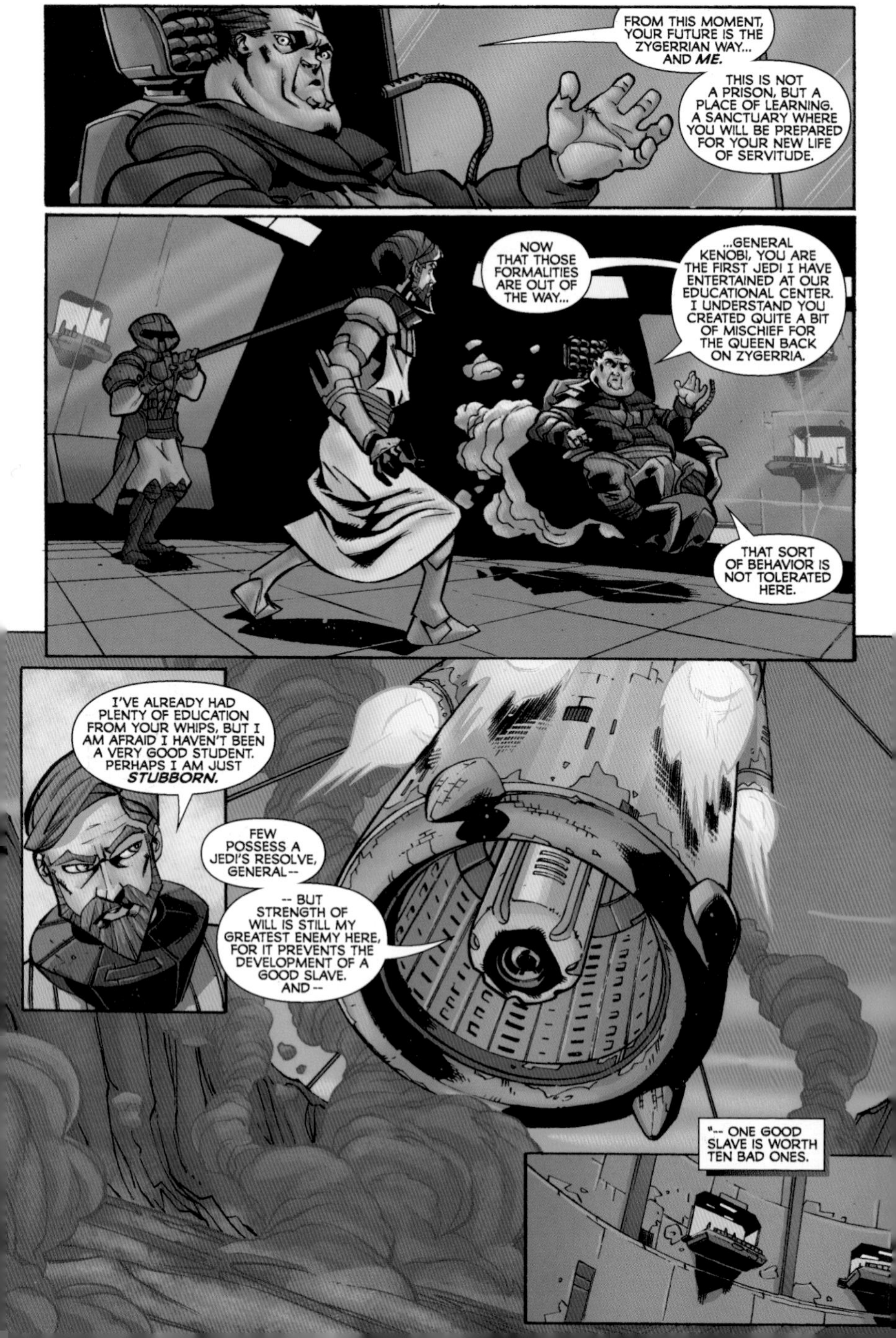
FROM THIS MOMENT, YOUR FUTURE IS THE ZYGERRIAN WAY... AND ***ME.***
THIS IS NOT A PRISON, BUT A PLACE OF LEARNING. A SANCTUARY WHERE YOU WILL BE PREPARED FOR YOUR NEW LIFE OF SERVITUDE.
NOW THAT THOSE FORMALITIES ARE OUT OF THE WAY...
...GENERAL KENOBI, YOU ARE THE FIRST JEDI I HAVE ENTERTAINED AT OUR EDUCATIONAL CENTER. I UNDERSTAND YOU CREATED QUITE A BIT OF MISCHIEF FOR THE QUEEN BACK ON ZYGERRIA.
THAT SORT OF BEHAVIOR IS NOT TOLERATED HERE.
I'VE ALREADY HAD PLENTY OF EDUCATION FROM YOUR WHIPS, BUT I AM AFRAID I HAVEN'T BEEN A VERY GOOD STUDENT. PERHAPS I AM JUST ***STUBBORN.***
FEW POSSESS A JEDI'S RESOLVE, GENERAL--
-- BUT STRENGTH OF WILL IS STILL MY GREATEST ENEMY HERE, FOR IT PREVENTS THE DEVELOPMENT OF A GOOD SLAVE. AND --
"-- ONE GOOD SLAVE IS WORTH TEN BAD ONES.

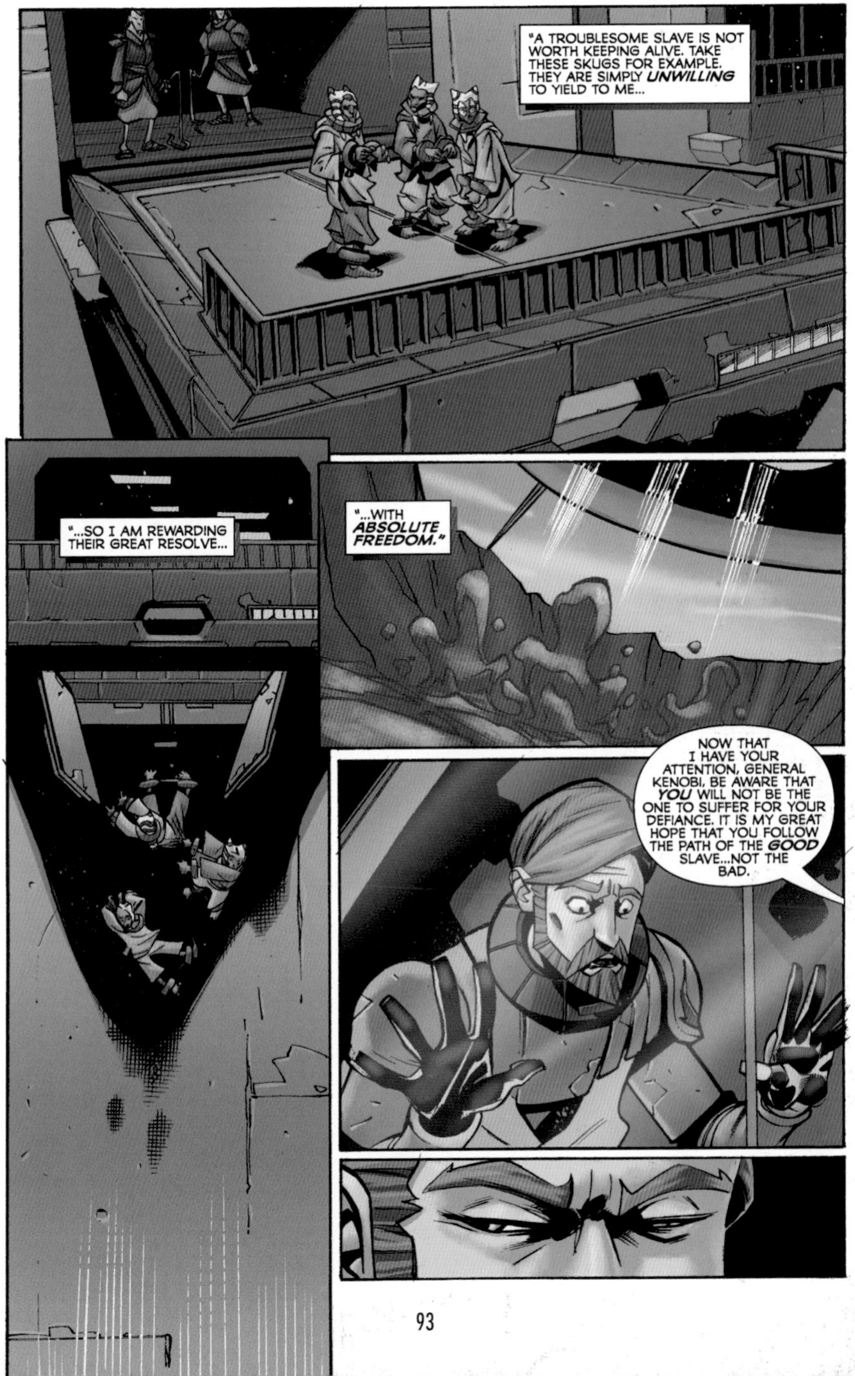
"A TROUBLESOME SLAVE IS NOT WORTH KEEPING ALIVE. TAKE THESE SKUGS FOR EXAMPLE. THEY ARE SIMPLY *UNWILLING* TO YIELD TO ME...
"...SO I AM REWARDING THEIR GREAT RESOLVE...
"...WITH *ABSOLUTE FREEDOM.*"
NOW THAT I HAVE YOUR ATTENTION, GENERAL KENOBI, BE AWARE THAT *YOU* WILL NOT BE THE ONE TO SUFFER FOR YOUR DEFIANCE. IT IS MY GREAT HOPE THAT YOU FOLLOW THE PATH OF THE *GOOD* SLAVE...NOT THE BAD.

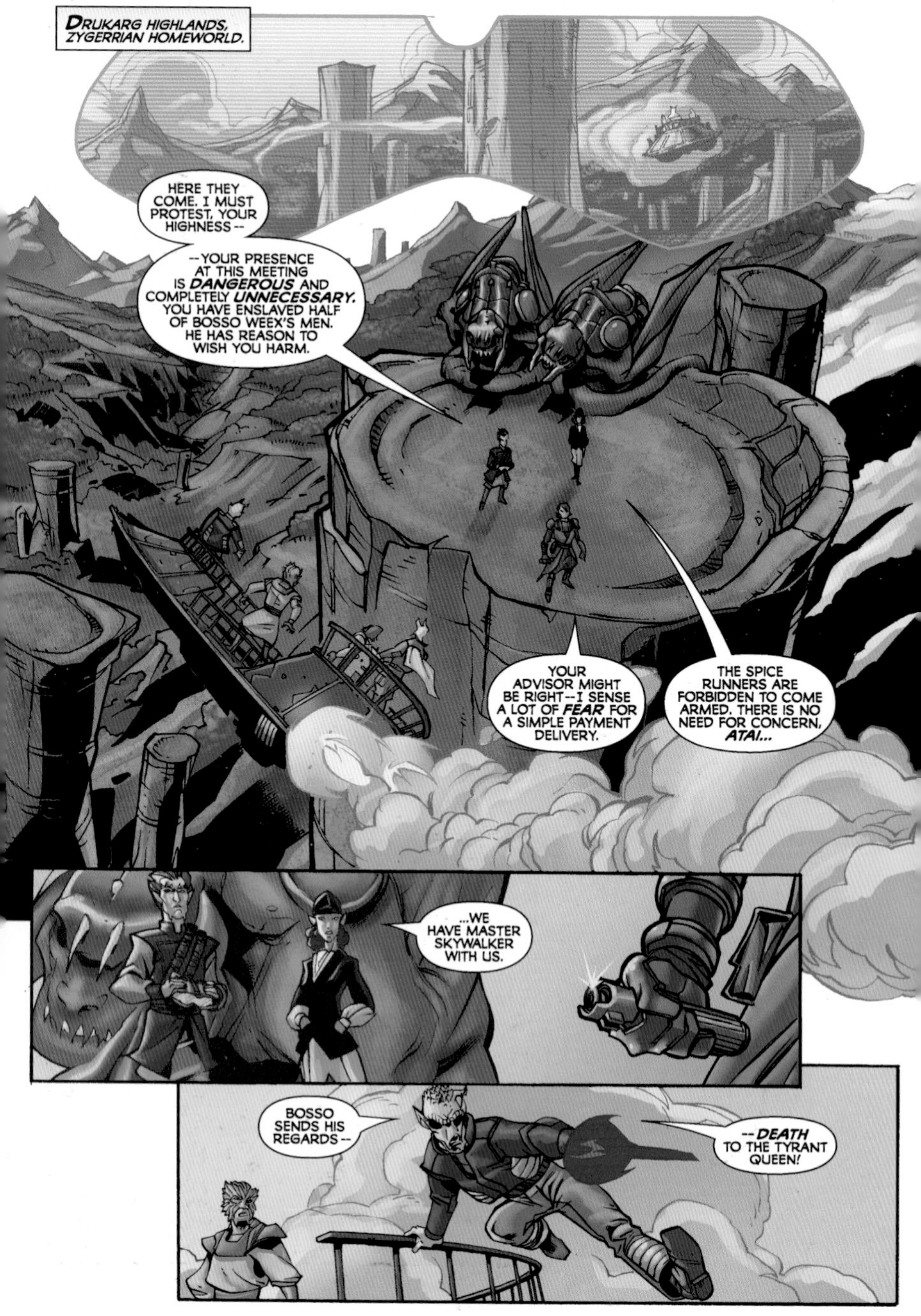
DRUKARG HIGHLANDS, ZYGERRIAN HOMEWORLD.
HERE THEY COME. I MUST PROTEST, YOUR HIGHNESS --
--YOUR PRESENCE AT THIS MEETING IS DANGEROUS AND COMPLETELY UNNECESSARY. YOU HAVE ENSLAVED HALF OF BOSSO WEEX'S MEN. HE HAS REASON TO WISH YOU HARM.
THE SPICE RUNNERS ARE FORBIDDEN TO COME ARMED. THERE IS NO NEED FOR CONCERN, ATAI...
YOUR ADVISOR MIGHT BE RIGHT--I SENSE A LOT OF FEAR FOR A SIMPLE PAYMENT DELIVERY.
...WE HAVE MASTER SKYWALKER WITH US.
BOSSO SENDS HIS REGARDS --
--DEATH TO THE TYRANT QUEEN!

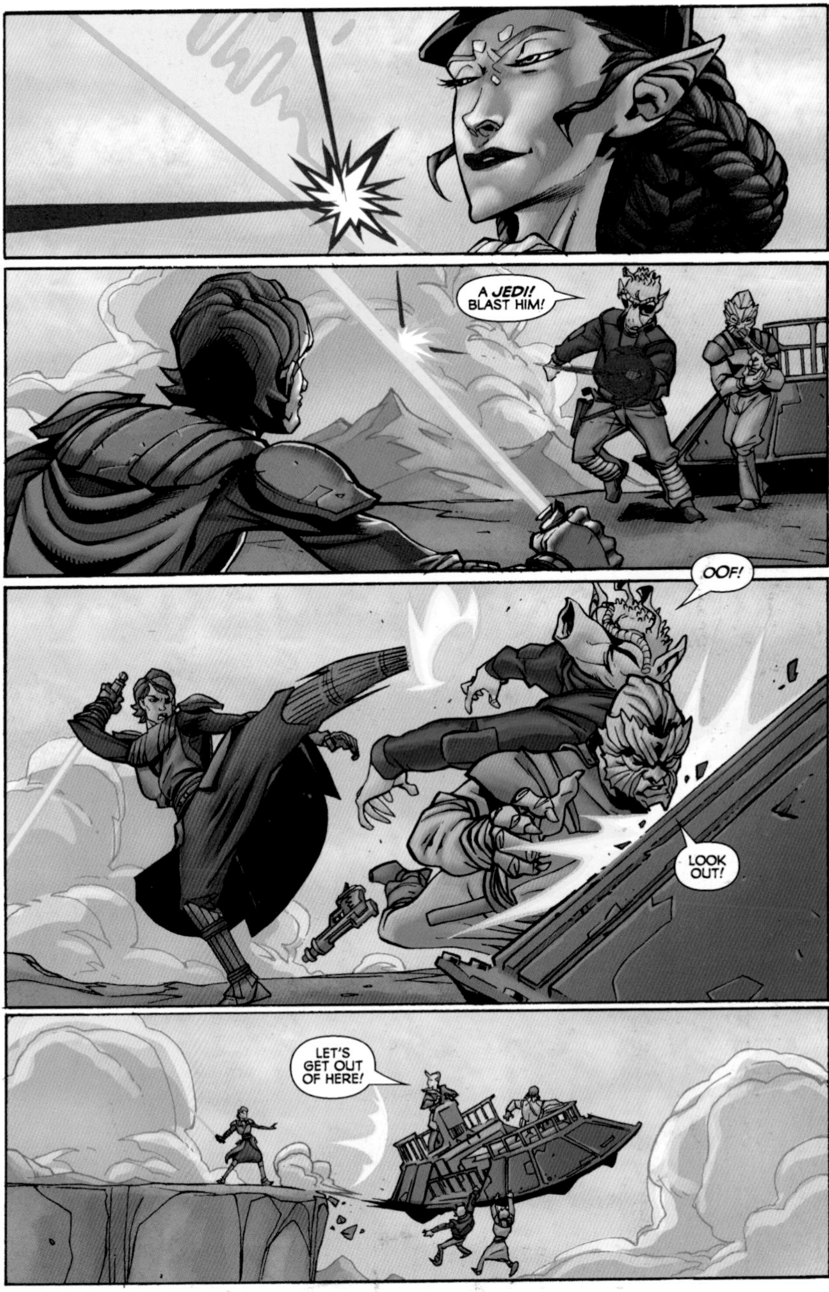
A JEDI! BLAST HIM!
OOF!
LOOK OUT!
LET'S GET OUT OF HERE!

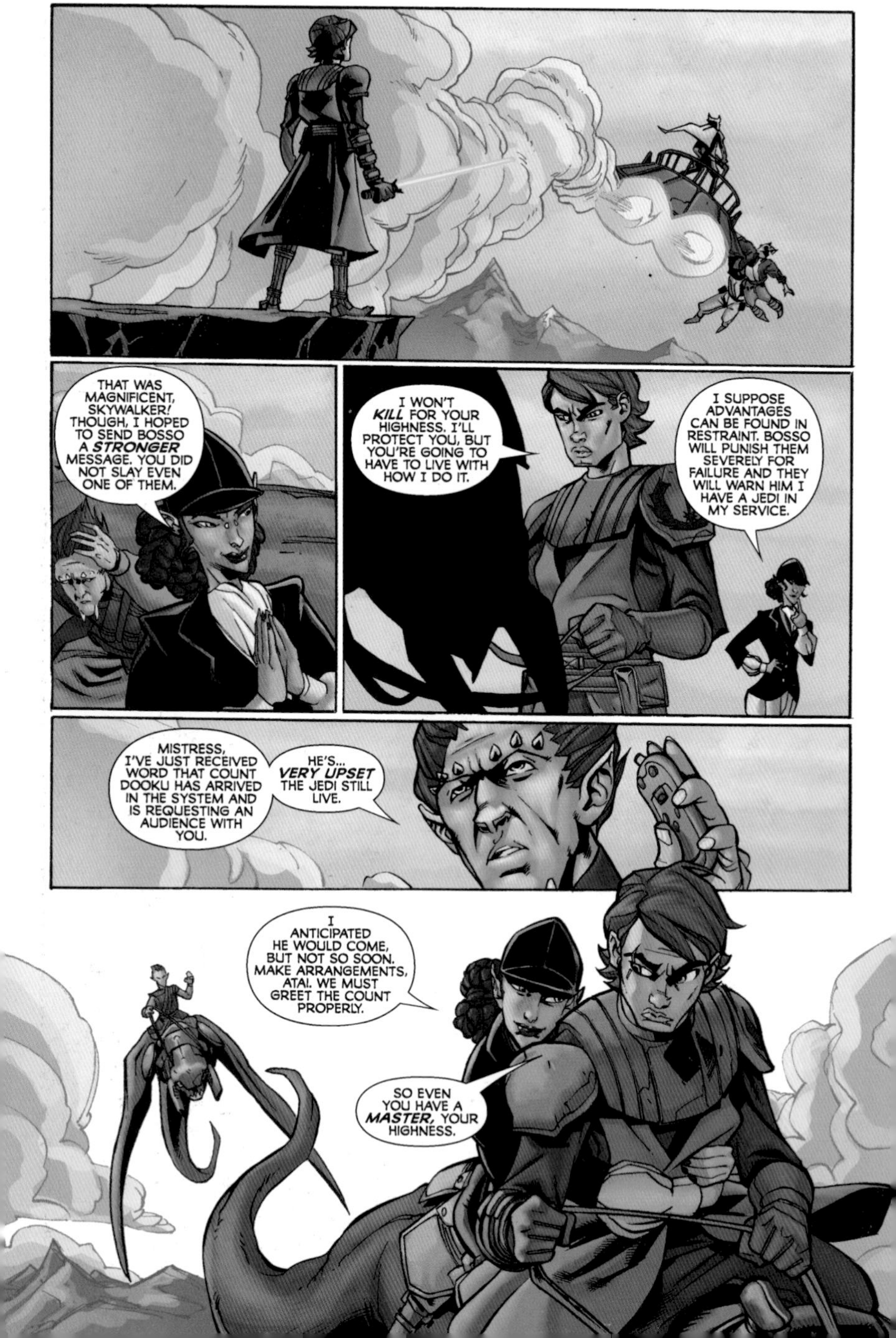
THAT WAS MAGNIFICENT, SKYWALKER! THOUGH, I HOPED TO SEND BOSSO A STRONGER MESSAGE. YOU DID NOT SLAY EVEN ONE OF THEM.
I WON'T KILL FOR YOUR HIGHNESS. I'LL PROTECT YOU, BUT YOU'RE GOING TO HAVE TO LIVE WITH HOW I DO IT.
I SUPPOSE ADVANTAGES CAN BE FOUND IN RESTRAINT. BOSSO WILL PUNISH THEM SEVERELY FOR FAILURE AND THEY WILL WARN HIM I HAVE A JEDI IN MY SERVICE.
MISTRESS, I'VE JUST RECEIVED WORD THAT COUNT DOOKU HAS ARRIVED IN THE SYSTEM AND IS REQUESTING AN AUDIENCE WITH YOU.
HE'S... VERY UPSET THE JEDI STILL LIVE.
I ANTICIPATED HE WOULD COME, BUT NOT SO SOON. MAKE ARRANGEMENTS, ATAI. WE MUST GREET THE COUNT PROPERLY.
SO EVEN YOU HAVE A MASTER, YOUR HIGHNESS.

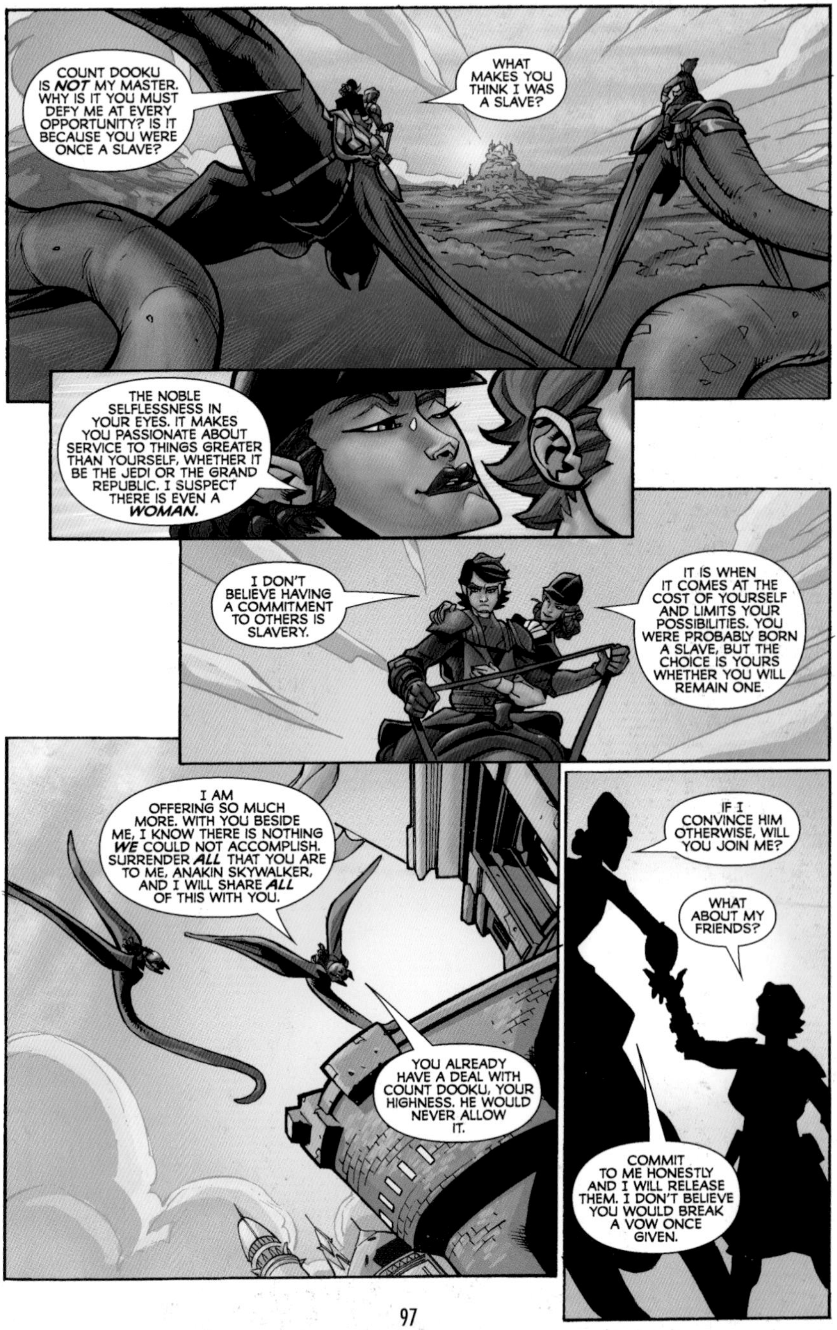
COUNT DOOKU IS NOT MY MASTER. WHY IS IT YOU MUST DEFY ME AT EVERY OPPORTUNITY? IS IT BECAUSE YOU WERE ONCE A SLAVE?
WHAT MAKES YOU THINK I WAS A SLAVE?
THE NOBLE SELFLESSNESS IN YOUR EYES. IT MAKES YOU PASSIONATE ABOUT SERVICE TO THINGS GREATER THAN YOURSELF, WHETHER IT BE THE JEDI OR THE GRAND REPUBLIC. I SUSPECT THERE IS EVEN A WOMAN.
I DON'T BELIEVE HAVING A COMMITMENT TO OTHERS IS SLAVERY.
IT IS WHEN IT COMES AT THE COST OF YOURSELF AND LIMITS YOUR POSSIBILITIES. YOU WERE PROBABLY BORN A SLAVE, BUT THE CHOICE IS YOURS WHETHER YOU WILL REMAIN ONE.
I AM OFFERING SO MUCH MORE. WITH YOU BESIDE ME, I KNOW THERE IS NOTHING WE COULD NOT ACCOMPLISH. SURRENDER ALL THAT YOU ARE TO ME, ANAKIN SKYWALKER, AND I WILL SHARE ALL OF THIS WITH YOU.
YOU ALREADY HAVE A DEAL WITH COUNT DOOKU, YOUR HIGHNESS. HE WOULD NEVER ALLOW IT.
IF I CONVINCE HIM OTHERWISE, WILL YOU JOIN ME?
WHAT ABOUT MY FRIENDS?
COMMIT TO ME HONESTLY AND I WILL RELEASE THEM. I DON'T BELIEVE YOU WOULD BREAK A VOW ONCE GIVEN.

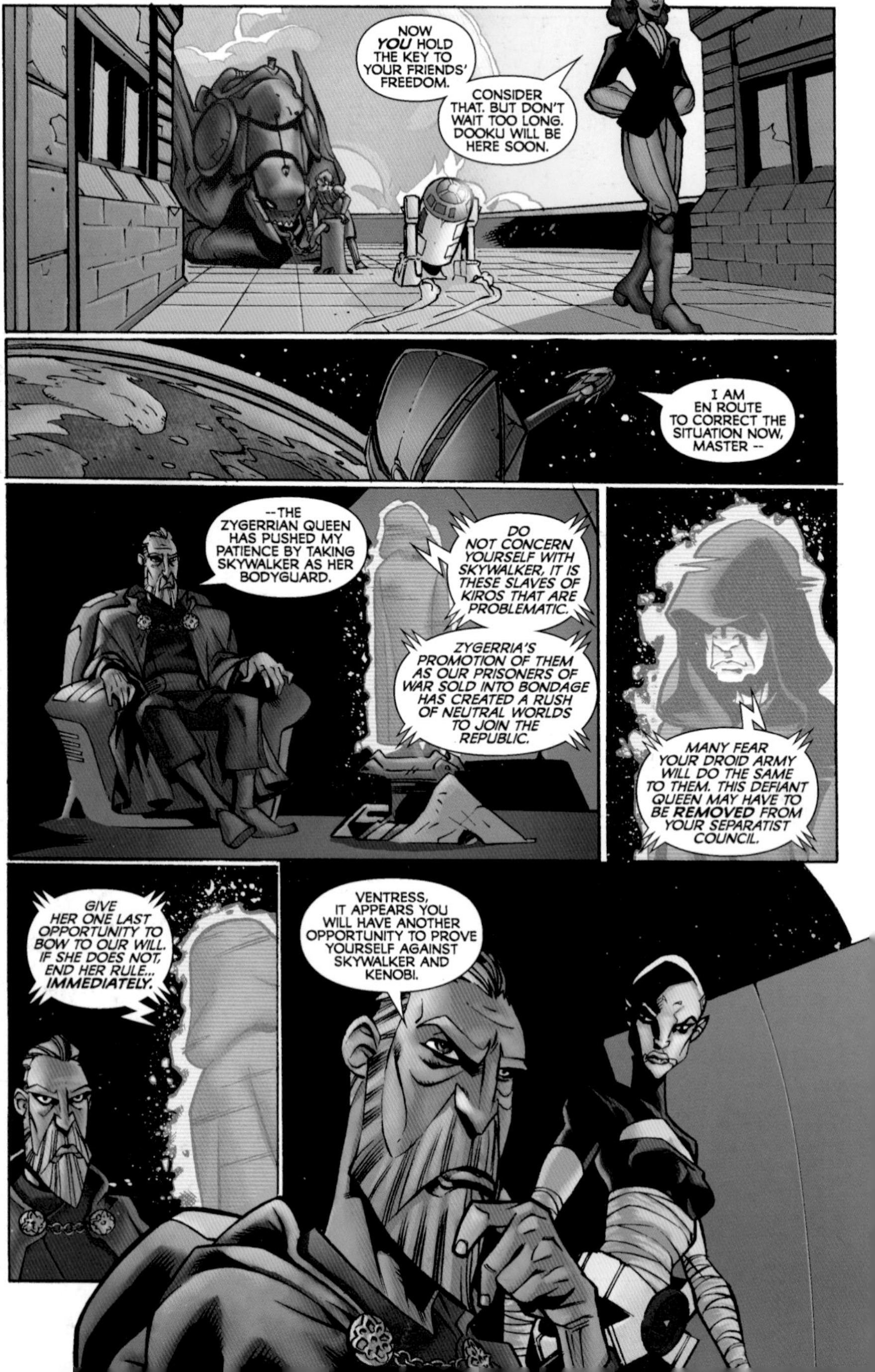

NOW *YOU* HOLD THE KEY TO YOUR FRIENDS' FREEDOM.
CONSIDER THAT. BUT DON'T WAIT TOO LONG. DOOKU WILL BE HERE SOON.
I AM EN ROUTE TO CORRECT THE SITUATION NOW, MASTER --
--THE ZYGERRIAN QUEEN HAS PUSHED MY PATIENCE BY TAKING SKYWALKER AS HER BODYGUARD.
DO NOT CONCERN YOURSELF WITH SKYWALKER, IT IS THESE SLAVES OF KIROS THAT ARE PROBLEMATIC.
ZYGERRIA'S PROMOTION OF THEM AS OUR PRISONERS OF WAR SOLD INTO BONDAGE HAS CREATED A RUSH OF NEUTRAL WORLDS TO JOIN THE REPUBLIC.
*MANY FEAR YOUR DROID ARMY WILL DO THE SAME TO THEM. THIS DEFIANT QUEEN MAY HAVE TO BE **REMOVED** FROM YOUR SEPARATIST COUNCIL.*
*GIVE HER ONE LAST OPPORTUNITY TO BOW TO OUR WILL. IF SHE DOES NOT, END HER RULE... **IMMEDIATELY.***
VENTRESS, IT APPEARS YOU WILL HAVE ANOTHER OPPORTUNITY TO PROVE YOURSELF AGAINST SKYWALKER AND KENOBI.

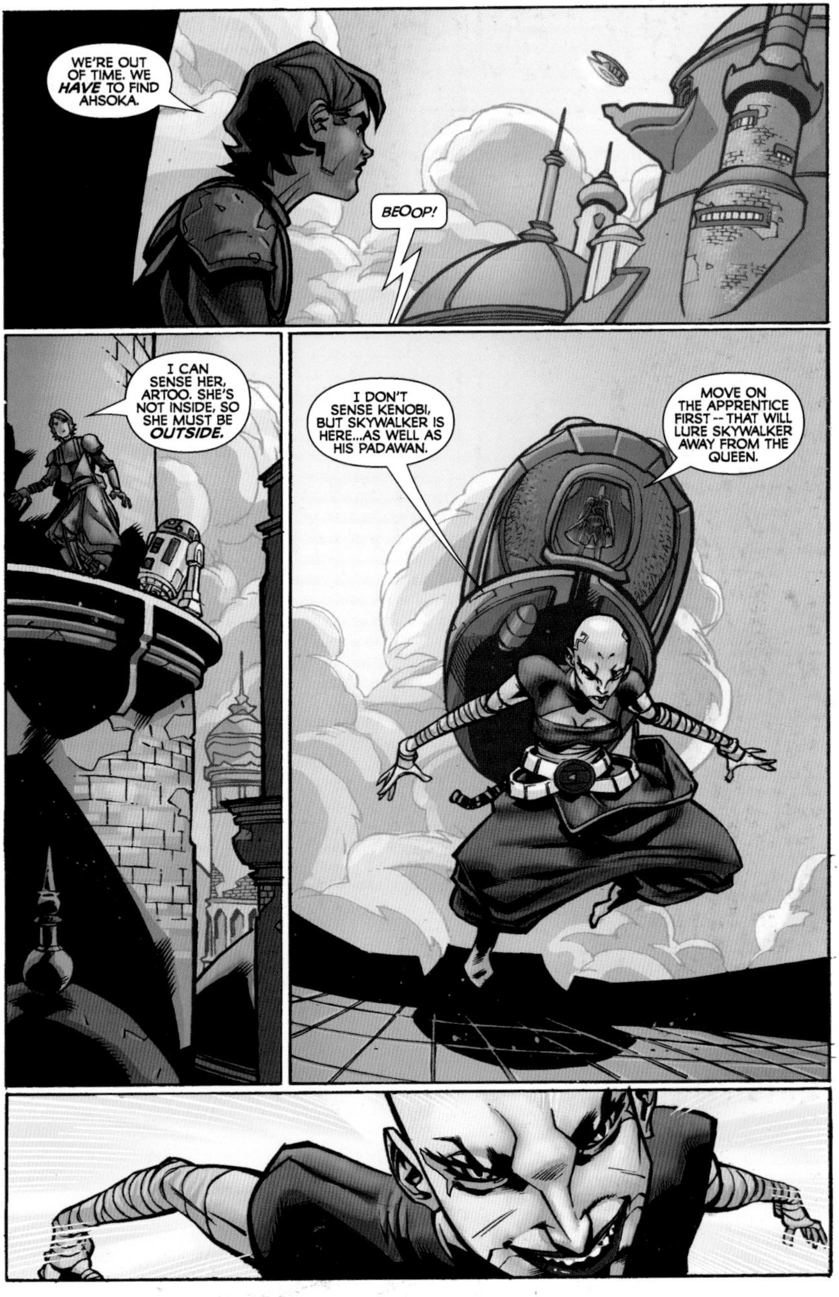
WE'RE OUT OF TIME. WE *HAVE* TO FIND AHSOKA.
BEOOP!
I CAN SENSE HER, ARTOO. SHE'S NOT INSIDE, SO SHE MUST BE *OUTSIDE.*
I DON'T SENSE KENOBI, BUT SKYWALKER IS HERE...AS WELL AS HIS PADAWAN.
MOVE ON THE APPRENTICE FIRST -- THAT WILL LURE SKYWALKER AWAY FROM THE QUEEN.

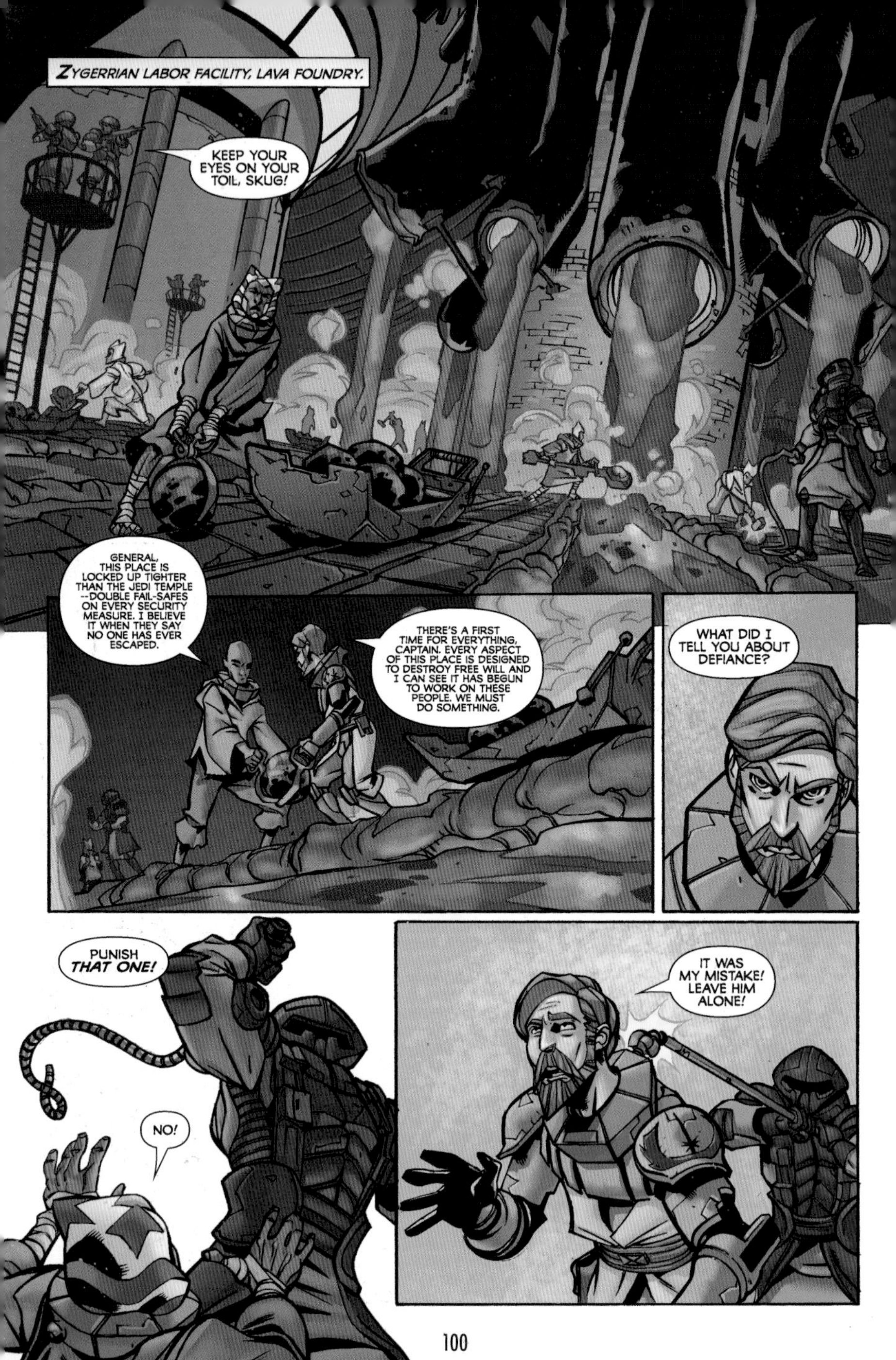

ZYGERRIAN LABOR FACILITY, LAVA FOUNDRY.
KEEP YOUR EYES ON YOUR TOIL, SKUG!
GENERAL, THIS PLACE IS LOCKED UP TIGHTER THAN THE JEDI TEMPLE --DOUBLE FAIL-SAFES ON EVERY SECURITY MEASURE. I BELIEVE IT WHEN THEY SAY NO ONE HAS EVER ESCAPED.
THERE'S A FIRST TIME FOR EVERYTHING, CAPTAIN. EVERY ASPECT OF THIS PLACE IS DESIGNED TO DESTROY FREE WILL AND I CAN SEE IT HAS BEGUN TO WORK ON THESE PEOPLE. WE MUST DO SOMETHING.
WHAT DID I TELL YOU ABOUT DEFIANCE?
PUNISH *THAT ONE!*
NO!
IT WAS MY MISTAKE! LEAVE HIM ALONE!

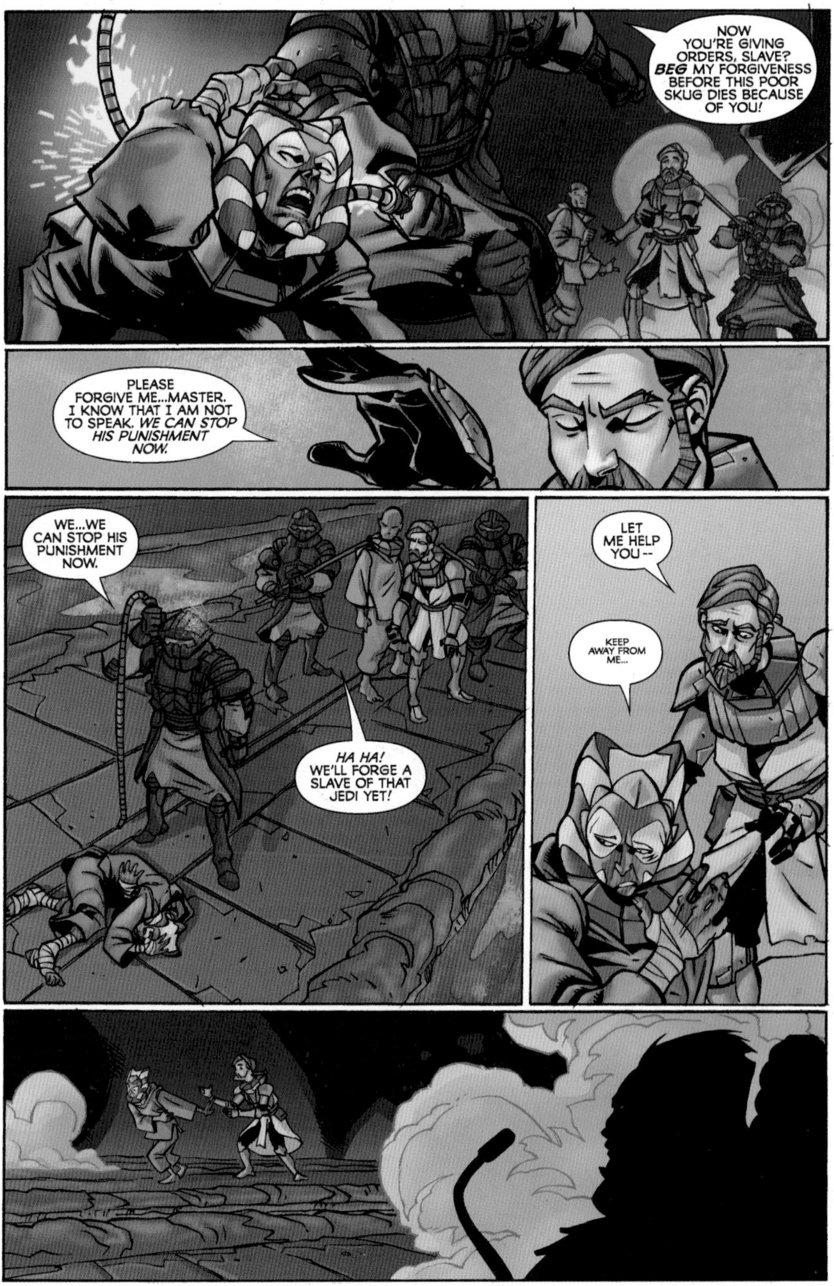
NOW YOU'RE GIVING ORDERS, SLAVE? BEG MY FORGIVENESS BEFORE THIS POOR SKUG DIES BECAUSE OF YOU!
PLEASE FORGIVE ME...MASTER. I KNOW THAT I AM NOT TO SPEAK. WE CAN STOP HIS PUNISHMENT NOW.
WE...WE CAN STOP HIS PUNISHMENT NOW.
HA HA! WE'LL FORGE A SLAVE OF THAT JEDI YET!
LET ME HELP YOU --
KEEP AWAY FROM ME...

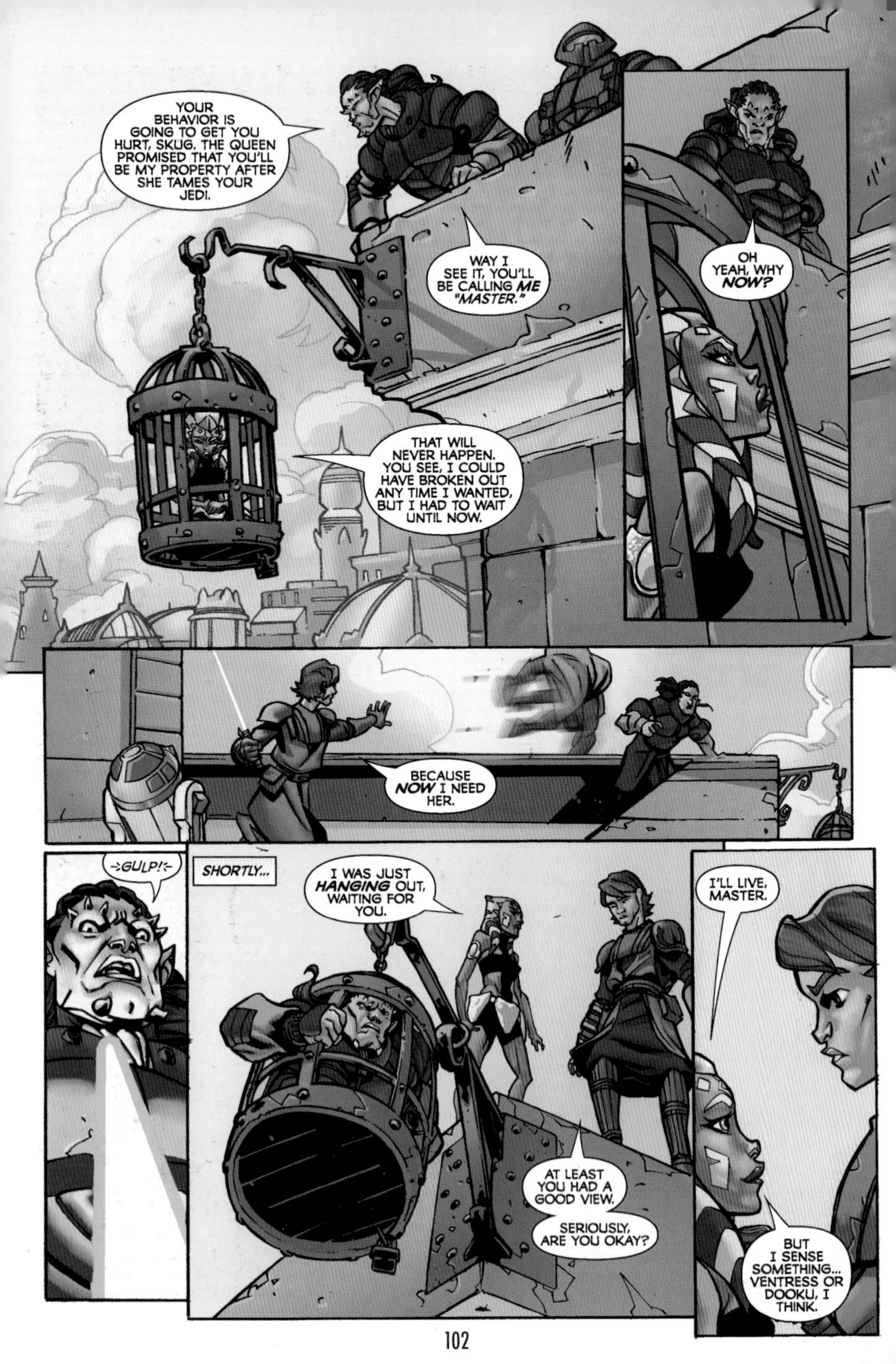
YOUR BEHAVIOR IS GOING TO GET YOU HURT, SKUG. THE QUEEN PROMISED THAT YOU'LL BE MY PROPERTY AFTER SHE TAMES YOUR JEDI.
WAY I SEE IT, YOU'LL BE CALLING *ME* "MASTER."
OH YEAH, WHY *NOW?*
THAT WILL NEVER HAPPEN. YOU SEE, I COULD HAVE BROKEN OUT ANY TIME I WANTED, BUT I HAD TO WAIT UNTIL NOW.
BECAUSE *NOW* I NEED HER.
-GULP!-
SHORTLY...
I WAS JUST *HANGING* OUT, WAITING FOR YOU.
AT LEAST YOU HAD A GOOD VIEW.
SERIOUSLY, ARE YOU OKAY?
I'LL LIVE, MASTER.
BUT I SENSE SOMETHING... VENTRESS OR DOOKU, I THINK.

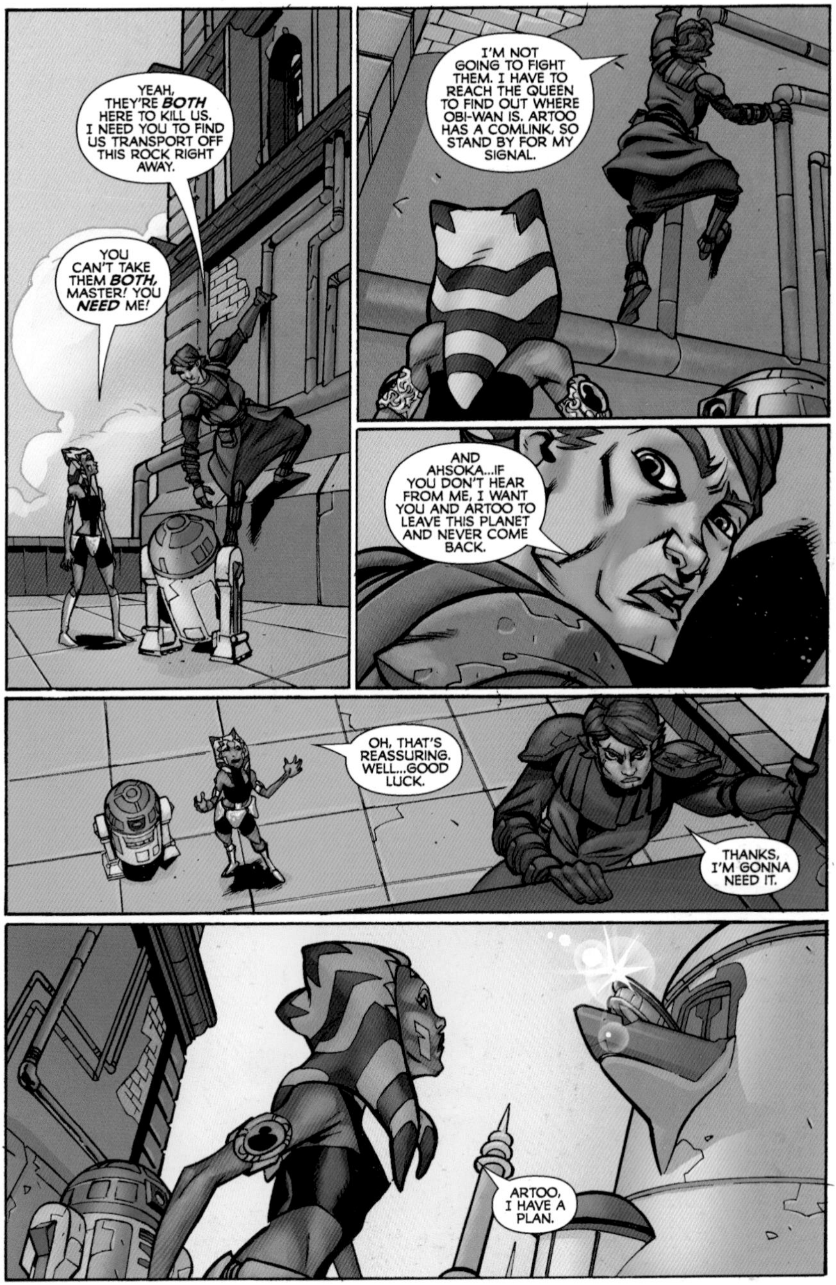

YEAH, THEY'RE *BOTH* HERE TO KILL US. I NEED YOU TO FIND US TRANSPORT OFF THIS ROCK RIGHT AWAY.
YOU CAN'T TAKE THEM *BOTH,* MASTER! YOU *NEED* ME!
I'M NOT GOING TO FIGHT THEM. I HAVE TO REACH THE QUEEN TO FIND OUT WHERE OBI-WAN IS. ARTOO HAS A COMLINK, SO STAND BY FOR MY SIGNAL.
AND AHSOKA...IF YOU DON'T HEAR FROM ME, I WANT YOU AND ARTOO TO LEAVE THIS PLANET AND NEVER COME BACK.
OH, THAT'S REASSURING. WELL...GOOD LUCK.
THANKS, I'M GONNA NEED IT.
ARTOO, I HAVE A PLAN.

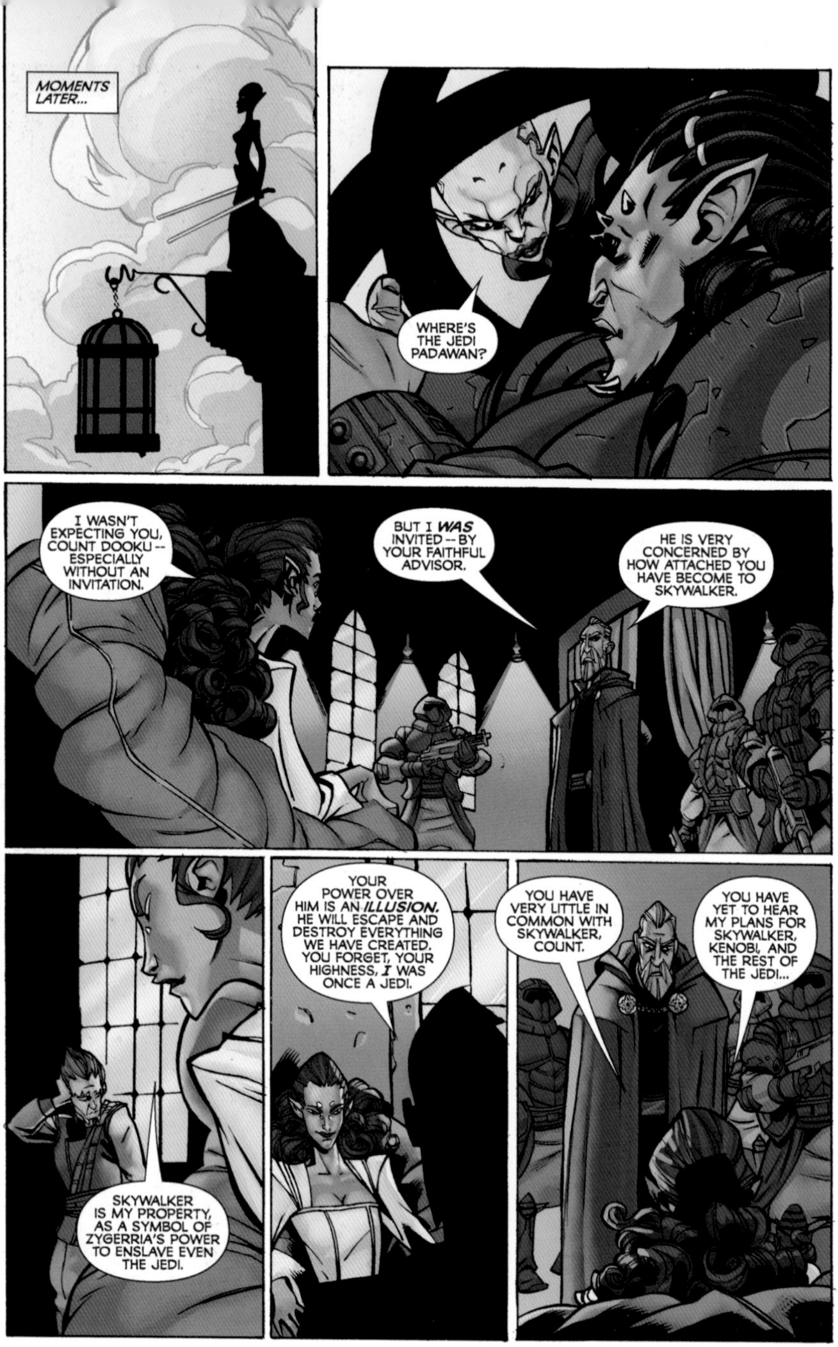
MOMENTS LATER...
WHERE'S THE JEDI PADAWAN?
I WASN'T EXPECTING YOU, COUNT DOOKU -- ESPECIALLY WITHOUT AN INVITATION.
BUT I WAS INVITED -- BY YOUR FAITHFUL ADVISOR.
HE IS VERY CONCERNED BY HOW ATTACHED YOU HAVE BECOME TO SKYWALKER.
SKYWALKER IS MY PROPERTY, AS A SYMBOL OF ZYGERRIA'S POWER TO ENSLAVE EVEN THE JEDI.
YOUR POWER OVER HIM IS AN ILLUSION. HE WILL ESCAPE AND DESTROY EVERYTHING WE HAVE CREATED. YOU FORGET, YOUR HIGHNESS, I WAS ONCE A JEDI.
YOU HAVE VERY LITTLE IN COMMON WITH SKYWALKER, COUNT.
YOU HAVE YET TO HEAR MY PLANS FOR SKYWALKER, KENOBI, AND THE REST OF THE JEDI...

"AT THIS MOMENT, FAR AWAY, MASTER KENOBI IS FEELING HELPLESS TO AID THE DESPERATELY NEEDY THAT SURROUND HIM.

"IT IS THE BEGINNING OF HIS SUBJUGATION -- HIS REALIZATION THAT PERHAPS FOR THE FIRST TIME IN HIS LIFE, HIS SELFLESS DESIRE TO HELP THE OPPRESSED MAKES HIM ONE TO BE *FEARED* BY THEM.

"YOU HAVE USED THE COMPASSION OF THE JEDI AGAINST THEM BEFORE, COUNT...

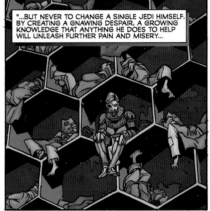

"...BUT NEVER TO CHANGE A SINGLE JEDI HIMSELF. BY CREATING A GNAWING DESPAIR, A GROWING KNOWLEDGE THAT ANYTHING HE DOES TO HELP WILL UNLEASH FURTHER PAIN AND MISERY...

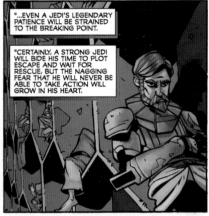

"...EVEN A JEDI'S LEGENDARY PATIENCE WILL BE STRAINED TO THE BREAKING POINT.

"CERTAINLY, A STRONG JEDI WILL BIDE HIS TIME TO PLOT ESCAPE AND WAIT FOR RESCUE, BUT THE NAGGING FEAR THAT HE WILL NEVER BE ABLE TO TAKE ACTION WILL GROW IN HIS HEART.

"AND SO, TO EASE THE BURDEN OF HIS FELLOW SLAVES, HIS DEFIANCE WILL CHANGE TO COMPLIANCE. HE WILL BEHAVE AS THE SLAVES DO FOR THEIR BENEFIT AND ALLOW HIS OWN WILL TO BE CRUSHED.

"WHEN HE IS NO DIFFERENT THAN THE OTHER SLAVES, HE WILL BE *MINE*."

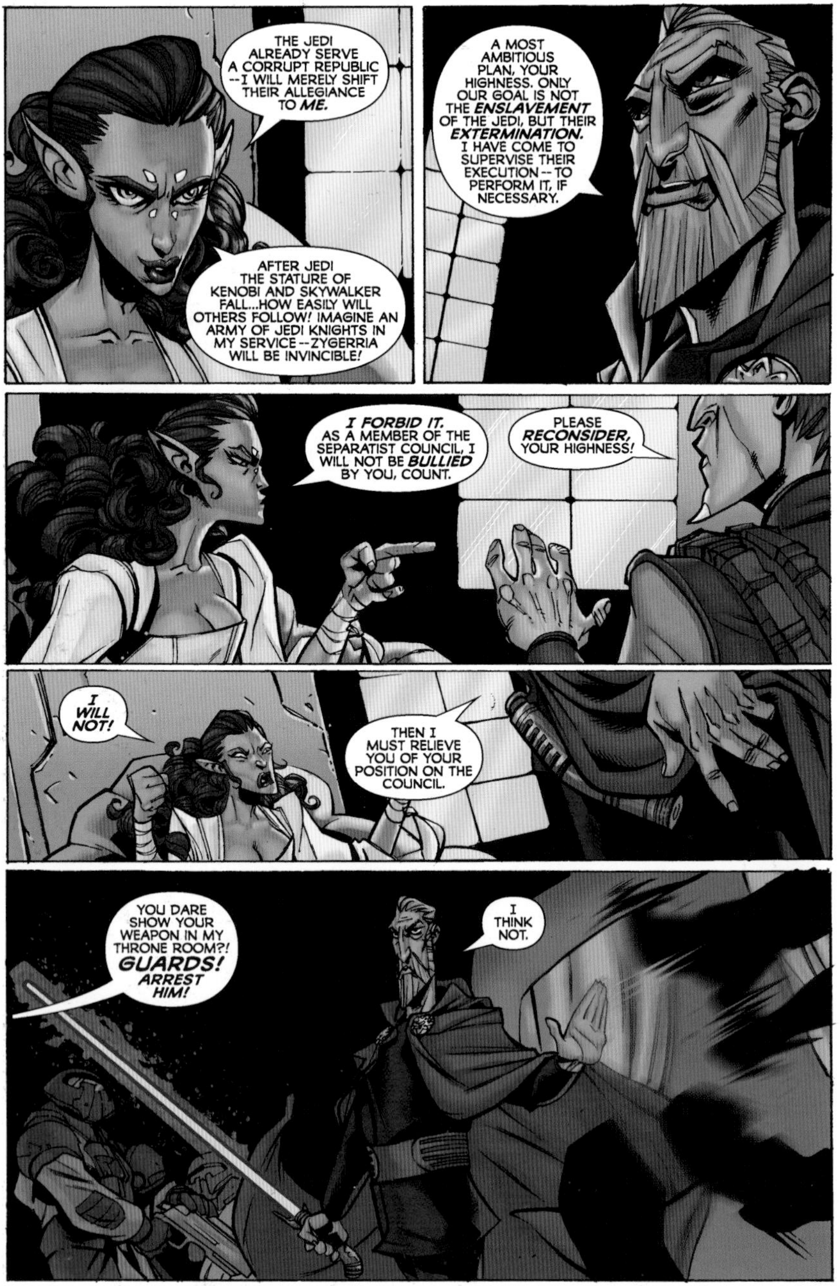
THE JEDI ALREADY SERVE A CORRUPT REPUBLIC --I WILL MERELY SHIFT THEIR ALLEGIANCE TO *ME.*
AFTER JEDI THE STATURE OF KENOBI AND SKYWALKER FALL...HOW EASILY WILL OTHERS FOLLOW! IMAGINE AN ARMY OF JEDI KNIGHTS IN MY SERVICE--ZYGERRIA WILL BE INVINCIBLE!
A MOST AMBITIOUS PLAN, YOUR HIGHNESS. ONLY OUR GOAL IS NOT THE *ENSLAVEMENT* OF THE JEDI, BUT THEIR *EXTERMINATION.* I HAVE COME TO SUPERVISE THEIR EXECUTION--TO PERFORM IT, IF NECESSARY.
I FORBID IT. AS A MEMBER OF THE SEPARATIST COUNCIL, I WILL NOT BE *BULLIED* BY YOU, COUNT.
PLEASE *RECONSIDER,* YOUR HIGHNESS!
I WILL NOT!
THEN I MUST RELIEVE YOU OF YOUR POSITION ON THE COUNCIL.
YOU DARE SHOW YOUR WEAPON IN MY THRONE ROOM?! ***GUARDS!*** ***ARREST HIM!***
I THINK NOT.

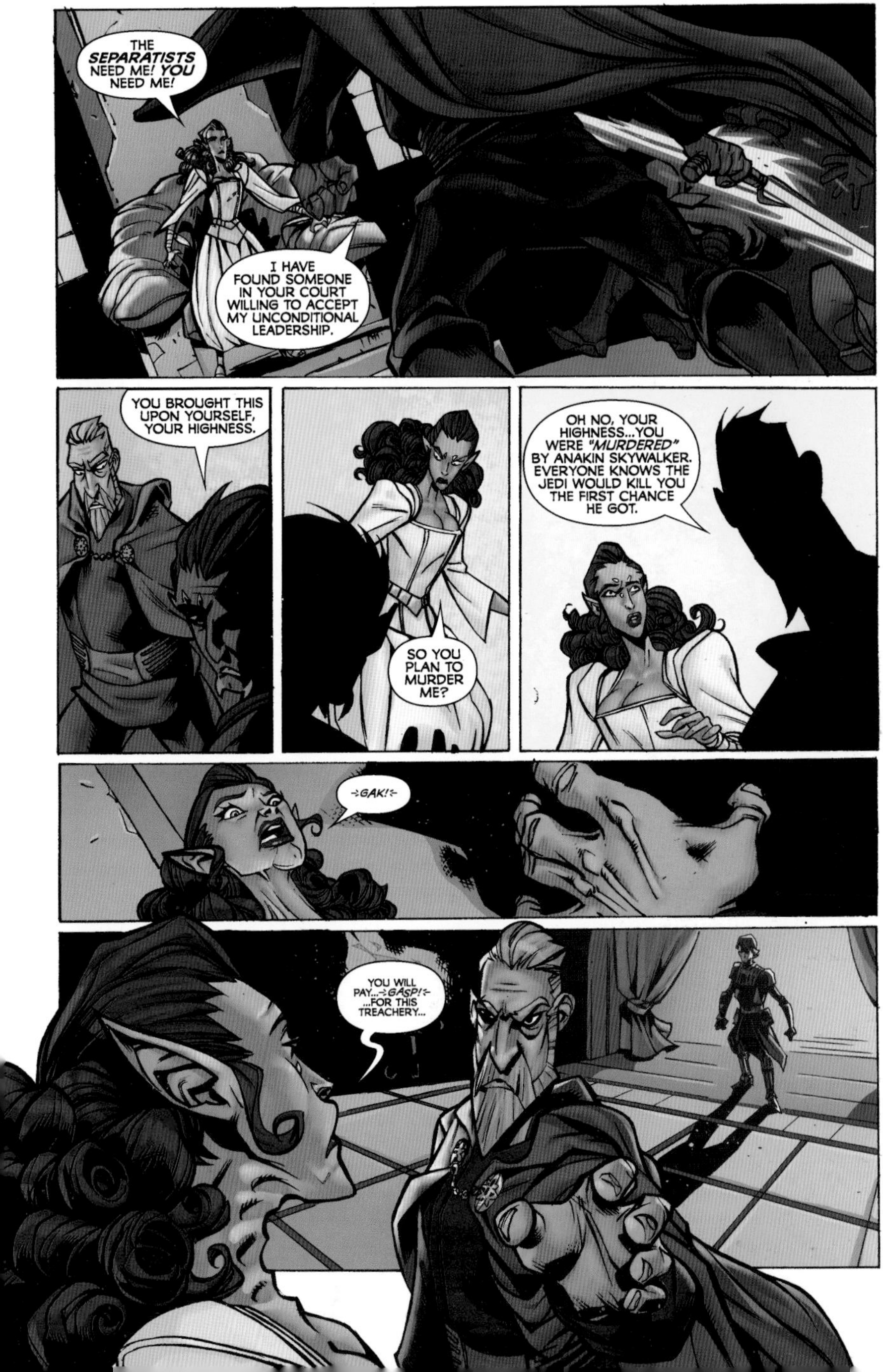
THE *SEPARATISTS* NEED ME! *YOU* NEED ME!
I HAVE FOUND SOMEONE IN YOUR COURT WILLING TO ACCEPT MY UNCONDITIONAL LEADERSHIP.
YOU BROUGHT THIS UPON YOURSELF, YOUR HIGHNESS.
SO YOU PLAN TO MURDER ME?
OH NO, YOUR HIGHNESS...YOU WERE *"MURDERED"* BY ANAKIN SKYWALKER. EVERYONE KNOWS THE JEDI WOULD KILL YOU THE FIRST CHANCE HE GOT.
GAK!
YOU WILL PAY...*GASP!* ...FOR THIS TREACHERY...

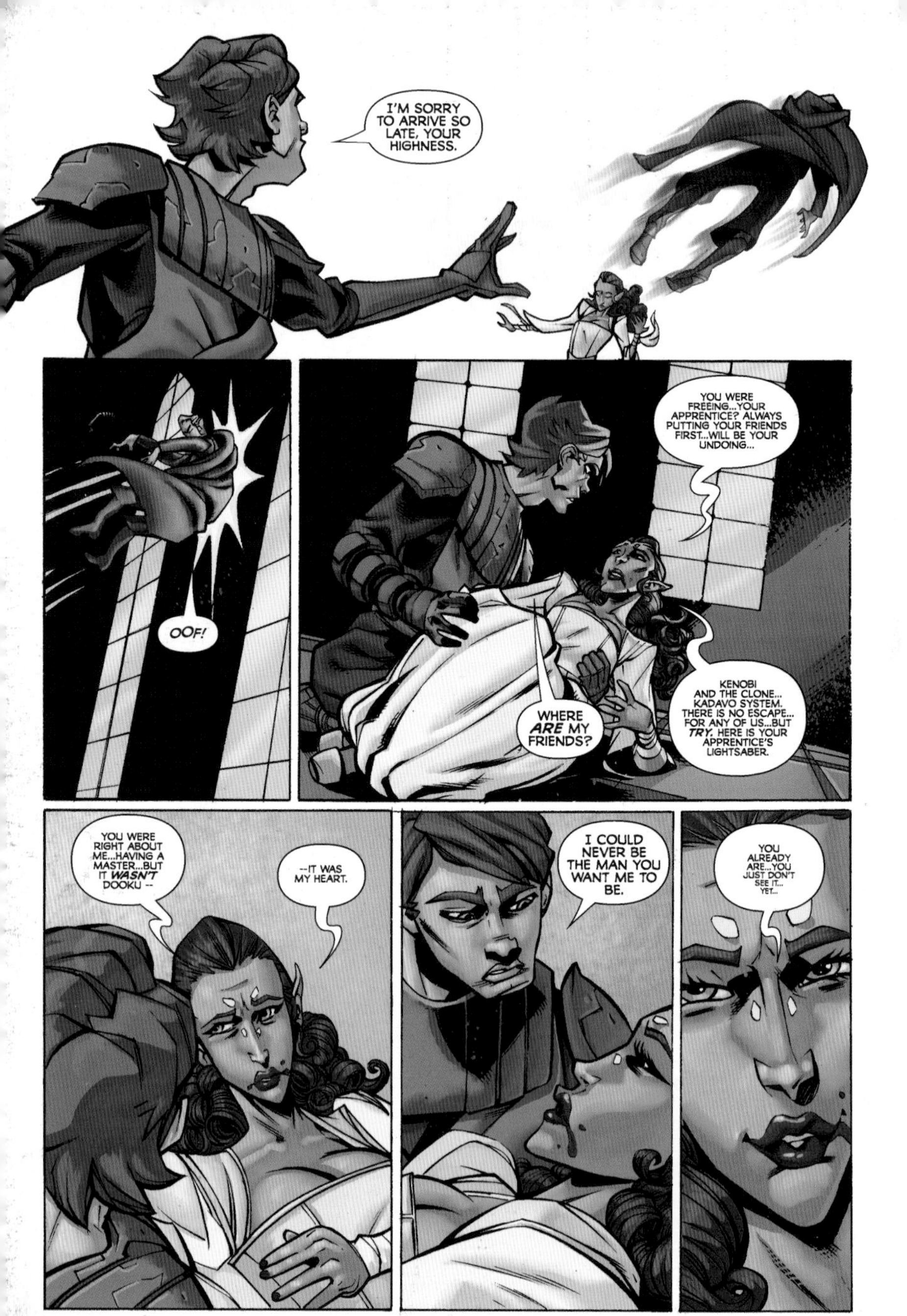

I'M SORRY TO ARRIVE SO LATE, YOUR HIGHNESS.
OOF!
YOU WERE FREEING...YOUR APPRENTICE? ALWAYS PUTTING YOUR FRIENDS FIRST...WILL BE YOUR UNDOING...
WHERE *ARE* MY FRIENDS?
KENOBI AND THE CLONE... KADAVO SYSTEM. THERE IS NO ESCAPE... FOR ANY OF US...BUT *TRY.* HERE IS YOUR APPRENTICE'S LIGHTSABER.
YOU WERE RIGHT ABOUT ME...HAVING A MASTER...BUT IT *WASN'T* DOOKU --
--IT WAS MY HEART.
I COULD NEVER BE THE MAN YOU WANT ME TO BE.
YOU ALREADY ARE...YOU JUST DON'T SEE IT... YET...

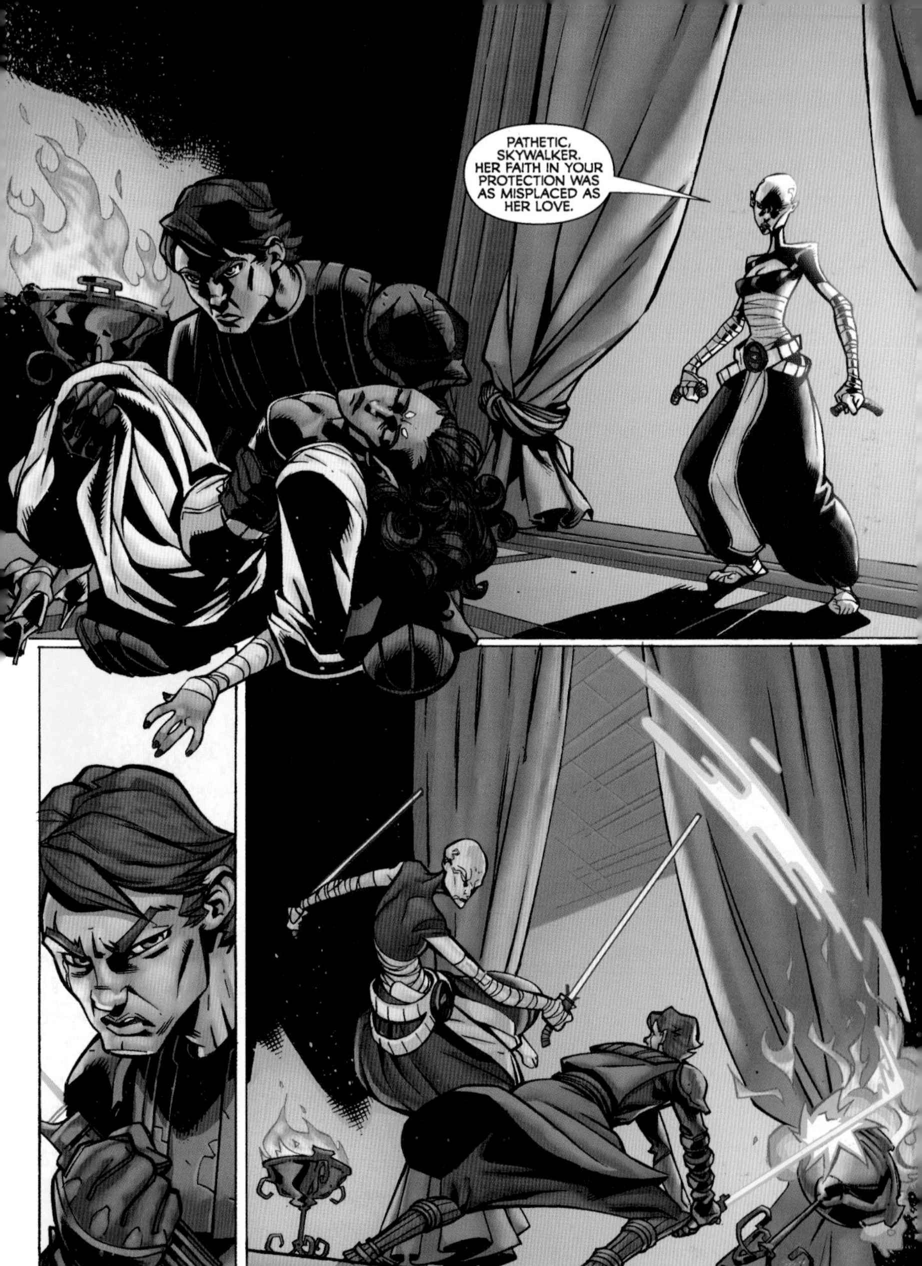
PATHETIC, SKYWALKER. HER FAITH IN YOUR PROTECTION WAS AS MISPLACED AS HER LOVE.

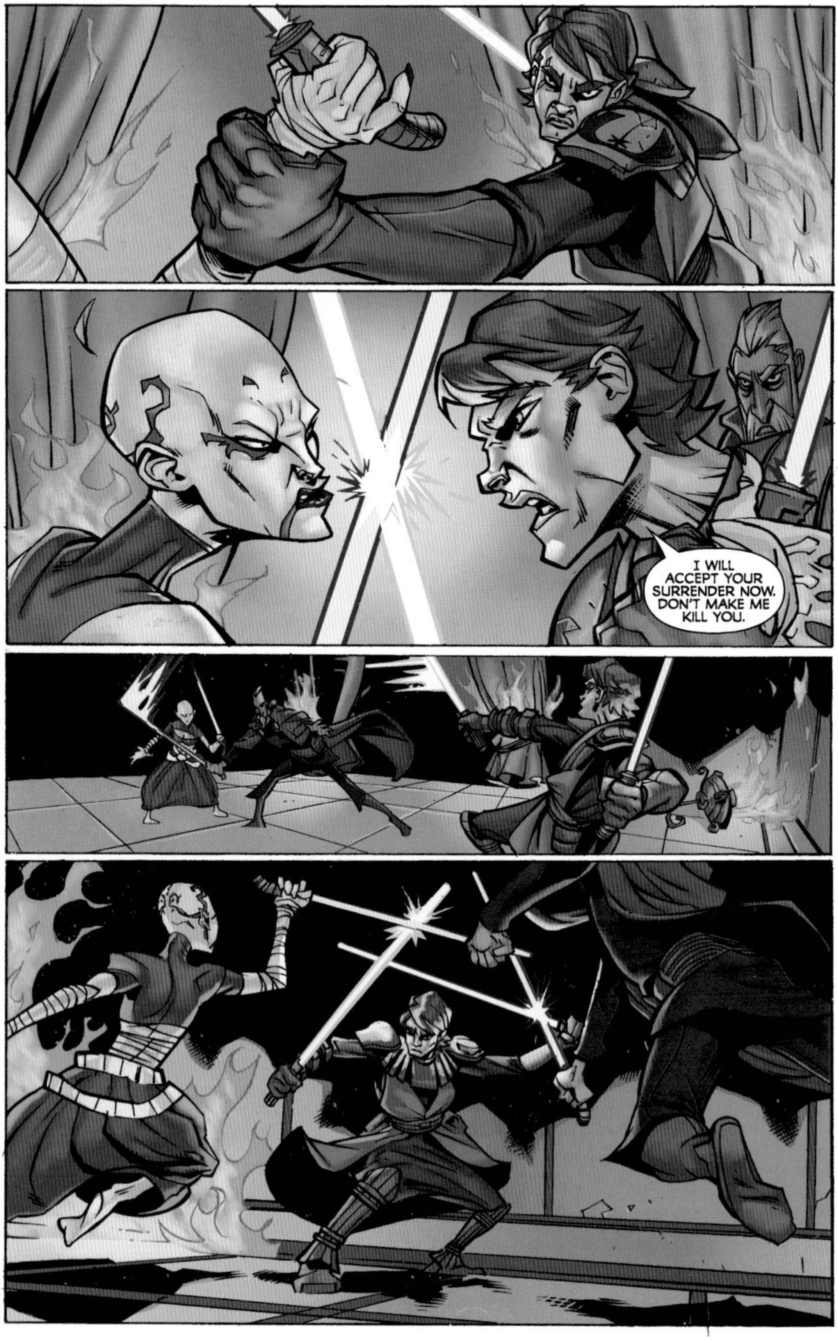
I WILL ACCEPT YOUR SURRENDER NOW. DON'T MAKE ME KILL YOU.

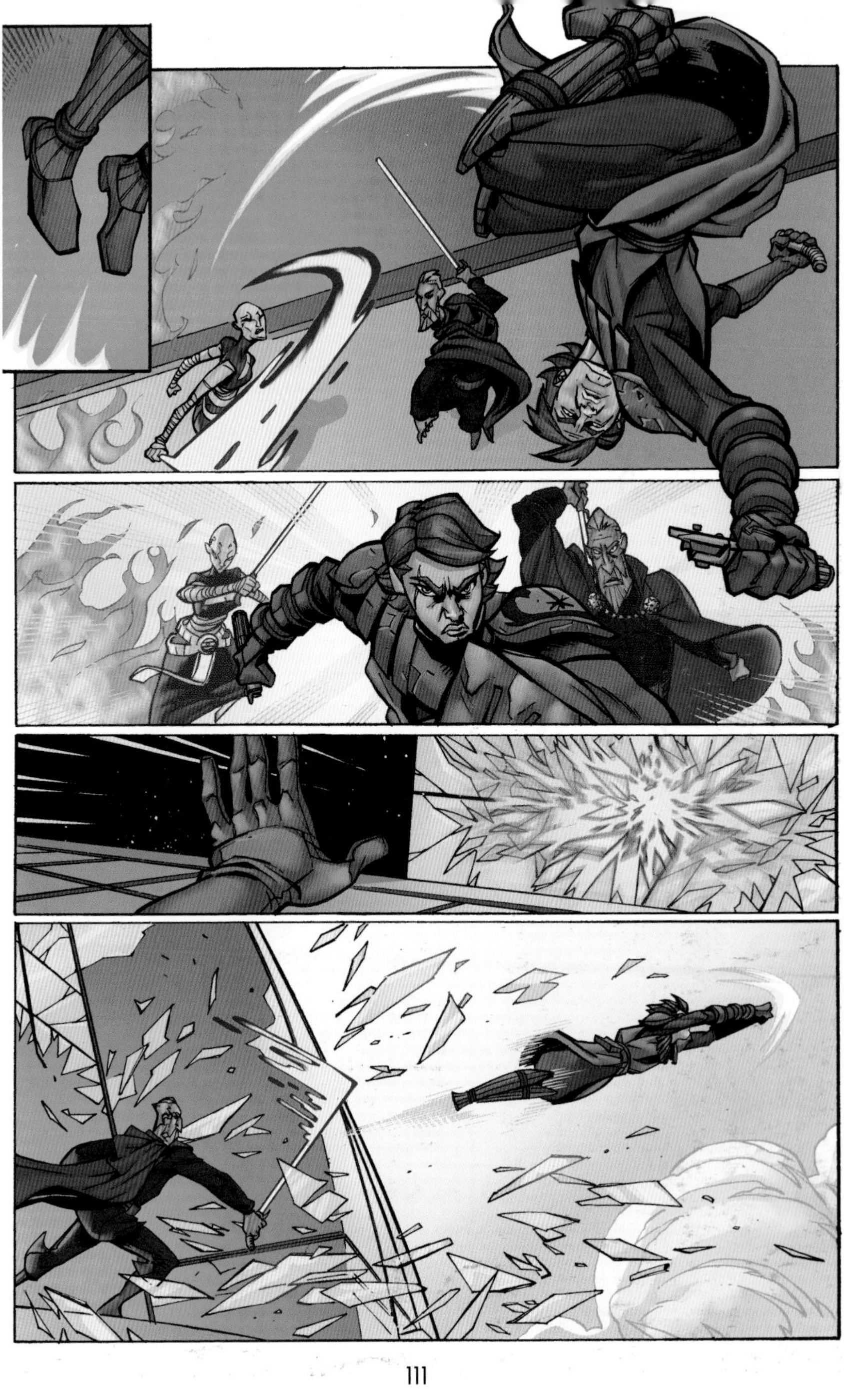

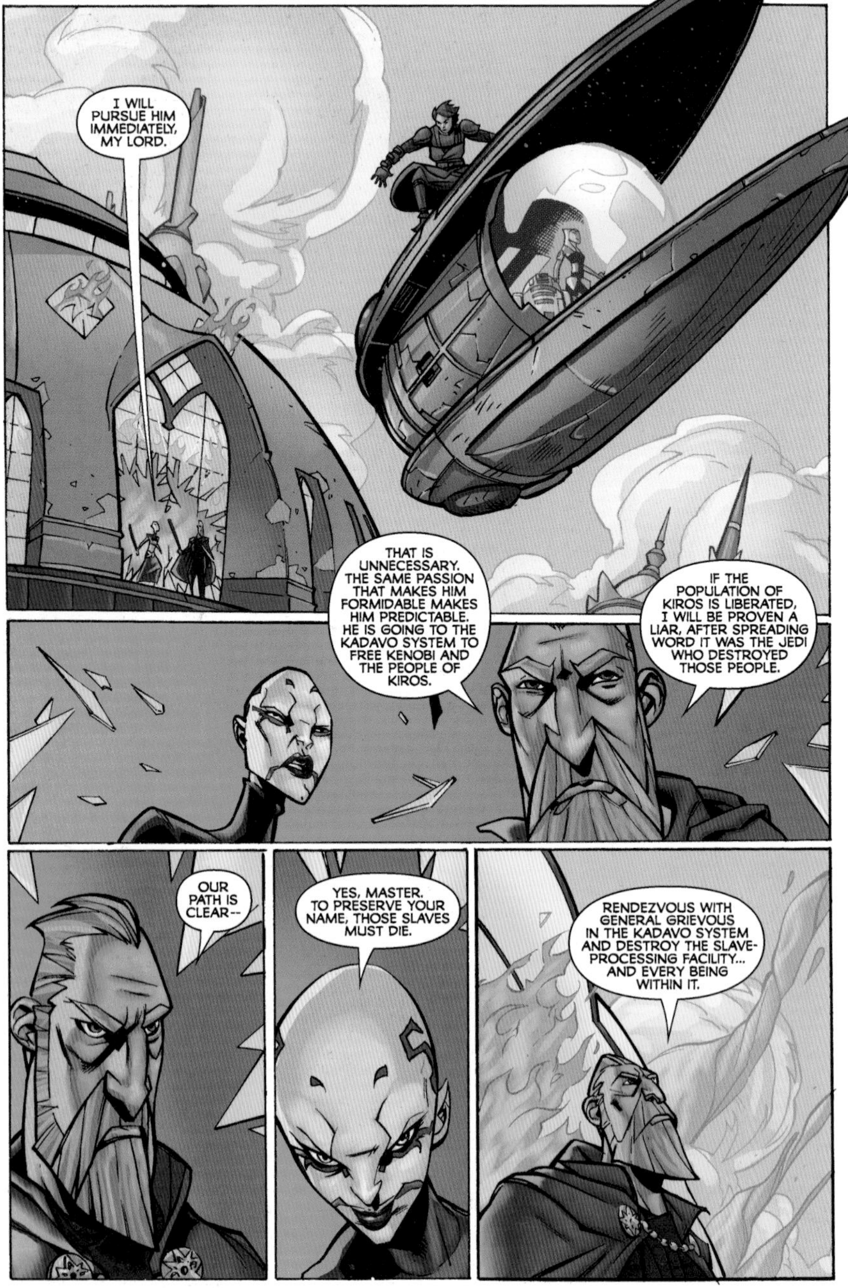
I WILL PURSUE HIM IMMEDIATELY, MY LORD.
THAT IS UNNECESSARY. THE SAME PASSION THAT MAKES HIM FORMIDABLE MAKES HIM PREDICTABLE. HE IS GOING TO THE KADAVO SYSTEM TO FREE KENOBI AND THE PEOPLE OF KIROS.
IF THE POPULATION OF KIROS IS LIBERATED, I WILL BE PROVEN A LIAR, AFTER SPREADING WORD IT WAS THE JEDI WHO DESTROYED THOSE PEOPLE.
OUR PATH IS CLEAR--
YES, MASTER. TO PRESERVE YOUR NAME, THOSE SLAVES MUST DIE.
RENDEZVOUS WITH GENERAL GRIEVOUS IN THE KADAVO SYSTEM AND DESTROY THE SLAVE-PROCESSING FACILITY... AND EVERY BEING WITHIN IT.

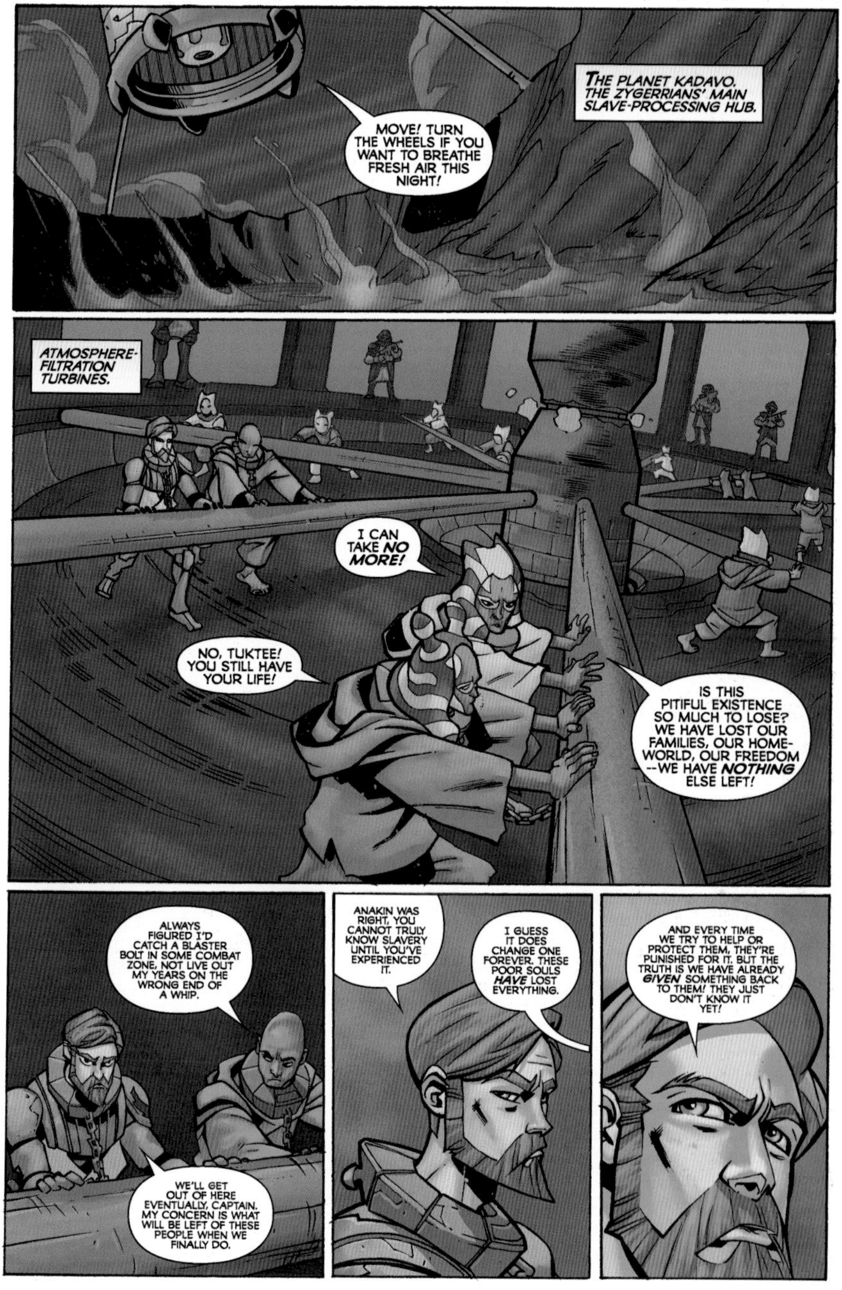
THE PLANET KADAVO. THE ZYGERRIANS' MAIN SLAVE-PROCESSING HUB.
MOVE! TURN THE WHEELS IF YOU WANT TO BREATHE FRESH AIR THIS NIGHT!
ATMOSPHERE-FILTRATION TURBINES.
I CAN TAKE NO MORE!
NO, TUKTEE! YOU STILL HAVE YOUR LIFE!
IS THIS PITIFUL EXISTENCE SO MUCH TO LOSE? WE HAVE LOST OUR FAMILIES, OUR HOME-WORLD, OUR FREEDOM --WE HAVE NOTHING ELSE LEFT!
ALWAYS FIGURED I'D CATCH A BLASTER BOLT IN SOME COMBAT ZONE, NOT LIVE OUT MY YEARS ON THE WRONG END OF A WHIP.
WE'LL GET OUT OF HERE EVENTUALLY, CAPTAIN. MY CONCERN IS WHAT WILL BE LEFT OF THESE PEOPLE WHEN WE FINALLY DO.
ANAKIN WAS RIGHT, YOU CANNOT TRULY KNOW SLAVERY UNTIL YOU'VE EXPERIENCED IT.
I GUESS IT DOES CHANGE ONE FOREVER. THESE POOR SOULS HAVE LOST EVERYTHING.
AND EVERY TIME WE TRY TO HELP OR PROTECT THEM, THEY'RE PUNISHED FOR IT. BUT THE TRUTH IS WE HAVE ALREADY GIVEN SOMETHING BACK TO THEM! THEY JUST DON'T KNOW IT YET!

QUIET, JEDI! FALSE HOPE IS WORSE THAN THE DESPAIR WE GET FROM THE LASH!

MY FRIENDS! YOU MAY HAVE LOST YOUR FREEDOM, BUT I KNOW OF ONE THING YOU CHERISH THAT HAS BEEN RETURNED TO YOU!

LET HIM SPEAK!

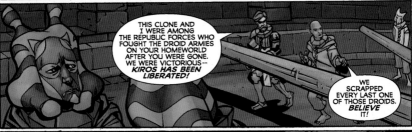

THIS CLONE AND I WERE AMONG THE REPUBLIC FORCES WHO FOUGHT THE DROID ARMIES ON YOUR HOMEWORLD AFTER YOU WERE GONE. WE WERE VICTORIOUS-- *KIROS HAS BEEN LIBERATED!*

WE SCRAPPED EVERY LAST ONE OF THOSE DROIDS. *BELIEVE* IT!

I DARED NOT DREAM IT!

IS IT POSSIBLE?

WE MUST *FIGHT!* IF WE *ALL* REBELLED--

THOUSANDS WOULD DIE! FIRST AND FOREMOST, YOU MUST *SURVIVE.* A CHANCE WILL COME TO FREE YOURSELVES, BUT IT WILL ONLY HAVE VALUE IF YOU ARE ALIVE TO USE IT.

SO LIVE THE LIFE OF A SLAVE. TOIL IN THE FOUNDRY OF THE MASTER, BUT SHARE YOUR HOPE WITH OTHERS SO THAT IT MAY GROW IN YOU ALL.

BELIEVE THAT AS BAD AS THINGS ARE HERE AND NOW, ACROSS THE STARS YOUR HOME AWAITS YOU. LIVE, AND YOU WILL BE REUNITED WITH YOUR LOVED ONES AND WALK ON KIROS AGAIN...*FREE!*

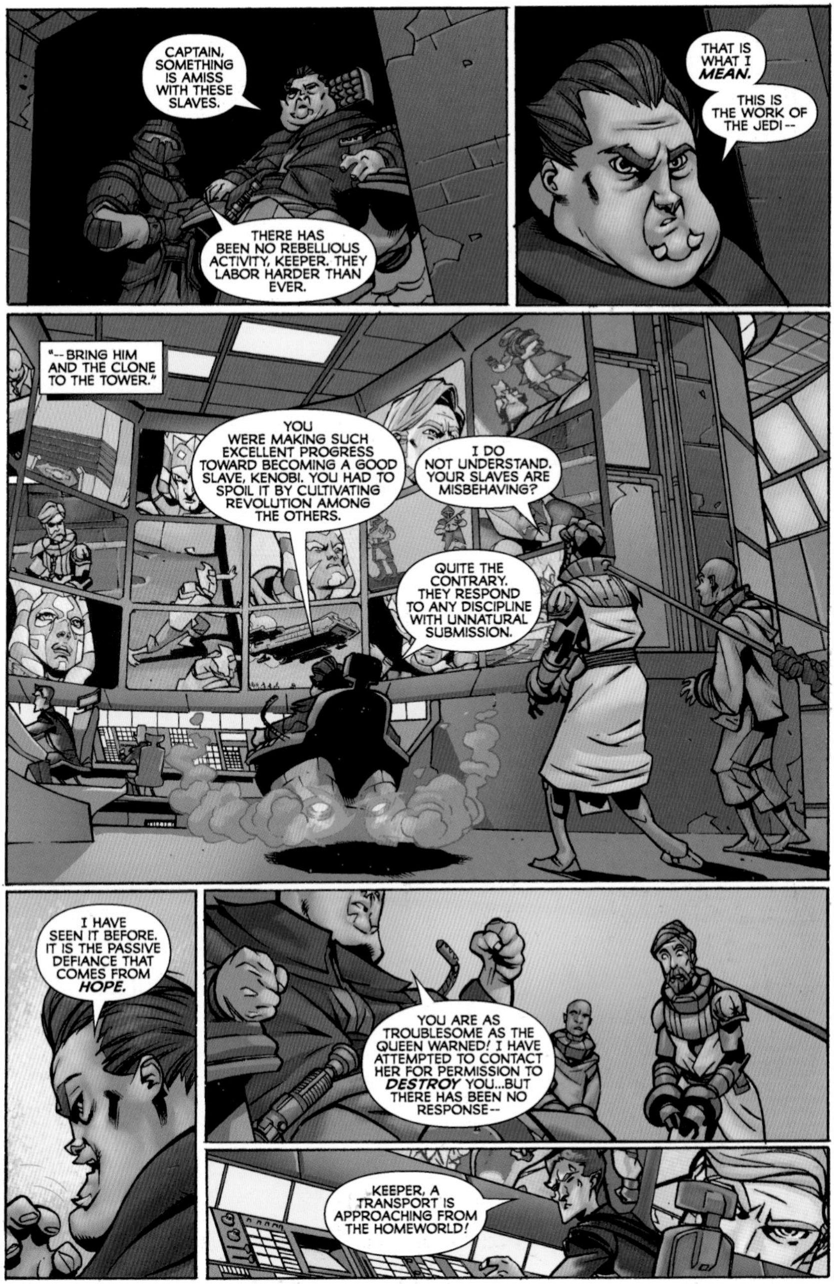

CAPTAIN, SOMETHING IS AMISS WITH THESE SLAVES.
THERE HAS BEEN NO REBELLIOUS ACTIVITY, KEEPER. THEY LABOR HARDER THAN EVER.
THAT IS WHAT I *MEAN.*
THIS IS THE WORK OF THE JEDI--
"--BRING HIM AND THE CLONE TO THE TOWER."
YOU WERE MAKING SUCH EXCELLENT PROGRESS TOWARD BECOMING A GOOD SLAVE, KENOBI. YOU HAD TO SPOIL IT BY CULTIVATING REVOLUTION AMONG THE OTHERS.
I DO NOT UNDERSTAND. YOUR SLAVES ARE MISBEHAVING?
QUITE THE CONTRARY. THEY RESPOND TO ANY DISCIPLINE WITH UNNATURAL SUBMISSION.
I HAVE SEEN IT BEFORE. IT IS THE PASSIVE DEFIANCE THAT COMES FROM *HOPE.*
YOU ARE AS TROUBLESOME AS THE QUEEN WARNED! I HAVE ATTEMPTED TO CONTACT HER FOR PERMISSION TO *DESTROY* YOU...BUT THERE HAS BEEN NO RESPONSE--
KEEPER, A TRANSPORT IS APPROACHING FROM THE HOMEWORLD!

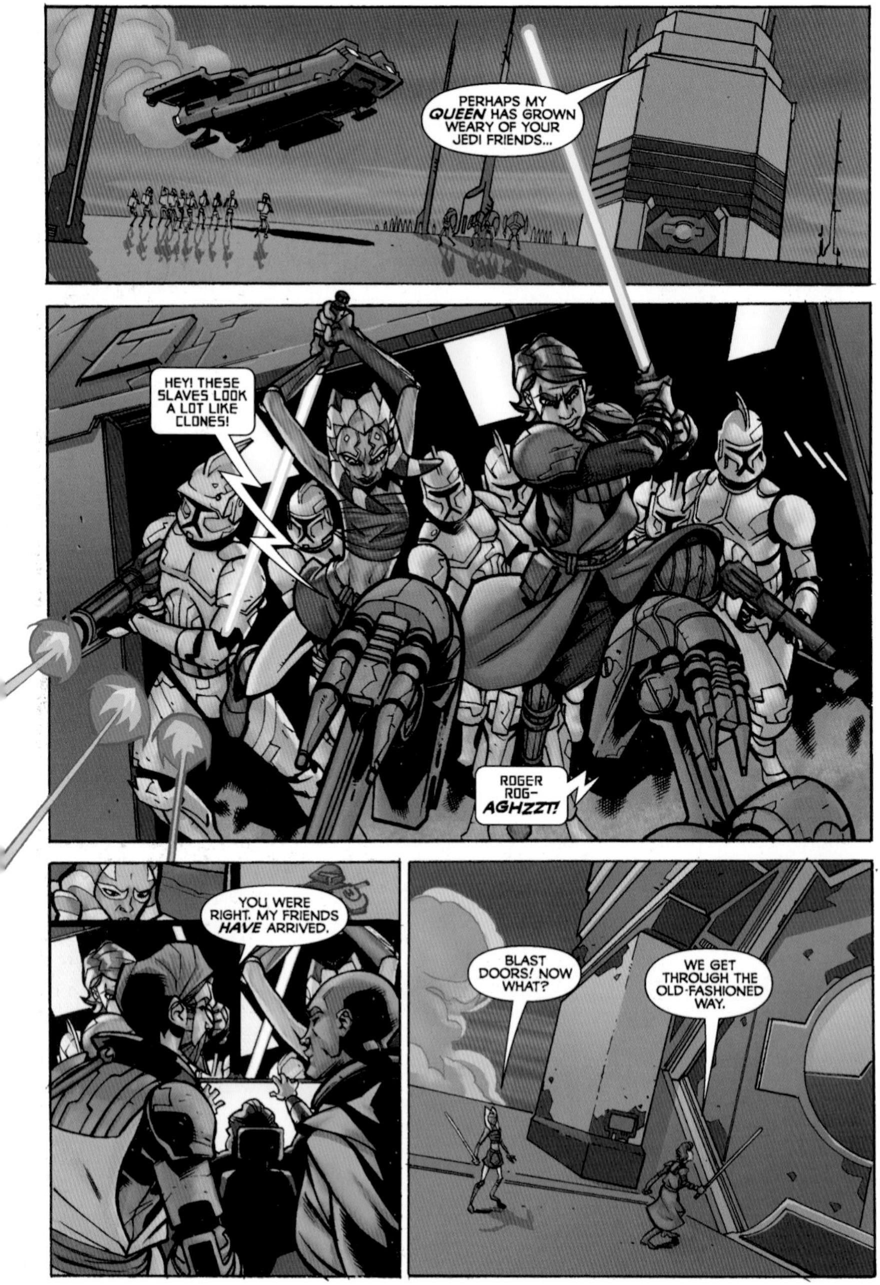
PERHAPS MY QUEEN HAS GROWN WEARY OF YOUR JEDI FRIENDS...
HEY! THESE SLAVES LOOK A LOT LIKE CLONES!
ROGER ROG- AGHZZT!
YOU WERE RIGHT. MY FRIENDS HAVE ARRIVED.
BLAST DOORS! NOW WHAT?
WE GET THROUGH THE OLD-FASHIONED WAY.

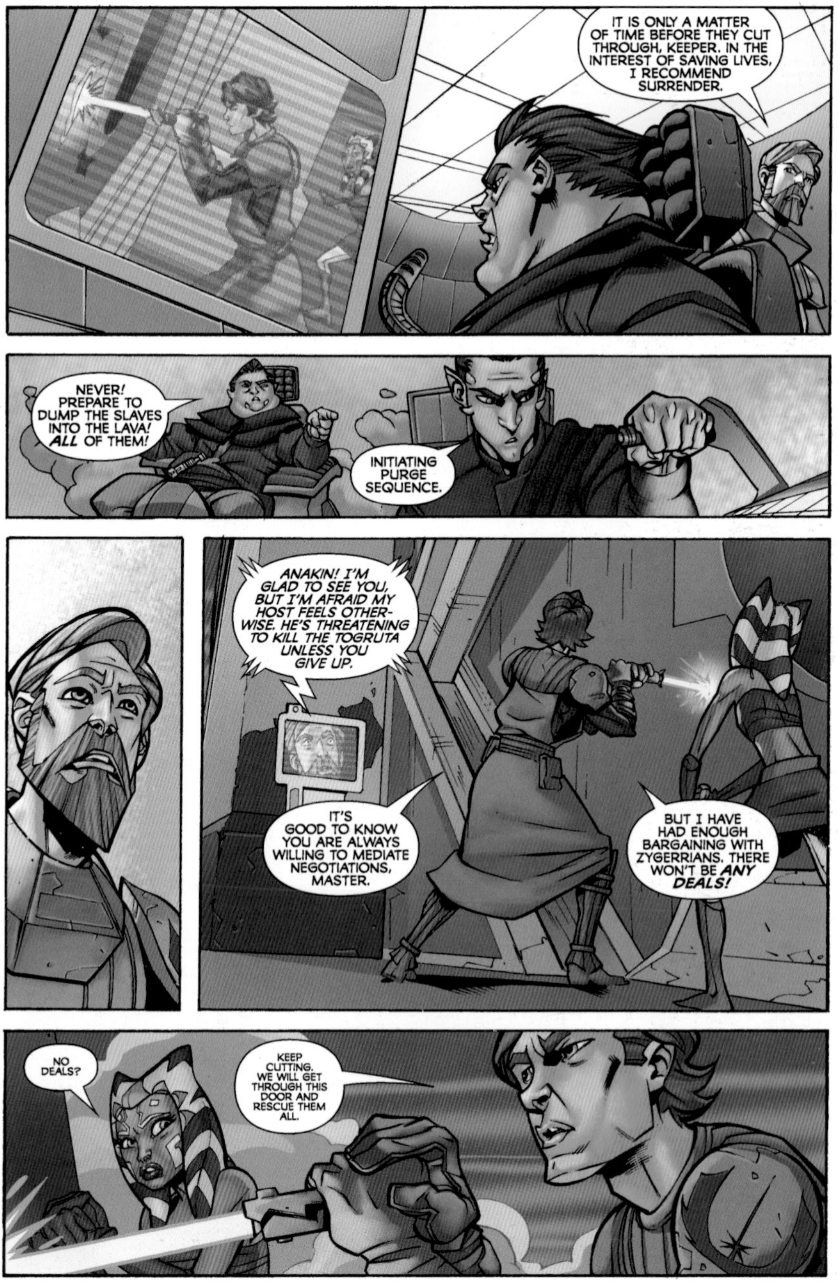
IT IS ONLY A MATTER OF TIME BEFORE THEY CUT THROUGH, KEEPER. IN THE INTEREST OF SAVING LIVES, I RECOMMEND SURRENDER.
NEVER! PREPARE TO DUMP THE SLAVES INTO THE LAVA! *ALL* OF THEM!
INITIATING PURGE SEQUENCE.
ANAKIN! I'M GLAD TO SEE YOU, BUT I'M AFRAID MY HOST FEELS OTHER-WISE. HE'S THREATENING TO KILL THE TOGRUTA UNLESS YOU GIVE UP.
IT'S GOOD TO KNOW YOU ARE ALWAYS WILLING TO MEDIATE NEGOTIATIONS, MASTER.
BUT I HAVE HAD ENOUGH BARGAINING WITH ZYGERRIANS. THERE WON'T BE ***ANY DEALS!***
NO DEALS?
KEEP CUTTING. WE WILL GET THROUGH THIS DOOR AND RESCUE THEM ALL.

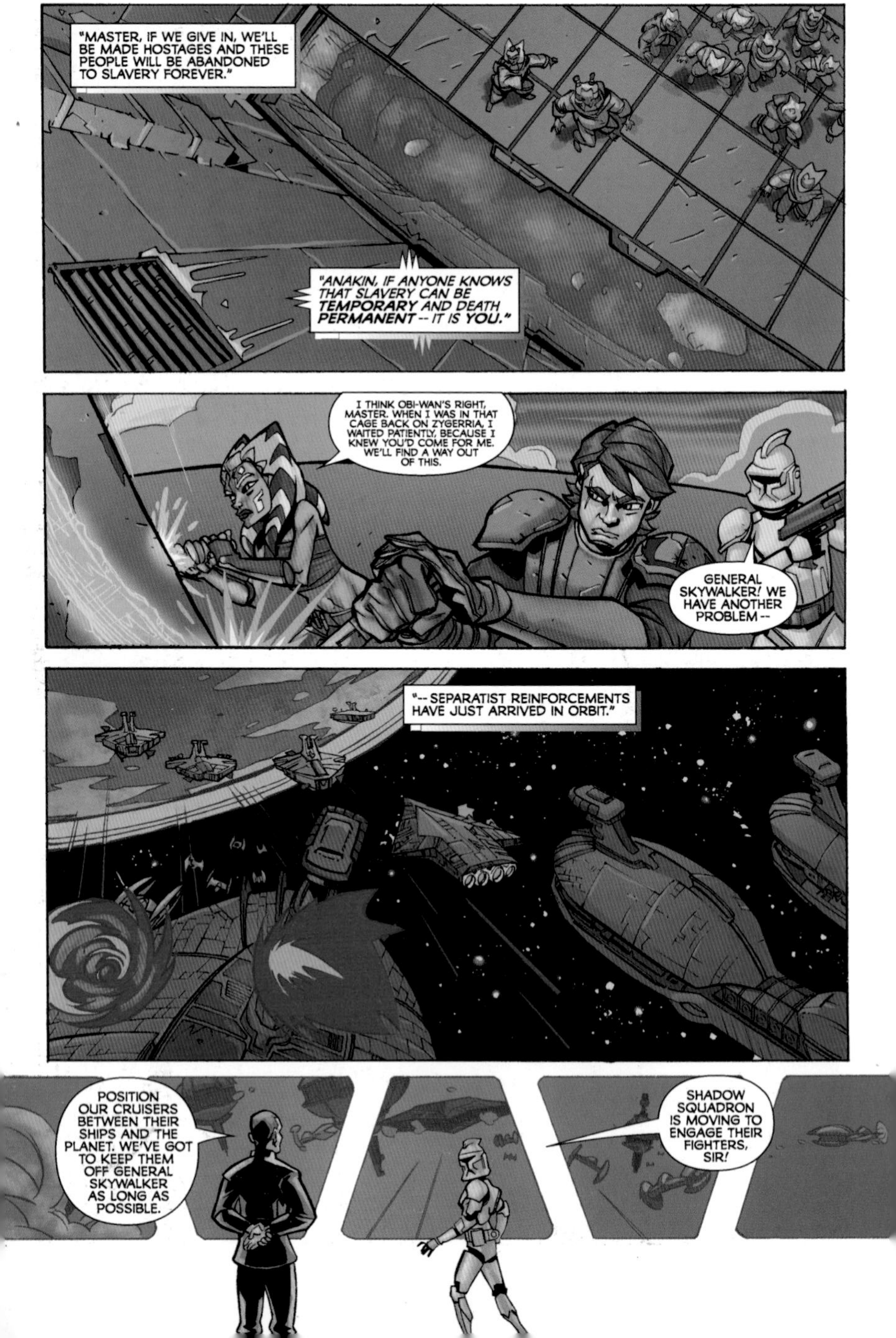
"MASTER, IF WE GIVE IN, WE'LL BE MADE HOSTAGES AND THESE PEOPLE WILL BE ABANDONED TO SLAVERY FOREVER."
"ANAKIN, IF ANYONE KNOWS THAT SLAVERY CAN BE TEMPORARY AND DEATH PERMANENT -- IT IS YOU."
I THINK OBI-WAN'S RIGHT, MASTER. WHEN I WAS IN THAT CAGE BACK ON ZYGERRIA, I WAITED PATIENTLY, BECAUSE I KNEW YOU'D COME FOR ME. WE'LL FIND A WAY OUT OF THIS.
GENERAL SKYWALKER! WE HAVE ANOTHER PROBLEM --
"-- SEPARATIST REINFORCEMENTS HAVE JUST ARRIVED IN ORBIT."
POSITION OUR CRUISERS BETWEEN THEIR SHIPS AND THE PLANET. WE'VE GOT TO KEEP THEM OFF GENERAL SKYWALKER AS LONG AS POSSIBLE.
SHADOW SQUADRON IS MOVING TO ENGAGE THEIR FIGHTERS, SIR!

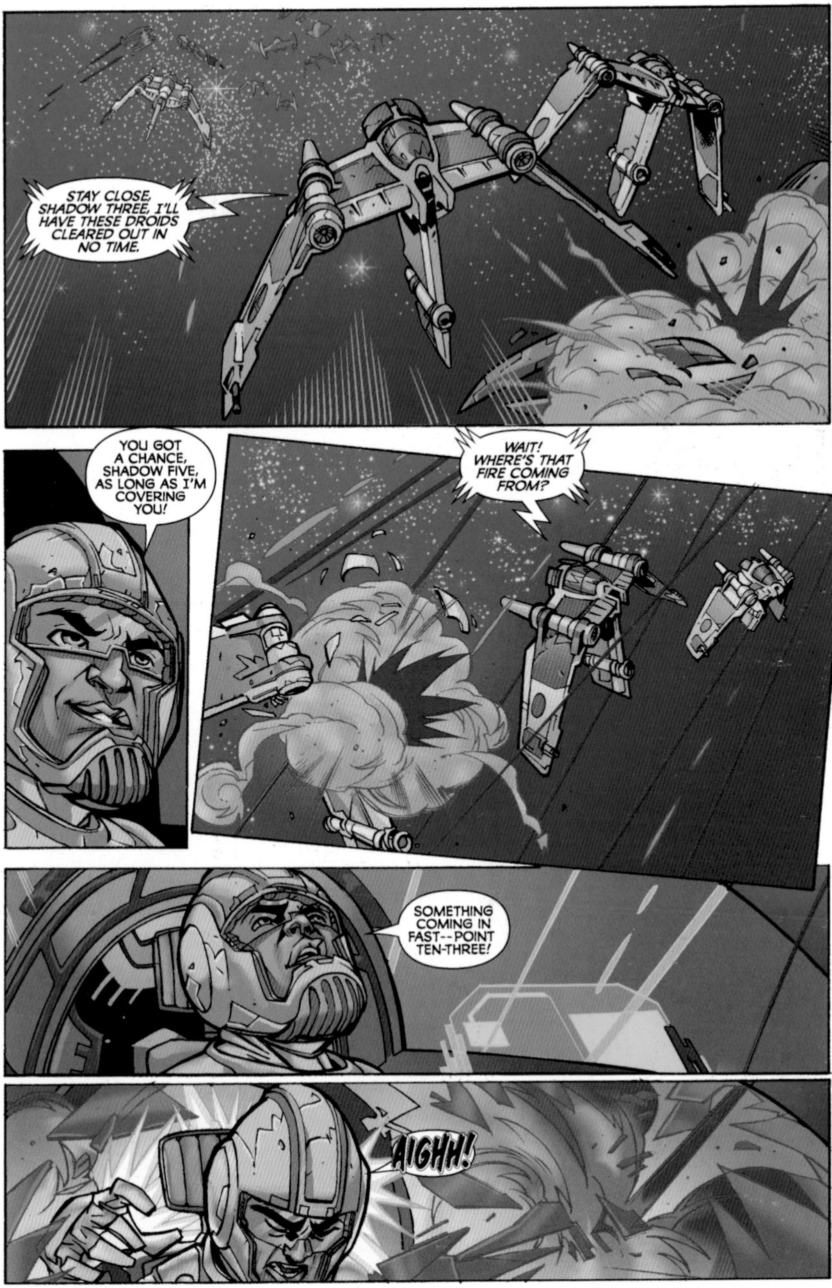
STAY CLOSE, SHADOW THREE, I'LL HAVE THESE DROIDS CLEARED OUT IN NO TIME.
YOU GOT A CHANCE, SHADOW FIVE, AS LONG AS I'M COVERING YOU!
WAIT! WHERE'S THAT FIRE COMING FROM?
SOMETHING COMING IN FAST--POINT TEN-THREE!
AIGHH!

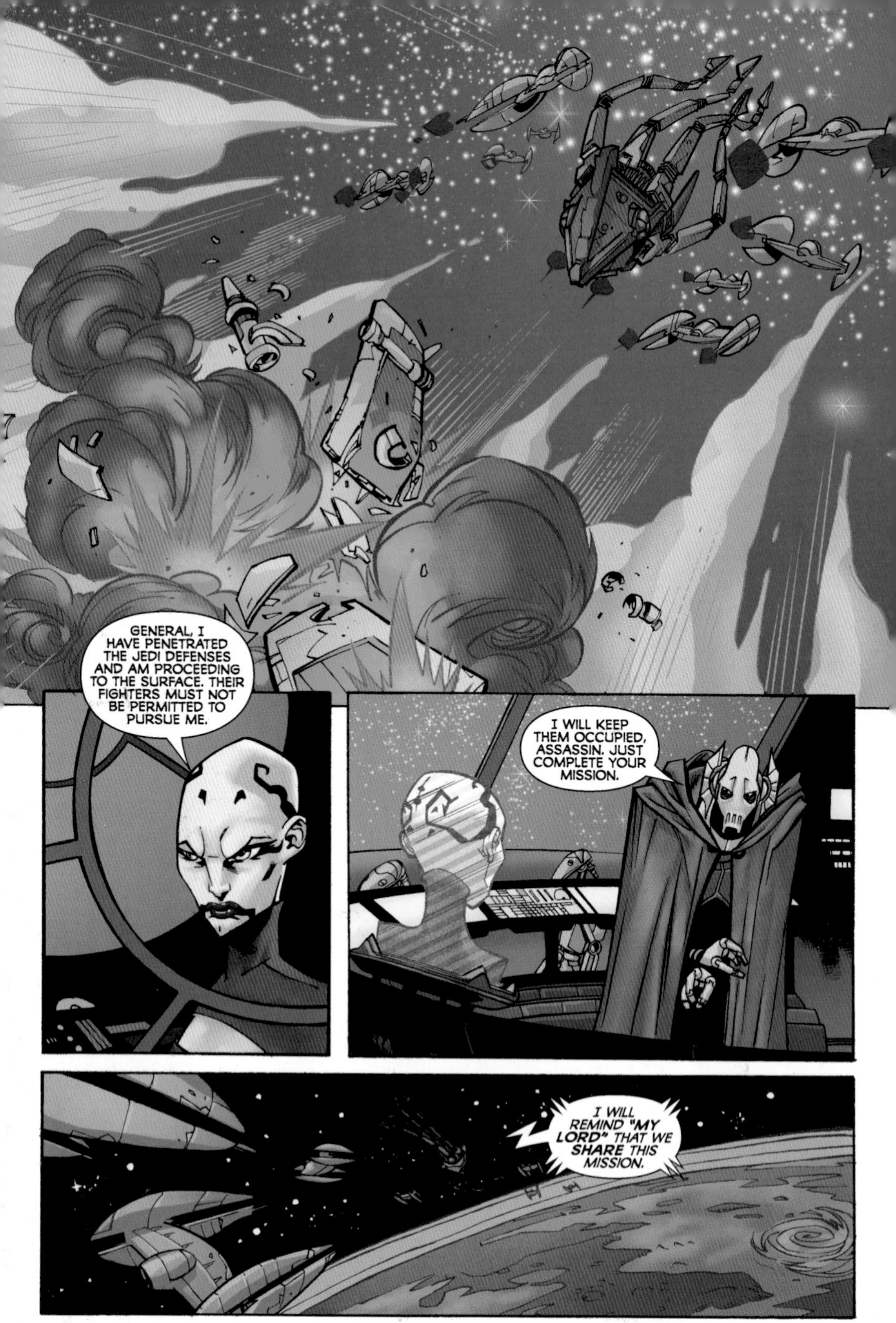
GENERAL, I HAVE PENETRATED THE JEDI DEFENSES AND AM PROCEEDING TO THE SURFACE. THEIR FIGHTERS MUST NOT BE PERMITTED TO PURSUE ME.
I WILL KEEP THEM OCCUPIED, ASSASSIN. JUST COMPLETE YOUR MISSION.
I WILL REMIND "MY LORD" THAT WE SHARE THIS MISSION.

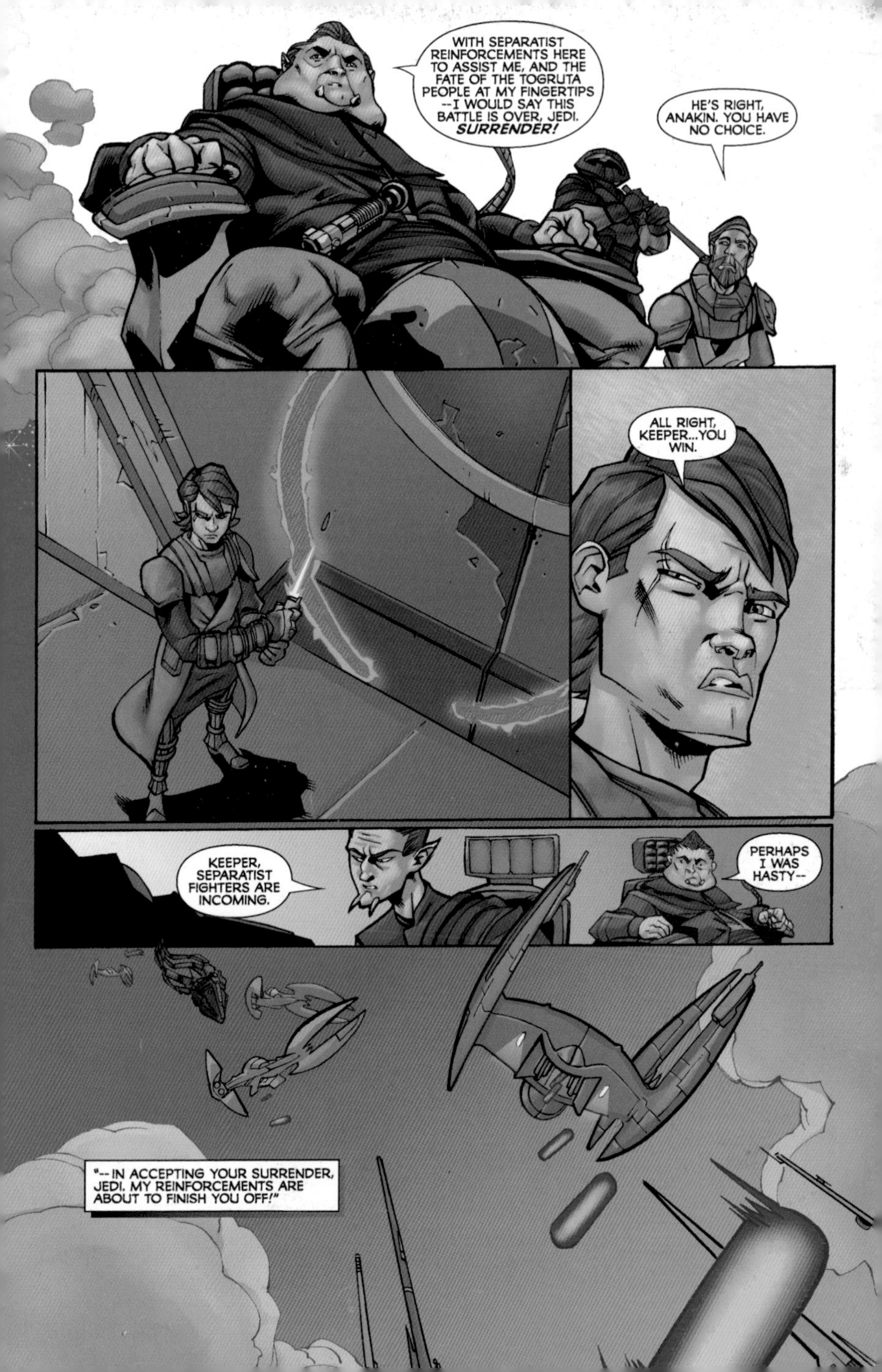
WITH SEPARATIST REINFORCEMENTS HERE TO ASSIST ME, AND THE FATE OF THE TOGRUTA PEOPLE AT MY FINGERTIPS --I WOULD SAY THIS BATTLE IS OVER, JEDI. SURRENDER!
HE'S RIGHT, ANAKIN. YOU HAVE NO CHOICE.
ALL RIGHT, KEEPER...YOU WIN.
KEEPER, SEPARATIST FIGHTERS ARE INCOMING.
PERHAPS I WAS HASTY--
"--IN ACCEPTING YOUR SURRENDER, JEDI. MY REINFORCEMENTS ARE ABOUT TO FINISH YOU OFF!"

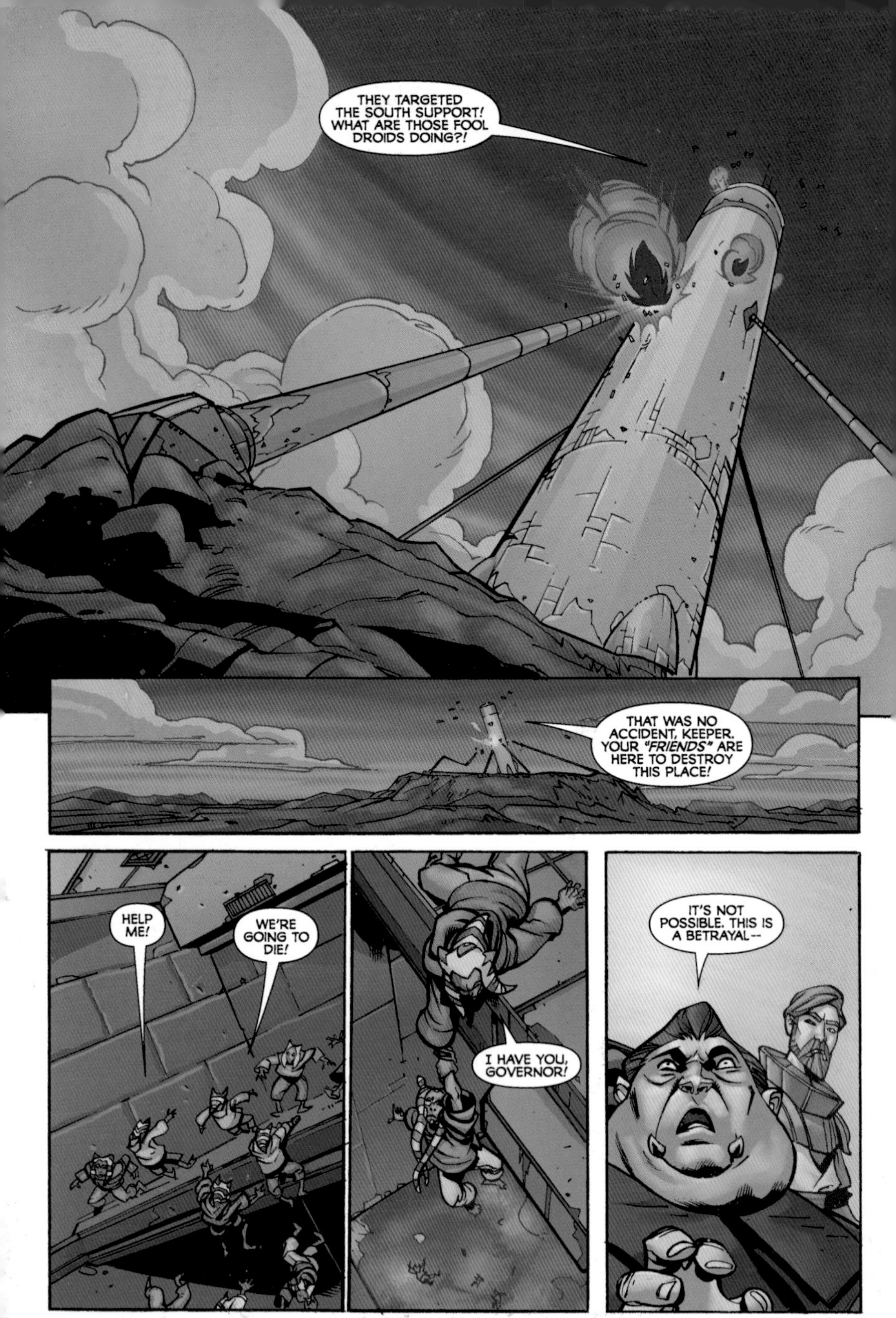
THEY TARGETED THE SOUTH SUPPORT! WHAT ARE THOSE FOOL DROIDS DOING?!
THAT WAS NO ACCIDENT, KEEPER. YOUR "FRIENDS" ARE HERE TO DESTROY THIS PLACE!
HELP ME!
WE'RE GOING TO DIE!
I HAVE YOU, GOVERNOR!
IT'S NOT POSSIBLE. THIS IS A BETRAYAL--

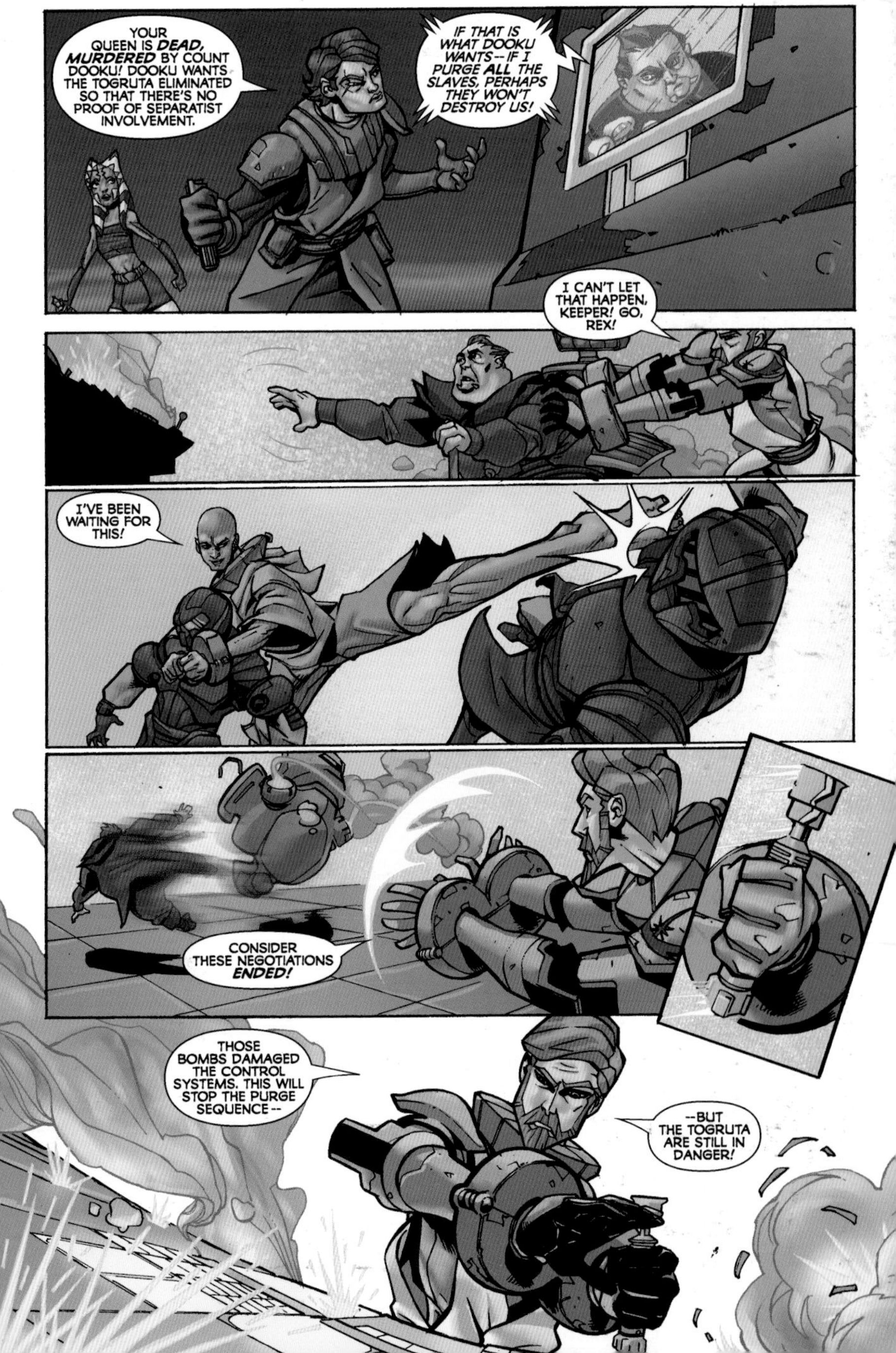
YOUR QUEEN IS DEAD, MURDERED BY COUNT DOOKU! DOOKU WANTS THE TOGRUTA ELIMINATED SO THAT THERE'S NO PROOF OF SEPARATIST INVOLVEMENT.
IF THAT IS WHAT DOOKU WANTS-- IF I PURGE ALL THE SLAVES, PERHAPS THEY WON'T DESTROY US!
I CAN'T LET THAT HAPPEN, KEEPER! GO, REX!
I'VE BEEN WAITING FOR THIS!
CONSIDER THESE NEGOTIATIONS ENDED!
THOSE BOMBS DAMAGED THE CONTROL SYSTEMS. THIS WILL STOP THE PURGE SEQUENCE--
--BUT THE TOGRUTA ARE STILL IN DANGER!

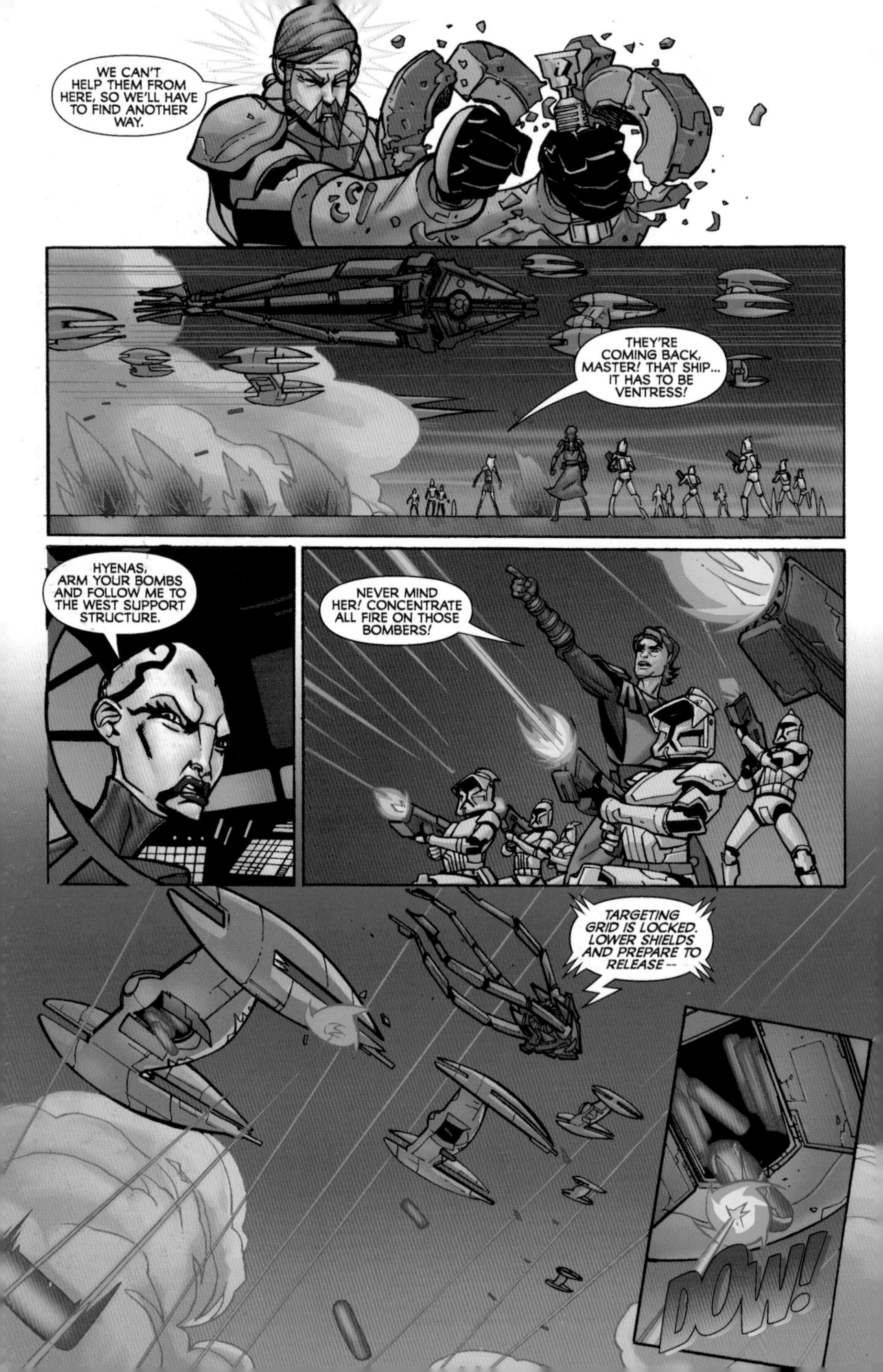
WE CAN'T HELP THEM FROM HERE, SO WE'LL HAVE TO FIND ANOTHER WAY.
THEY'RE COMING BACK, MASTER! THAT SHIP... IT HAS TO BE VENTRESS!
HYENAS, ARM YOUR BOMBS AND FOLLOW ME TO THE WEST SUPPORT STRUCTURE.
NEVER MIND HER! CONCENTRATE ALL FIRE ON THOSE BOMBERS!
TARGETING GRID IS LOCKED. LOWER SHIELDS AND PREPARE TO RELEASE --
DOW!

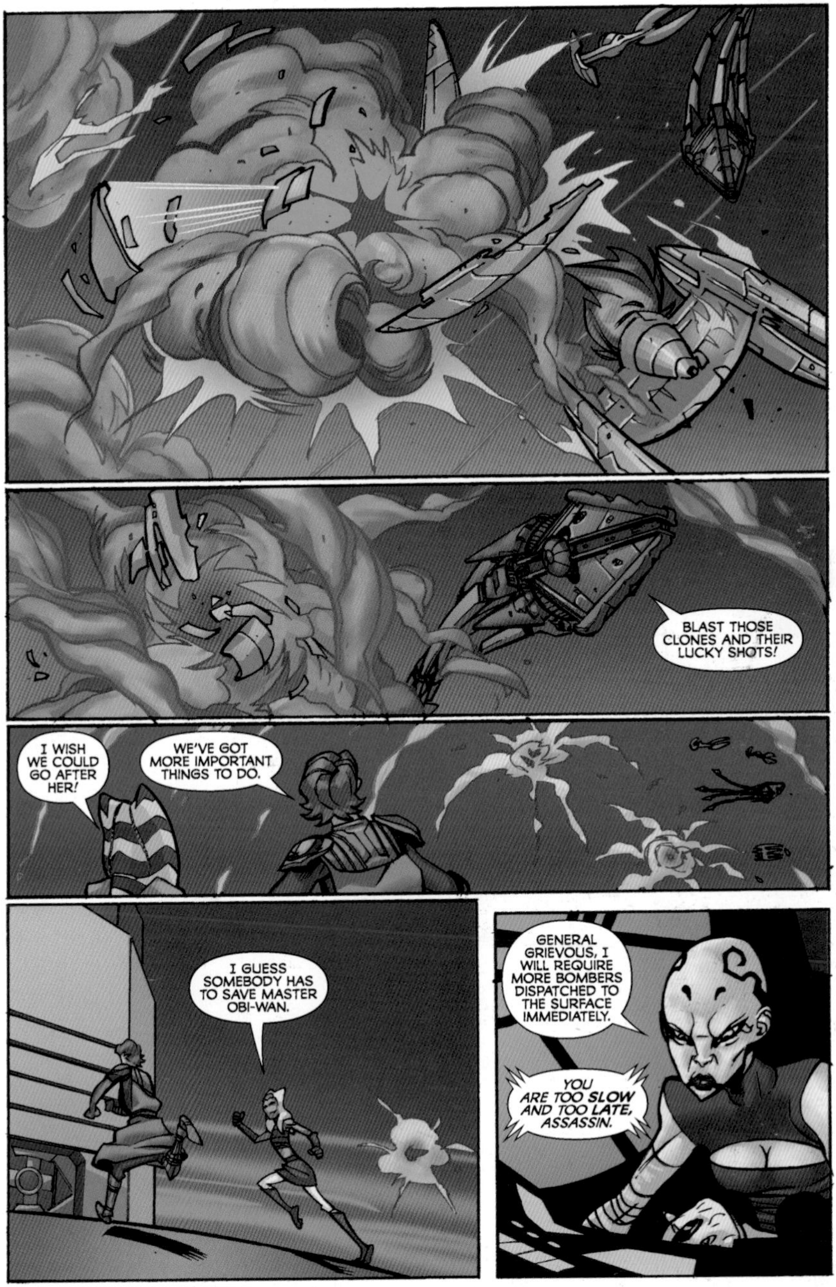
BLAST THOSE CLONES AND THEIR LUCKY SHOTS!
I WISH WE COULD GO AFTER HER!
WE'VE GOT MORE IMPORTANT THINGS TO DO.
I GUESS SOMEBODY HAS TO SAVE MASTER OBI-WAN.
GENERAL GRIEVOUS, I WILL REQUIRE MORE BOMBERS DISPATCHED TO THE SURFACE IMMEDIATELY.
YOU ARE TOO SLOW AND TOO LATE, ASSASSIN.

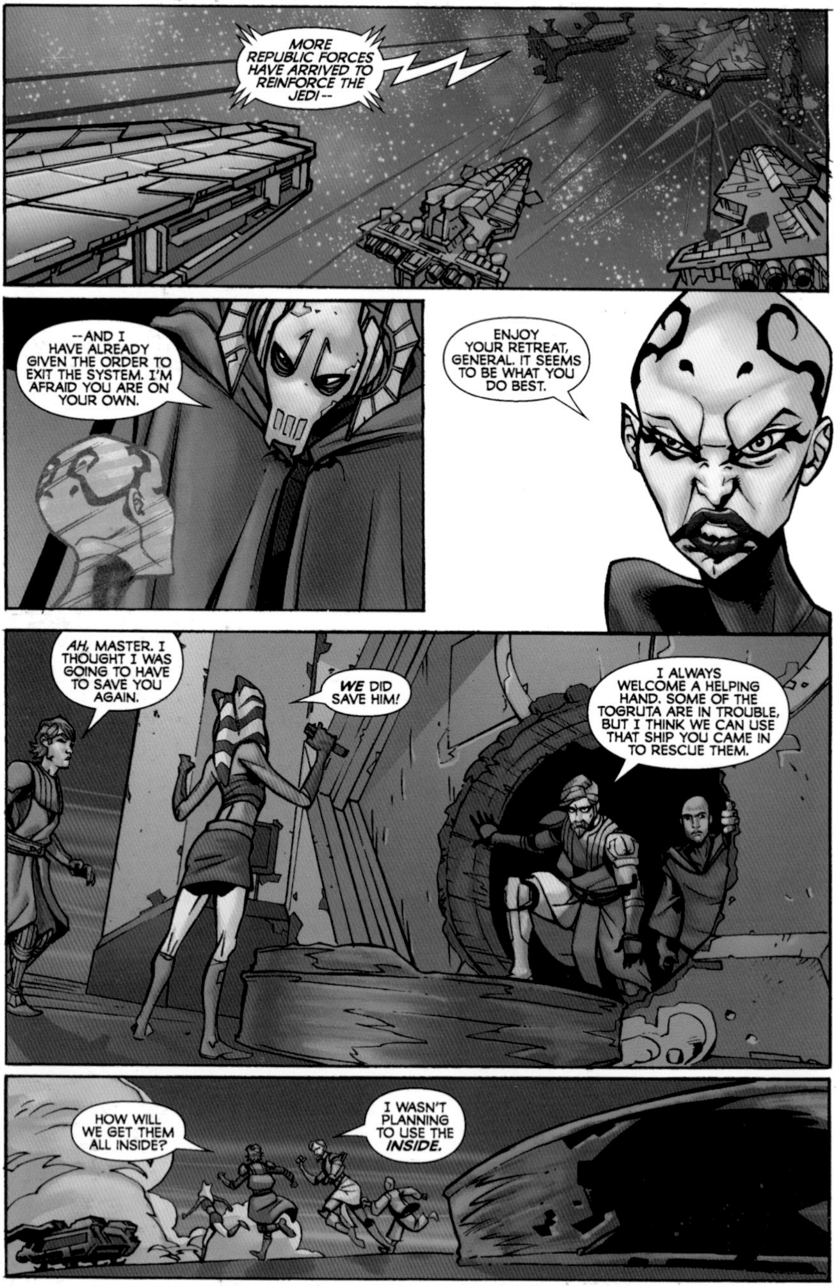
MORE REPUBLIC FORCES HAVE ARRIVED TO REINFORCE THE JEDI--
--AND I HAVE ALREADY GIVEN THE ORDER TO EXIT THE SYSTEM. I'M AFRAID YOU ARE ON YOUR OWN.
ENJOY YOUR RETREAT, GENERAL. IT SEEMS TO BE WHAT YOU DO BEST.
AH, MASTER. I THOUGHT I WAS GOING TO HAVE TO SAVE YOU AGAIN.
WE DID SAVE HIM!
I ALWAYS WELCOME A HELPING HAND. SOME OF THE TOGRUTA ARE IN TROUBLE, BUT I THINK WE CAN USE THAT SHIP YOU CAME IN TO RESCUE THEM.
HOW WILL WE GET THEM ALL INSIDE?
I WASN'T PLANNING TO USE THE INSIDE.

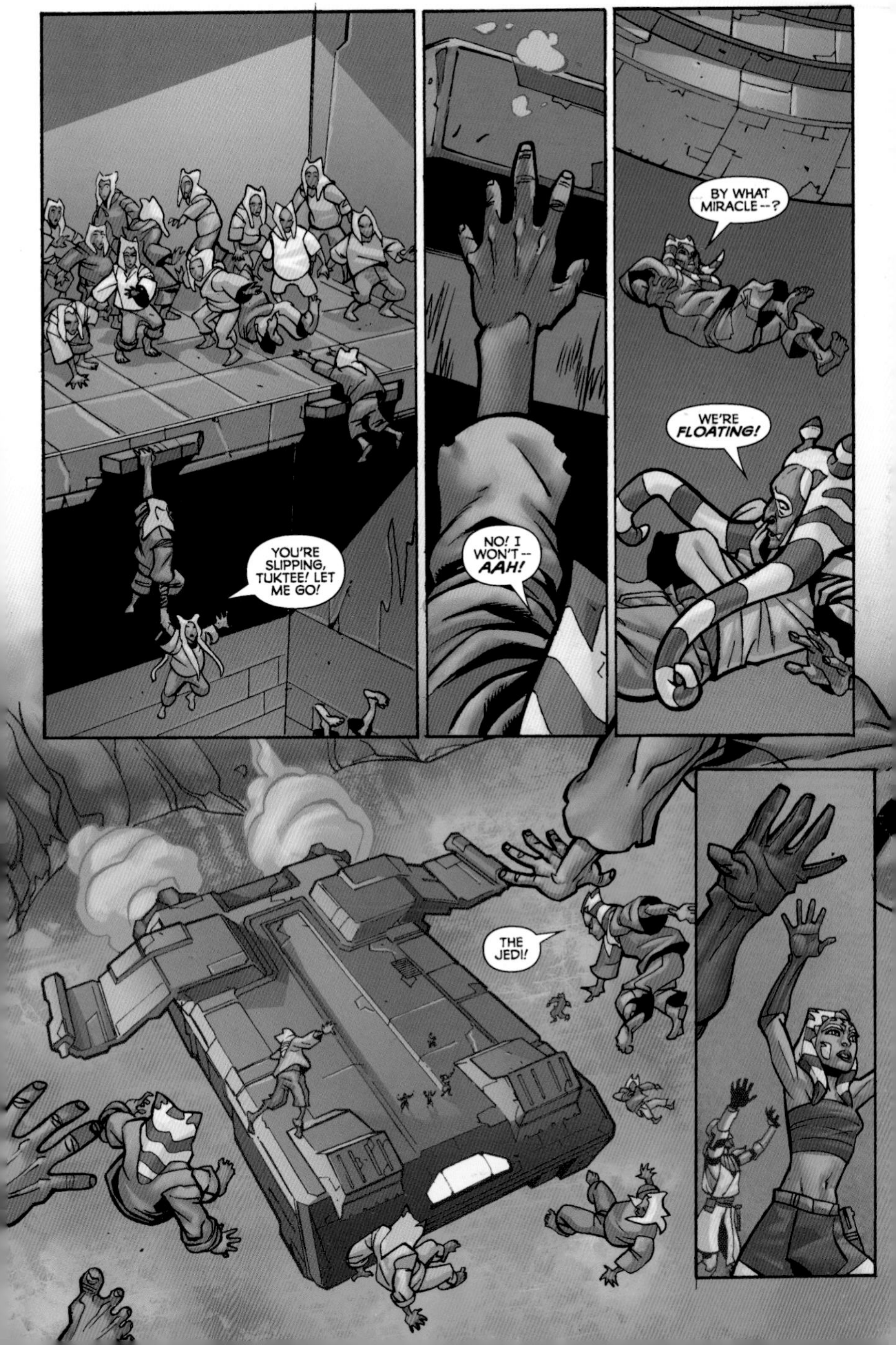
YOU'RE SLIPPING, TUKTEE! LET ME GO!
NO! I WON'T -- AAH!
BY WHAT MIRACLE --?
WE'RE FLOATING!
THE JEDI!

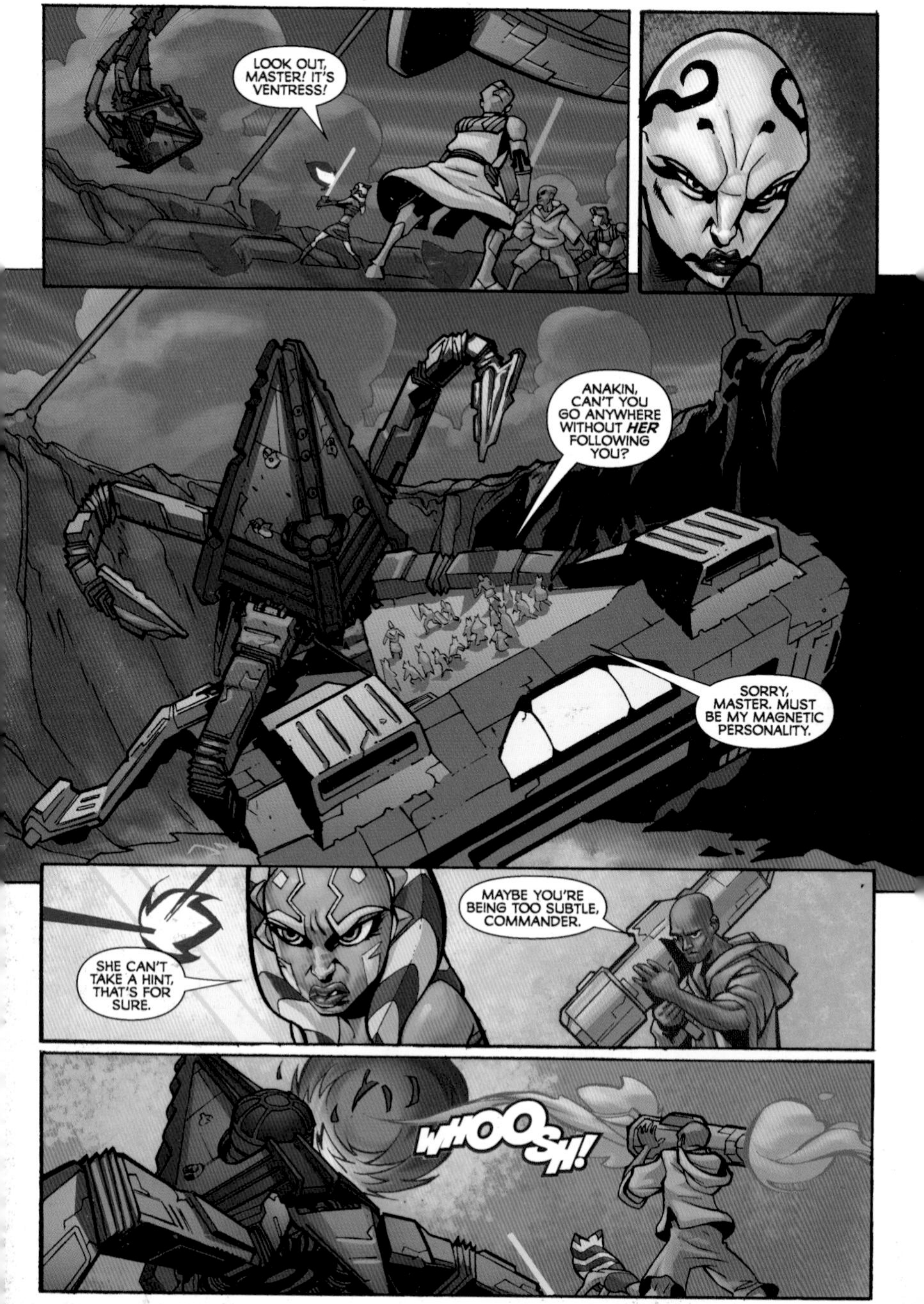
LOOK OUT, MASTER! IT'S VENTRESS!
ANAKIN, CAN'T YOU GO ANYWHERE WITHOUT HER FOLLOWING YOU?
SORRY, MASTER. MUST BE MY MAGNETIC PERSONALITY.
MAYBE YOU'RE BEING TOO SUBTLE, COMMANDER.
SHE CAN'T TAKE A HINT, THAT'S FOR SURE.
WHOOSH!

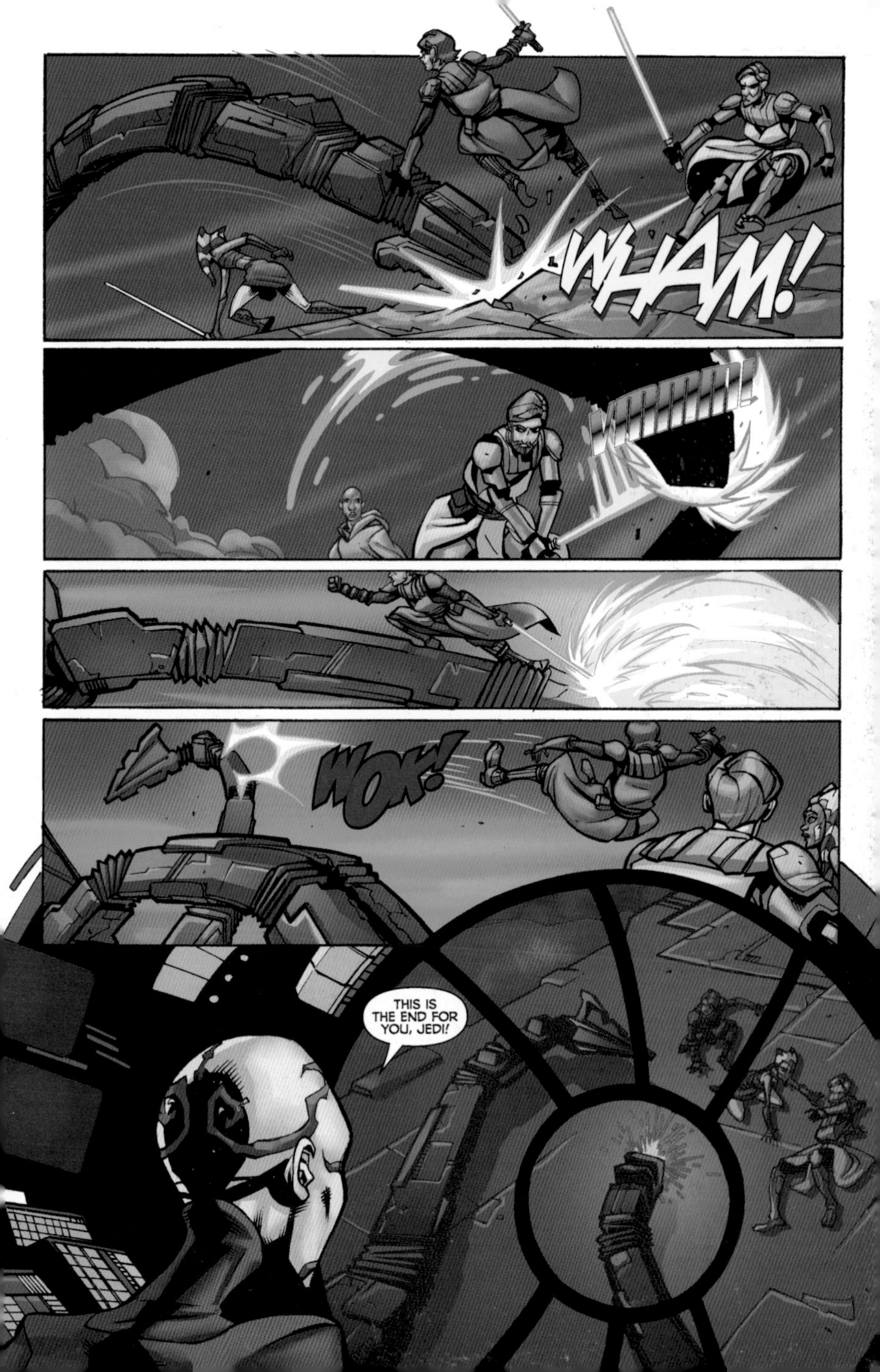
WHAM!
VMMM!
WOK!
THIS IS THE END FOR YOU, JEDI!

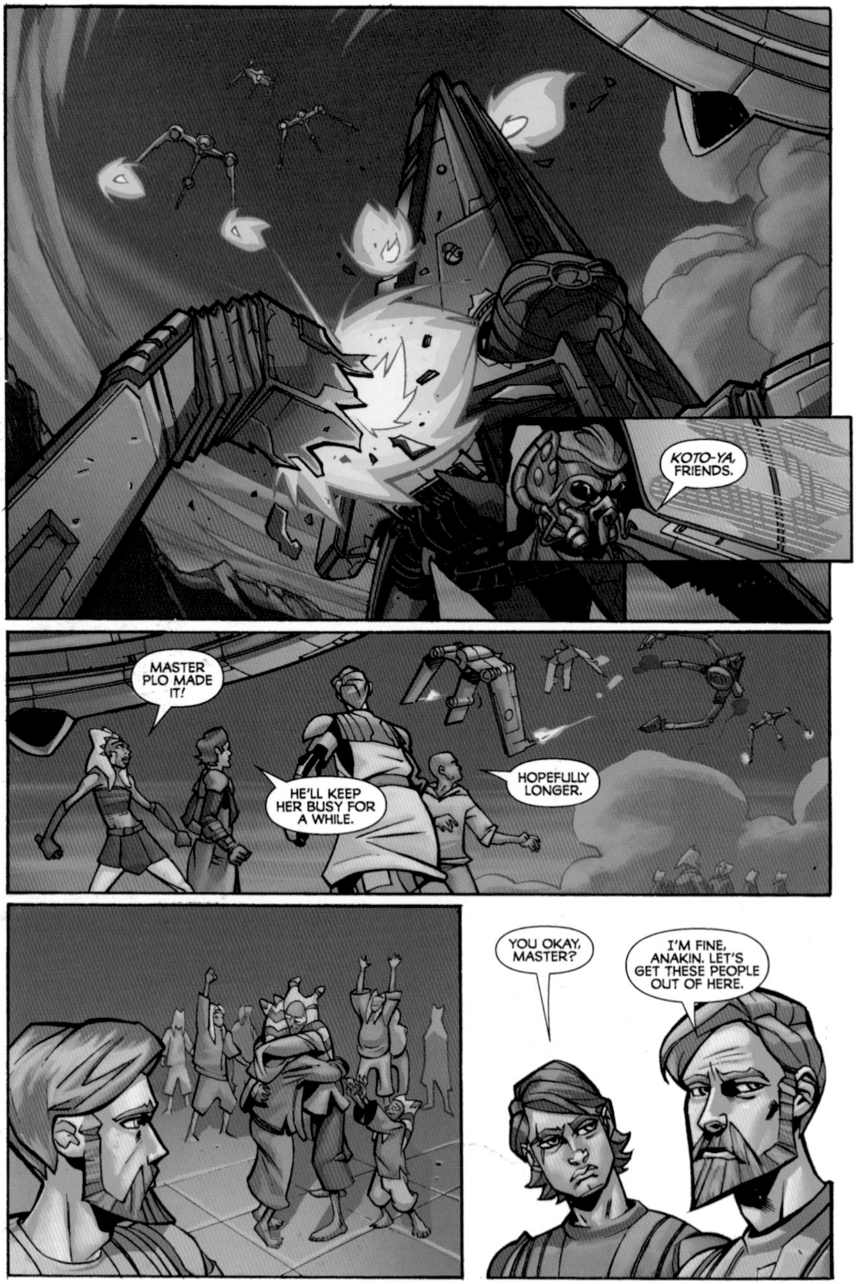
KOTO-YA, FRIENDS.
MASTER PLO MADE IT!
HE'LL KEEP HER BUSY FOR A WHILE.
HOPEFULLY LONGER.
YOU OKAY, MASTER?
I'M FINE, ANAKIN. LET'S GET THESE PEOPLE OUT OF HERE.

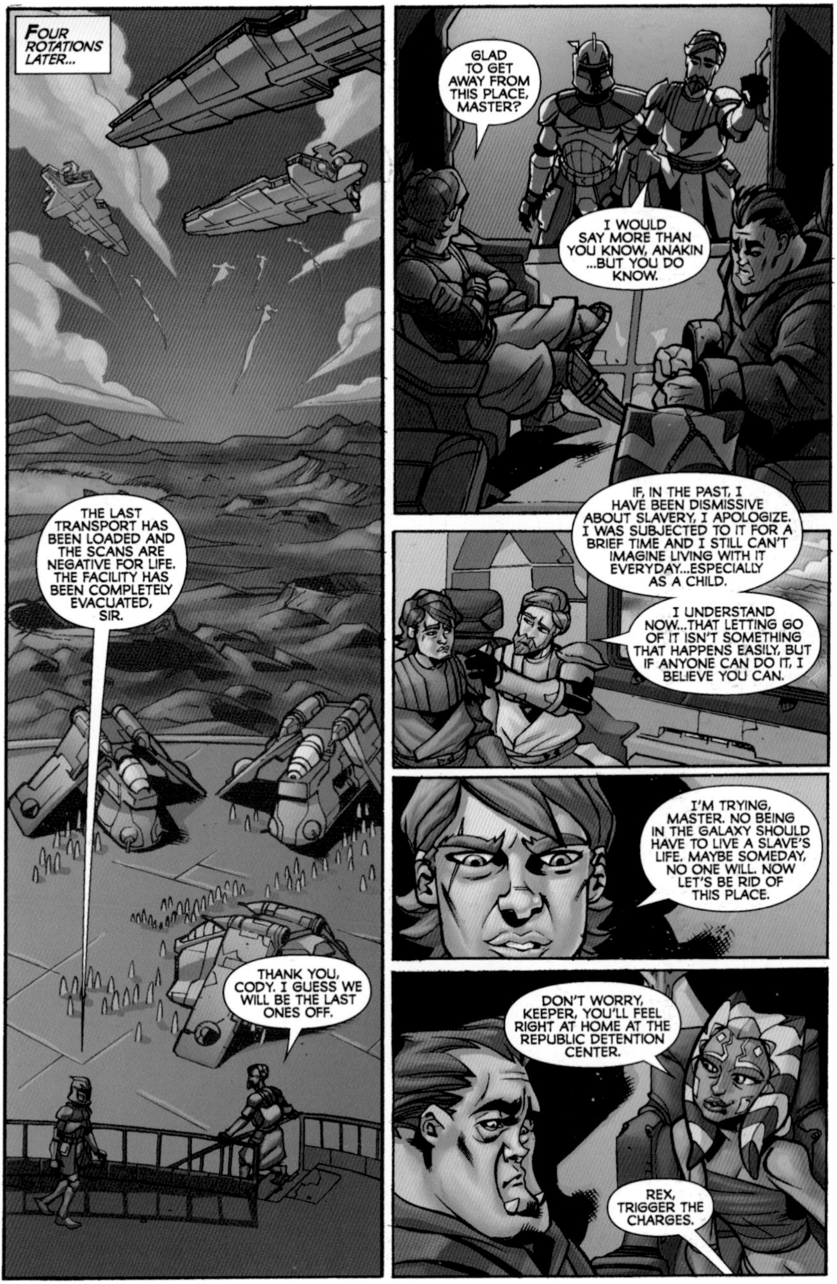
FOUR ROTATIONS LATER...
THE LAST TRANSPORT HAS BEEN LOADED AND THE SCANS ARE NEGATIVE FOR LIFE. THE FACILITY HAS BEEN COMPLETELY EVACUATED, SIR.
THANK YOU, CODY. I GUESS WE WILL BE THE LAST ONES OFF.
GLAD TO GET AWAY FROM THIS PLACE, MASTER?
I WOULD SAY MORE THAN YOU KNOW, ANAKIN ...BUT YOU DO KNOW.
IF, IN THE PAST, I HAVE BEEN DISMISSIVE ABOUT SLAVERY, I APOLOGIZE. I WAS SUBJECTED TO IT FOR A BRIEF TIME AND I STILL CAN'T IMAGINE LIVING WITH IT EVERYDAY...ESPECIALLY AS A CHILD.
I UNDERSTAND NOW...THAT LETTING GO OF IT ISN'T SOMETHING THAT HAPPENS EASILY, BUT IF ANYONE CAN DO IT, I BELIEVE YOU CAN.
I'M TRYING, MASTER. NO BEING IN THE GALAXY SHOULD HAVE TO LIVE A SLAVE'S LIFE. MAYBE SOMEDAY, NO ONE WILL. NOW LET'S BE RID OF THIS PLACE.
DON'T WORRY, KEEPER, YOU'LL FEEL RIGHT AT HOME AT THE REPUBLIC DETENTION CENTER.
REX, TRIGGER THE CHARGES.

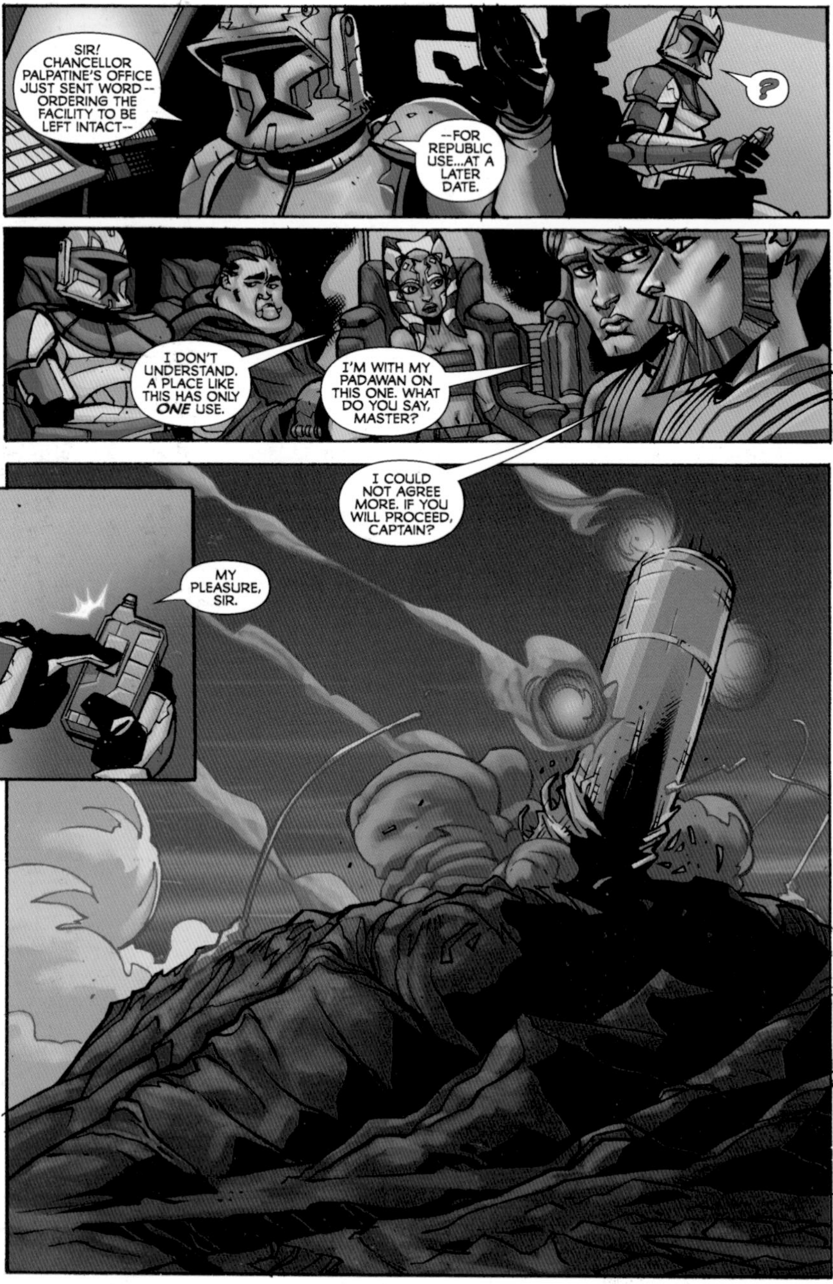
SIR! CHANCELLOR PALPATINE'S OFFICE JUST SENT WORD-- ORDERING THE FACILITY TO BE LEFT INTACT--
--FOR REPUBLIC USE...AT A LATER DATE.
?
I DON'T UNDERSTAND. A PLACE LIKE THIS HAS ONLY *ONE* USE.
I'M WITH MY PADAWAN ON THIS ONE. WHAT DO YOU SAY, MASTER?
I COULD NOT AGREE MORE. IF YOU WILL PROCEED, CAPTAIN?
MY PLEASURE, SIR.

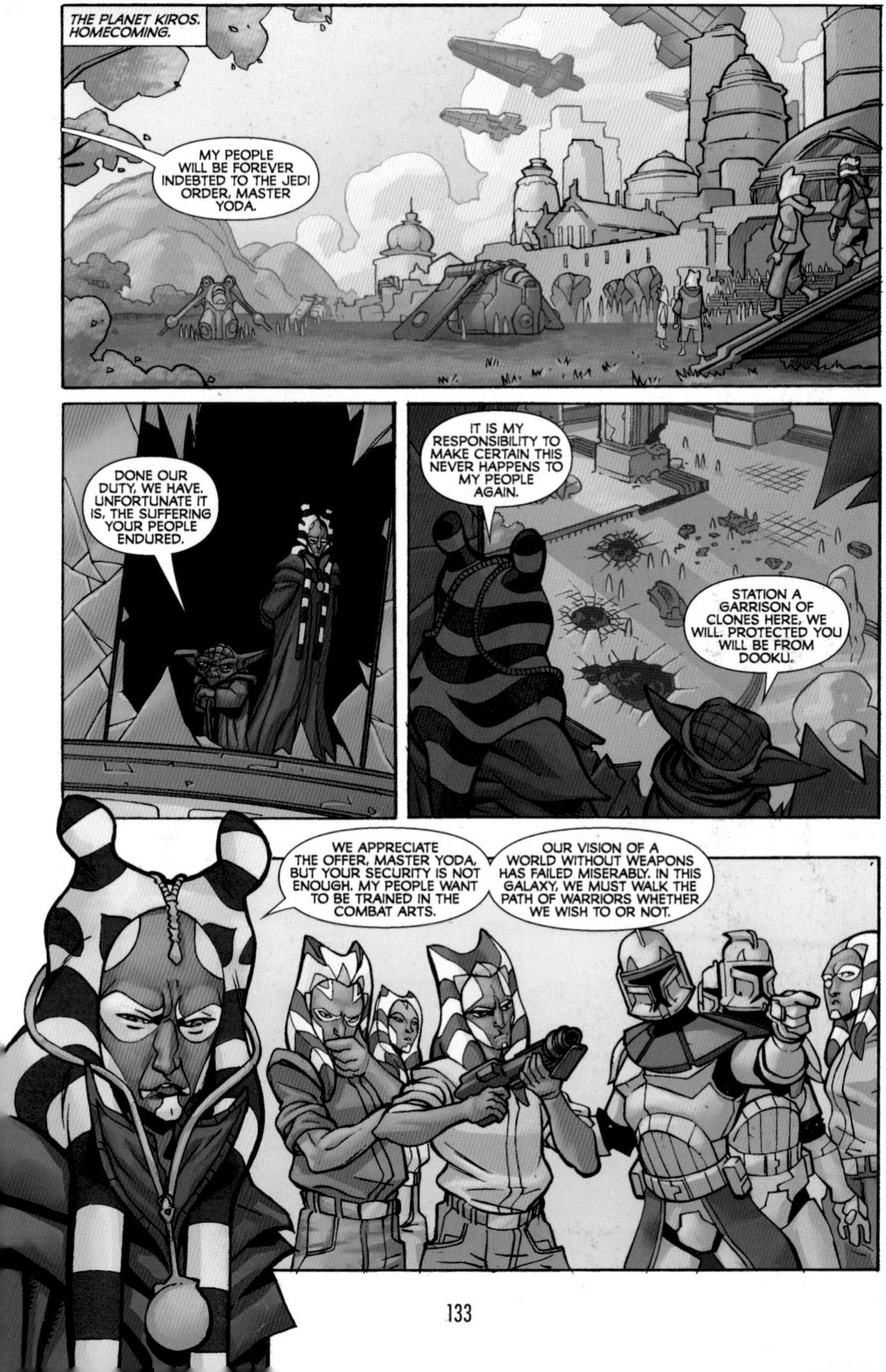
THE PLANET KIROS. HOMECOMING.
MY PEOPLE WILL BE FOREVER INDEBTED TO THE JEDI ORDER, MASTER YODA.
DONE OUR DUTY, WE HAVE. UNFORTUNATE IT IS, THE SUFFERING YOUR PEOPLE ENDURED.
IT IS MY RESPONSIBILITY TO MAKE CERTAIN THIS NEVER HAPPENS TO MY PEOPLE AGAIN.
STATION A GARRISON OF CLONES HERE, WE WILL. PROTECTED YOU WILL BE FROM DOOKU.
WE APPRECIATE THE OFFER, MASTER YODA, BUT YOUR SECURITY IS NOT ENOUGH. MY PEOPLE WANT TO BE TRAINED IN THE COMBAT ARTS.
OUR VISION OF A WORLD WITHOUT WEAPONS HAS FAILED MISERABLY. IN THIS GALAXY, WE MUST WALK THE PATH OF WARRIORS WHETHER WE WISH TO OR NOT.

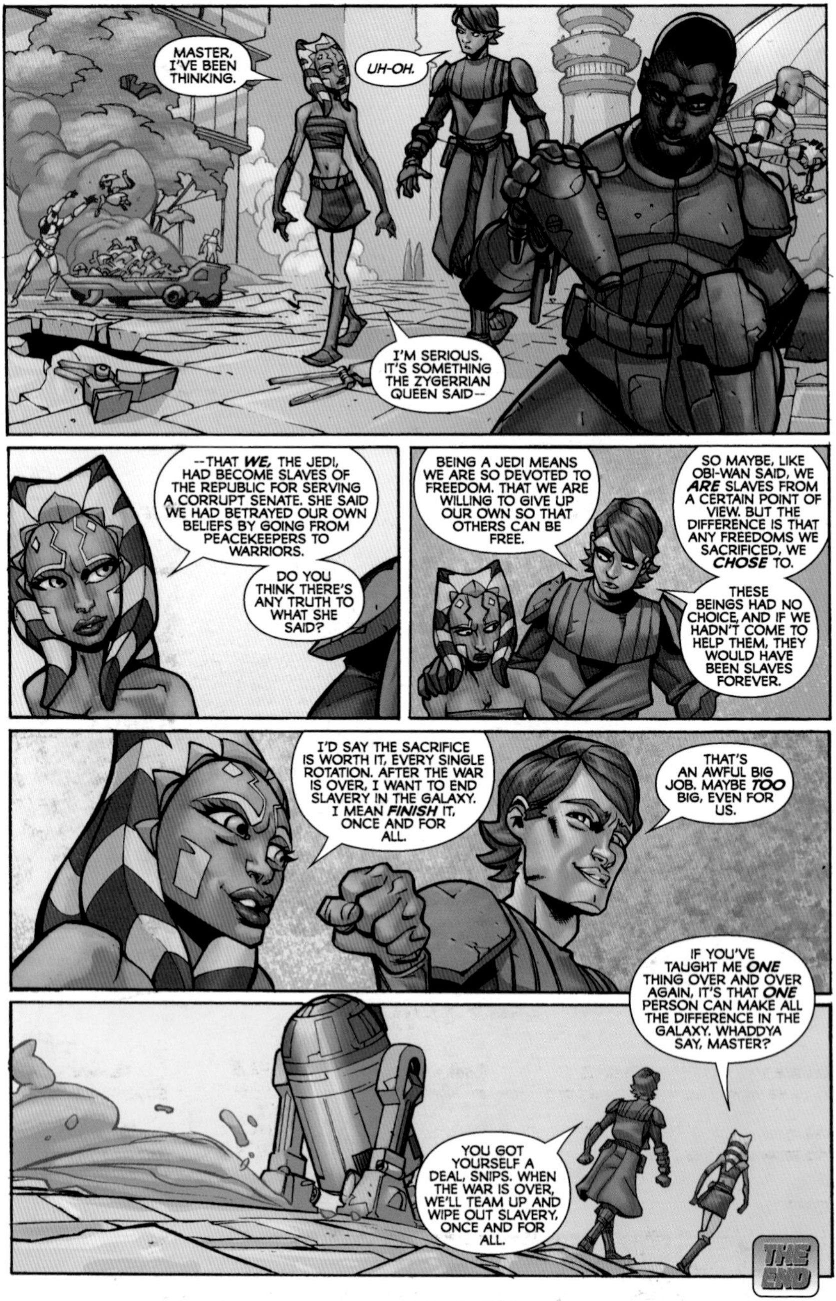
MASTER, I'VE BEEN THINKING.
UH-OH.
I'M SERIOUS. IT'S SOMETHING THE ZYGERRIAN QUEEN SAID--
--THAT WE, THE JEDI, HAD BECOME SLAVES OF THE REPUBLIC FOR SERVING A CORRUPT SENATE. SHE SAID WE HAD BETRAYED OUR OWN BELIEFS BY GOING FROM PEACEKEEPERS TO WARRIORS.
DO YOU THINK THERE'S ANY TRUTH TO WHAT SHE SAID?
BEING A JEDI MEANS WE ARE SO DEVOTED TO FREEDOM. THAT WE ARE WILLING TO GIVE UP OUR OWN SO THAT OTHERS CAN BE FREE.
SO MAYBE, LIKE OBI-WAN SAID, WE ARE SLAVES FROM A CERTAIN POINT OF VIEW. BUT THE DIFFERENCE IS THAT ANY FREEDOMS WE SACRIFICED, WE CHOSE TO.
THESE BEINGS HAD NO CHOICE, AND IF WE HADN'T COME TO HELP THEM, THEY WOULD HAVE BEEN SLAVES FOREVER.
I'D SAY THE SACRIFICE IS WORTH IT, EVERY SINGLE ROTATION. AFTER THE WAR IS OVER, I WANT TO END SLAVERY IN THE GALAXY. I MEAN FINISH IT, ONCE AND FOR ALL.
THAT'S AN AWFUL BIG JOB. MAYBE TOO BIG, EVEN FOR US.
IF YOU'VE TAUGHT ME ONE THING OVER AND OVER AGAIN, IT'S THAT ONE PERSON CAN MAKE ALL THE DIFFERENCE IN THE GALAXY. WHADDYA SAY, MASTER?
YOU GOT YOURSELF A DEAL, SNIPS. WHEN THE WAR IS OVER, WE'LL TEAM UP AND WIPE OUT SLAVERY, ONCE AND FOR ALL.
THE END

STAR WARS®
CLONE WARS ADVENTURES

Don't miss any of the action-packed adventures of your favorite STAR WARS® characters, available at comics shops and bookstores in a galaxy near you!

STAR WARS
CLONE WARS
ADVENTURES
Vol 4
STAR WARS
CLONE WARS
ADVENTURES
Vol 1
THREE NEW STORIES! ALL-JEDI ACTION!
STAR WARS
CLONE WARS
ADVENTURES
CLONES, DROIDS, AND BOUNTY HUNTERS IN FOUR FANTASTIC TALES!
Vol 10

$6.95 each!

Volume 1	**Volume 2**	**Volume 3**	**Volume 4**	**Volume 5**
ISBN 978-1-59307-243-8	ISBN 978-1-59307-271-1	ISBN 978-1-59307-307-7	ISBN 978-1-59307-402-9	ISBN 978-1-59307-483-8
Volume 6	**Volume 7**	**Volume 8**	**Volume 9**	**Volume 10**
ISBN 978-1-59307-567-5	ISBN 978-1-59307-678-8	ISBN 978-1-59307-680-1	ISBN 978-1-59307-832-4	ISBN 978-1-59307-878-2

AVAILABLE AT YOUR LOCAL COMICS SHOP OR BOOKSTORE
To find a comics shop in your area, call 1-888-266-4226
For more information or to order direct: • On the web: darkhorse.com • Phone: 1-800-862-0052 Mon.–Fri. 9 AM to 5 PM Pacific Time.
• E-mail: mailorder@darkhorse.com *Prices and availability subject to change without notice.

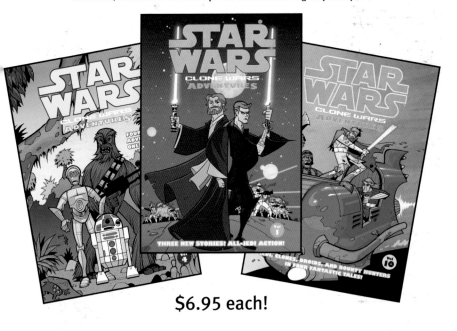